PRAISE FOR
AUDIO BRANDING

'*Audio Branding: Using sound to build your brand* expertly combines the theory and practice of sensory branding in a guide that will be essential to every marketer. I highly recommend this book for your library.' **Martin Lindstrom, *New York Times* bestselling author of *Small Data* and *Buyology***

'This book rings true. Written by marketers, not musicians, it makes it clear why a brand needs its own tailor-made musical vocabulary to thrive. Full of stories and tips, supported by academic studies, and illustrated with cases, it's a great read. A must for anyone who is building or defending a brand today.' **Angela Johnson, EVP, Worldwide Managing Director, Ogilvy**

'If you can conjure up Intel's audio logo, you can start to understand the power of distinctive proprietary sounds, strategically employed across your experiences with that brand, cueing you to recall it with an emotionally positive response. Just as a visual identity creates coherence across trans-media touchpoints, so does an audio identity. Minsky and Fahey deliver a comprehensive guide to conceiving and designing audio branding in the digital age. This book will help you design with sound.' **Robin Landa, Distinguished Professor, Michael Graves College at Kean University, author of *Graphic Design Solutions*, fifth edition, *Designing Brand Experiences*, and *Advertising by Design*, third edition**

'We've created scores of audio branding concepts in our ideation sessions, but it never occurred to me – nor did I have the tools – to create an audio branding *strategy* for our clients. The heavens have opened up and the trumpets have sounded, now that I understand the how and why of *Audio Branding*!' **Bryan Mattimore, author of *21 Days to a Big Idea*, and Cofounder and Chief Idea Guy, The Growth Engine Co, An Innovation Agency**

'*Audio Branding: Using sound to build your brand* is a well-written, practical guide, to a (curiously) nascent field, sprinkled with enough real-world case studies and academic references to provide the reassurance you are on the right path. Music and sound, congruent with other sensory experiences, have long played a critical role in shaping our emotions, aiding recall, and affecting our decisions. Why is it so few marketers sufficiently recognize this? Reading this book might just give your brand that competitive edge you are looking for.' **Andrew Wilson, Executive Vice President and Chief Marketing Officer, Atlanta Convention & Visitors Bureau**

'Pardon the misappropriation of Lennon and McCartney, but brands today must work harder than ever to be "Here, There and Everywhere". In *Audio Branding*, Minsky and Fahey offer a detailed look at why sound is an essential element in this multi-modal, ever-changing effort. Through approachable prose punctuated by a wide range of real-world examples, the authors explain the many creative ways audio can be employed to better identify, differentiate and communicate your brands, all while enhancing the core brand experience. As a long-time advertising writer, brand strategist and sometimes tunesmith, I applaud their performance in these pages.' **Chuck Kent, Contributing Editor, *Branding Magazine* and Creator and Moderator of *Branding Magazine*'s The Branding Roundtable**

'Minsky and Fahey provide a strategy for simply conveying brand essence in an often overlooked, yet ubiquitous medium – sound. And at Siegel+Gale, we know that simple brand experiences win customers' hearts and wallets.' **Howard Belk, Co-CEO, Chief Creative Officer, Siegel+Gale**

'Laurence Minksy and Colleen Fahey remind us that not only are brands multisensory but of just how important sound is – in all its variations – to creating those powerful communities that we call brands.' **Patrick Hanlon, Founder and CEO, Thinktopia, and author of *Primal Branding: Create zealots for your brand, your company, and your future***

'What Minsky and Fahey have done is moved audio branding from an afterthought in the creative process to a preeminent position which must be considered forcefully whenever we sit down to make a campaign.' **Stan Richards, Principal, The Richards Group**

'A highly practical and fun-to-read guide on a topic that really isn't thought about enough. Full of great ideas and examples that will really get you thinking.' **Daniel Rowles, CEO, Target Internet, author of *Digital Branding* and *Mobile Marketing*, and co-author of *Building Digital Culture***

'Marketing doesn't have a blind spot. It's *deaf*! Too many operate with the audio dimension totally unleveraged. Read this book. Then listen for your own unique audio opportunities.' **Bruce Bendinger, The Copy Workshop**

Audio Branding

Using sound to build your brand

Laurence Minsky
Colleen Fahey

Publisher's note

Every possible effort has been made to ensure that the information contained in this book is accurate at the time of going to press, and the publisher and authors cannot accept responsibility for any errors or omissions, however caused. No responsibility for loss or damage occasioned to any person acting, or refraining from action, as a result of the material in this publication can be accepted by the editor, the publisher or the authors.

First published in Great Britain and the United States in 2017 by Kogan Page Limited

Apart from any fair dealing for the purposes of research or private study, or criticism or review, as permitted under the Copyright, Designs and Patents Act 1988, this publication may only be reproduced, stored or transmitted, in any form or by any means, with the prior permission in writing of the publishers, or in the case of reprographic reproduction in accordance with the terms and licences issued by the CLA. Enquiries concerning reproduction outside these terms should be sent to the publishers at the undermentioned addresses:

2nd Floor, 45 Gee Street	c/o Martin P Hill Consulting	4737/23 Ansari Road
London	122 W 27th St, 10th Floor	Daryaganj
EC1V 3RS	New York, NY 10001	New Delhi 110002
United Kingdom	USA	India

www.koganpage.com

© Laurence Minsky and Colleen Fahey, 2017

The right of Laurence Minsky and Colleen Fahey to be identified as the authors of this work has been asserted by them in accordance with the Copyright, Designs and Patents Act 1988.

ISBN   978 0 7494 7857 5
E-ISBN   978 0 7494 7858 2

British Library Cataloguing-in-Publication Data

A CIP record for this book is available from the British Library.

Library of Congress Cataloging-in-Publication Data

Names: Minsky, Laurence, author. | Fahey, Colleen, author.
Title: Audio branding : using sound to build your brand / Laurence Minsky, Colleen Fahey.
Description: 1st Edition. | New York : Kogan Page Ltd, [2017] | Includes bibliographical references and index.
Identifiers: LCCN 2016058930 (print) | LCCN 2017003807 (ebook) | ISBN 9780749478575 (alk. paper) | ISBN 9780749478582 (ebook)
Subjects: LCSH: Branding (Marketing) | Music in advertising. | Advertising–Brand name products. | Advertising–Psychological aspects.
Classification: LCC HF5415.1255 .M56 2017 (print) | LCC HF5415.1255 (ebook) | DDC 658.8/27–dc23

Typeset by Integra Software Services, Pondicherry
Print production managed by Jellyfish
Printed and bound by CPI Group (UK) Ltd, Croydon, CR0 4YY

CONTENTS

About the authors ix
Foreword xi
Preface xiii
Acknowledgements xvii

01 Wake up to the power of audio branding 1
You have an audio identity – whether you're managing it or not 2
Audio branding: it's not just a sound – or a jingle – but a system 3
Welcome to your worldwide language 7
On the horizon: the sound of the lifestyle gains on the sound of the product 8
The easiest big thing a company can do for a brand 10
Guest perspective: Michaël Boumendil 11
Case: SNCF 16
References 17

02 Audio branding in the digital age 19
Welcome to the new marketing landscape 20
Defining the brand 24
The value of branding: some initial ways to determine it for your brand 30
Guest perspective: Ben DiSanti and Ken Hicks 31
Case: Huggies 40
References 42

03 It's time we came to our sensory marketing 45
Marketers have already set their sights on visual branding 46
What does taste mean in the world of sensory branding? 47
Let's get in touch with the key idea behind tactile branding 48
Time to sniff out the status of olfactory branding 48
And now for some sound thoughts on auditory branding 50

So who should consider audio branding and why? **51**
Guest perspective: Charles Spence **52**
Case: Nestlé, La Roche-Posay and Louis XIII Cognac **59**
References **61**

04 Welcome to the world of audio branding 65

Resilience within a defined structure **66**
Identify your brand's touchpoints – especially where sound design can improve the experience **66**
Guest perspective: Ramón Vives Xiol **77**
Case: MICHELIN **81**
References **82**

05 The search for your sound 85

Symbols, sounds, and structure **86**
Universal vs local. Consistent vs varied **88**
Six audio-branding dos and don'ts for marketers **89**
Guest perspective: Mickey Brazeal **92**
Case: Roland Garros/The French Tennis Open **97**
References **99**

06 What gets measured 103

Deconstruction and layering **105**
Which creative execution? **106**
A simple online questionnaire **108**
Guest perspective: Gene Topper **111**
Case: Intel **116**
References **118**

07 The audio-branding process 121

A familiar process but an exciting one **122**
Brand briefing and analysis **122**
Guest perspective: Neil Gains **131**
Case: Atlanta Convention & Visitors Bureau (ACVB) **134**
References **137**

08   How to launch your audio brand 139
Launch approaches 140
More on the mighty Audio Style Guide 143
Audio Style Guide: an example 144
Guest perspective: Ellen Byron 149
Case: Renault 152
References 156

09   Maintaining and evolving your audio brand 157
United Airlines: a long off-and-on-again relationship with *Rhapsody in Blue* 158
Counter-intuitive but true: protect your audio brand by not playing it 160
Guest perspective: Janet Borgerson and Jonathan Schroeder 162
Case: AXA 171
References 175

10   Music and sound design in environments 177
The trapped audience for environmental music: the staff 178
What to do? Sorry to sound like a broken record: it's all about values 180
Bringing the shopper back to the spirit of the brand 182
Zoning and dayparting: creating specific moods within the same environment 184
Environmental sounds: great opportunities for wit and humour 186
Guest perspective: Mickey Brazeal 187
Case: Barnes-Jewish Hospital 198
References 200

Glossary 203
Index 207

ABOUT THE AUTHORS

Laurence Minsky is recognized in both professional and academic circles for his strategic and creative leadership, his broad-reaching industry experience and expertise in brand foundational development, brand advertising, and brand activation, and for developing effective cross-channel solutions that boost marketing ROI. He serves as an associate professor in the Communication and Media Innovation Department of the School of Media Arts at Columbia College Chicago and as a consultant for agencies, corporations, and nonprofits across the globe.

Laurence is also the co-author of *The Activation Imperative: How to build brands and business by inspiring action*, executive editor of *The Get a Job Workshop: How to find your way to a creative career in advertising, branding, collateral, digital, experiential and more*, the author of *How to Succeed in Advertising When All You Have is Talent*, Second Edition; and a co-author of *Advertising and the Business of Brands* (Media Revolution Edition). As an industry thought-leader, he has been published by the *Harvard Business Review*, MarketingProfs, and others.

He has created marketing and communications solutions for many blue-chip clients, including Laila Ali, Amazon, Bay Valley Foods, Beltone, Black+Decker Spacemaker, Fleetwood Homes, Frito-Lay, George Foreman, The Lakeside Collection, Lamin-Art, Mayo Medical Laboratories, McDonald's, Motorola, PetSmart, Spacelabs Healthcare, Taiwan External Trade Development Council, United Airlines, United States Postal Service, Westinghouse, Vita Foods, and more.

An award-winning creative with over 125 industry accolades to date, he has served on the juries of many leading industry award shows and is a long-standing member of the One Club for Art and Copy, the Authors Guild, and the American Academy of Advertising.

Colleen Fahey Managing Director, Sixième Son USA, is a seasoned creative executive with deep expertise in branding and marketing at multiple touchpoints.

When she learned of Sixième Son, a Paris audio branding agency that had created over 300 audio brands, she approached them about expanding their borders to North America. Three years ago, she opened Sixième Son in the US. Since then she has led Sixième Son's audio branding initiatives for the Atlanta Convention & Visitors Bureau, Huggies, a major research hospital, a college, a top-ten pharmaceutical company, and a global vaccine launch.

Throughout her career, Colleen has worked for major marketing organizations as well as leading brands in the US, Europe, Latin America, and Asia. Her past and present clients include: Atlanta, Huggies, McDonald's, Frito-Lay, Visa, Target Stores, Citibank, US Centers for Disease Control, Kellogg's, and many brands in the Nestlé portfolio, including Purina, Nesquik, Maggi, Nido, Pure Life Waters, Wonka, and Nestlé Ice Creams.

She began her career with Frankel, where she became Executive Creative Director. She also ran a thriving business unit and simultaneously carried executive responsibility for Human Resources and Employee Development, managing over 150 mostly right-brained people.

Post the sale of Frankel to Publicis, Colleen moved onto a global Publicis Worldwide strategic team based in Paris, where her role was to support the network of agencies with branding, path-to-purchase, activation, and kids marketing initiatives, with the goal of building the Nestlé's business around the world.

Raised in Madrid, she speaks fluent Spanish as well as conversational French and pathetic Portuguese.

FOREWORD
Audio branding: a sound investment

Many brands are still operating in the past. As more ways of delivering messages burst onto the scene, the need to offer coherent brand experiences becomes more urgent. In the search for differential advantage, brands need to take advantage of every opportunity to make their values understood.

Years ago, I wrote about the need to manage your atmospherics, discussing the idea that sales of your products are influenced, not just by your reputation, but also by emotional and sensual cues in the environment.

Today the shopping environment has leaked out of physical spaces and into your pocket, your lap, and onto your kitchen table. With this subtraction of the senses found in physical environments, the job of creating a multifaceted brand connection gets even harder. It is critical that brand values, position and personality find their way into all the places and environments in which brand influence takes place.

Enter the mostly untapped language of sound and music. Sound and music can deliver brand meaning and offer both functional cues and emotional connections. Sound and music is available on all the new devices that have supplanted or joined our physical environments.

As a result, today's atmospherics must be designed for devices as well as spaces.

Marketers have accepted that music and sound have key roles to play in their integrated communications, but haven't figured out how to devise an auditory strategy – yet alone how to integrate distinctive soundscapes into their marketing landscape.

That's what this book aims to correct. Minsky and Fahey offer a tested process by which to plan and implement the auditory atmospherics into your brand. The case studies bring texture to their process. And the guest perspectives help round out the academic support as well as demonstrate opportunities for creating your audio brand.

So sit back and read on, because if you care about your brands and getting the most out of them, getting up to speed in the latest thinking in audio branding will be well worth your time.

Philip Kotler, SC Johnson Distinguished Professor
of International Marketing,
Kellogg School of Management, Northwestern University

PREFACE
Why audio branding?

Laurence's story

More than a decade ago, I started working on a campaign to revitalize a regional pickle brand. Searching for a solution, research found an interesting fact: our brand defied the normal lifecycle of pickles. You see, in the typical lifecycle, a consumer opens a jar of pickles and enjoys or serves some of them and then refrigerates. Occasionally, they return to enjoy more, but slowly, the jar makes it to the back of the refrigerator and sits as the pickles get soggy and tossed.

Then the pickle lifecycle started all over again with the purchase of the next jar.

On the other hand, the brand I was to work on didn't experience this lifecycle. Rather, its primary consumers tended to eat up the entire jar, so there was less waste. We decided to launch a campaign based on the idea of 'the emptiest jar in the house'.

As part of this campaign, we also decided to run on radio rather than on TV, with a heavier media buy on Thursdays as the key shopping days approached. To bring our idea to life, the owner of the agency suggested we develop an 'audio icon' of a fork dropping into the empty jar, which ended every spot.

Needless to say, the campaign was a success. We took the failing brand, turned it around, and made it the regional leader. It would even go on to earn a 40 per cent share in some markets. Research showed that when our competitors ran TV spots, consumers would credit these spots to us.

I was hooked.

The academic side of me took over and wanted to learn more about the use of sound to build a brand.

In around 2012, I heard what Colleen was doing as the US managing director of Sixième Son, the world's leading audio-branding firm. I had known her back in the 1990s when we both worked at an agency called Frankel (now Arc Worldwide).

At Frankel, Colleen served as the executive creative director and was considered one of the world's leading experts in kids' marketing.

I was much lower on the agency totem pole, but then working to launch the concept of marketing to employees – and the broader area of employee branding – as a leader of an agency initiative called the 'Walking Brand'.

I learned of Colleen's activities through my then publisher, Bruce Bendinger of the Copy Workshop, while I was working with him to develop the book *The Get a Job Workshop*, a collection of essays from leading professionals as well as exercises designed to serve as 'a roadmap for the new career landscape' in the creative areas of advertising and related marketing disciplines.

My publisher suggested I ask Colleen to donate an essay.

When we met about her essay, I asked Colleen to collaborate with me on a digital article on audio branding for the *Harvard Business Review*. It was my sneaky way of learning more about this intriguing area. (In fact, I continually seek to collaborate with people who are smarter than me as a way to learn and grow.)

Working with Colleen on the first article, I learned that my view of audio branding was still very limited. The abilities and practice of audio branding was much bigger, parallel to visual branding. I knew I needed to learn more about this fascinating and effective yet vastly underutilized field.

We then co-wrote additional articles on audio branding, which were published by places like MarketingProfs.com and the Data Driven Network.

I said that we should write a book on audio branding, particularly given the lack of them on its benefits – and the process on how to create one. Colleen said she was never really motivated to write a book, but when Kogan Page came along, she came on board.

I hope you learn as much about audio branding as I have from Colleen. It's an interesting area and a truly powerful branding tool for smart marketers.

Join us and your brand story might be singing a whole new song.

(And, in the meantime, beyond the acknowledgements, I'd like to thank Colleen for her dedication, drive, and willingness to share her expertise and her husband for letting me steal her time – and my family for their understanding and giving me the time to write this book.)

Colleen's story

At the tail end of 2011, I attended the first Audio Branding Congress ever held in the USA. To be honest, I had no idea what to expect, but someone had offered me a free admission and I had planned to be in New York anyway.

Upon entering the hall at the Colombia University Faculty House, I felt a surge of excitement. The bustling space was echoing with a din of enthusiastic conversation, which I soon realized was in English spoken in many accents that had become familiar to me since my time on the global Nestlé team at Publicis. I could identify the shadings of Dutch, French, British, Brazilian Portuguese, Spanish, Indian, Scandinavian (I can't distinguish among the accents of the different Scandinavian nationalities) and German and/or Austrian. Except for the people who had checked us in, I didn't detect any North American accents.

My trend-seeking antennae went up. What was going on here?

The first presentation outlined the state of the emerging audio-branding world. Frankly, it was far from earth shattering, and the budgets were nothing to write home about. I still couldn't quite understand what exactly was the point, but, as a marketer, I remained politely interested.

It was when the cases started to be presented that my spine began to tingle. I had spent years teaching innovative marketing ideas, leading workshops and giving speeches to brand marketers and agencies all around the world and I had completely missed this powerful concept: the idea that a brand's audio identity could and should be designed to be as meaningful and coherent as its visual identity.

I felt as if I had been living in a cave. This way of thinking struck me as a dead simple but profound and far-reaching idea that had been hiding in the light of the sun.

A Brazilian audio-branding company, Zanna, had created an identity for an over-the-counter pharmaceutical that conveyed a sense of maternal caring and embedded a suggestion of the three-syllable name, Airela, into its audio signature, and a sound for the national water company, Sabesp, which suggested natural sources by making use of the instruments played by indigenous rainforest peoples.

Audio Consulting Group from Germany presented the rich audio brand they had created for UBS in a system that was so thorough that even the 'pink noise' as they called it (music that covered up the transaction conversations but could only be heard if you listened closely) was part of the unified audio identity. Their system included jazz, pop and several classical variations, all beautifully related to each other.

The City of Vienna danced their presentation – and explained that the casual nature of their city, along with its rich musical heritage, inspired them to include the sound of an orchestra tuning up as part of their audio brand.

ING-DiBa-HC had a well-known and well-liked audio logo called 'DiBa-DiBa-Du' based on 'Strangers in the Night'. They had evolved and modernized their audio brand by reinterpreting the melody and adding rhythm surprise as well as a warm voice. This ensured that their new customer orientation was communicated with an audio brand that wasn't too abrupt a change for the audience.

And Sixième Son presented the SNCF French railroad audio identity with its familiar train station signal. The fact that this sound was created with sensitivity toward the anxious mood of the traveller touched me. I began to realize that with this discipline you could not only generate clearer brand understanding but could improve people's experience. I've always believed that the core of good marketing is empathy and I felt that this company was speaking my language.

I was on the edge of my seat. A former colleague who had joined me in the mid-morning wasn't experiencing the same epiphany. His interest was drawn to the entertainment side of the music world. He fidgeted in his chair, checked his messages, stepped out to make phone calls and, eventually, made arrangements to meet some friends in the suburbs and left early. I, in contrast, decided to stop every other marketing pursuit and dedicate the rest of my career to audio branding.

Michaël Boumendil of Sixième Son and I came to an agreement the following year, and I opened Sixième Son in the US in September 2012. This arrangement has given me plenty more chances to hear the SNCF station signal and to aspire to create something equally iconic.

This book is based on our crash course in audio branding that has continually taken place over the four years that followed. It's not intended to be academic or philosophical but to share the stories, the processes, the applications and the best practices that will be helpful to a brand marketer or agency partner who's trying to gain an advantage in a competitive marketplace.

See for yourself – or should we say hear? – and start discovering your audio brand today. It might just be the difference you need to stand out in a highly crowded marketplace and achieve your marketing goals.

ACKNOWLEDGEMENTS

Special thanks to Giannella Alvarez, Paul Bennett, Jane Berliss-Vincent, Janet Borgerson, Casey Brazeal, Mickey Brazeal, Ellen Byron, Courtney Cashman, Laurent Cochini, Ben DiSanti, Ella Duda, Caroline Fabrigas, Philippa Fiszzon, Eric Freedman, Neil Gains, Julien Goris, Delphine Guerin, Anne Hayward, Patrick Herron, Ken Hicks, Wilbert Hirsch, Brian Hodes, Susan Hodgson, David Houle, Molly James-Lundak, Angela Johnson, Ivy Joseph, Colin Kennedy, Kwang-Ku Kim, Philip Kotler, Carrie Leinonen, James Lucas, Suzanne McBride, Alex de Miranda Silva, Margaret Murphy, Jasmin Naim, Charlotte Owen, Andy Peart, Ariella Phillipo, Jonathan Phillipo, Jonathon Price, Traci Ray, Uli Reese, Christopher Richert, Jonathan Schroeder, Victor Siegel, Craig Sigele, Jodee Sorrentino, Charles Spence, Herman Tiemans, Daina Todorovic, Gene Topper, Natasha Tulett, Ramón Vives Xiol, Jennifer Volich, Joe Walsh, John Walther, Stanley Wearden, Claire White, Andrew Wilson, Shelby Yastrow and, of course, our families, the blind peer reviewers (some of whom we will never know, but who helped shape the content in ways they'll never know through their feedback on our proposal and manuscript), as well as the Paris Sixième Son team who keep our spirits up by sending new music files almost daily.

*Dedicated to Michaël Boumendil, the founder of modern audio branding.
Without his vision, insight, and innovations, this book would not exist.*

Wake up to the power of audio branding

01

Brand-oriented companies across the world are just beginning to realize that they must use logos wherever they come into contact with their prospects and customers.

Obvious, you say?

Not entirely. Because while most – if not all – brand marketers are using visual logos, it is still the dawn of the age of the audio logo.

Though there are a few audio logos that most people can recognize, like those for Intel, and even fewer that they can hum, like McDonald's, many companies have overlooked the fact that, as media has moved into the digital age, it has become audio-enabled. Gone is the sales flipchart, replaced by an app with a dashboard. Lost is the morning printed newspaper, replaced by a news site. Moved aside are paper posters, replaced by digital signage. And, most importantly, the fastest-growing marketing platform right now is an ever-present audio-enabled computer that fits in a pocket: the smartphone.

The time has come for brands to take sound seriously and to use its exceptional power to be recognized and understood across all the points that they come in contact with: their prospects, customers, employees, and other key constituents.

In today's world, brands must now treat sound with the same care and discipline as they do their graphic standards and visual brand-building.

Because, just as graphics do, sound carries meaning. And just like properly employed visual branding programmes, the strategic use of sound can play a pivotal role in positively differentiating a product or service, enhancing recall, creating preference, building trust, and perhaps most importantly, increasing sales and marketing return on investment (ROI).

If you're stuck in the visual-only branding world, you are competing with one hand tied behind your back, weakening your efforts, because, as you'll see, cognitive studies show that relevant sounds and musical cues can truly influence people in ways marketers want.

You have an audio identity – whether you're managing it or not

Take a tour of your company in your mind. What music is playing on your customer service line? What music is in your training videos? Your YouTube videos? What ringtones do the sales reps use? Which songs were played at your company meeting? What music played in your advertising last year? Is it different this year?

Think of a typical brand. They probably used *Chariots of Fire*, *Hunger Games*, or *Star Wars* themes for their sales or annual meetings, Vivaldi's *Four Seasons* for their on-hold music, an 80s' or 90s' pop song for their commercials, the *Dragnet* theme for one training video and 'Rock Around the Clock' for yet another, and perhaps a startling metallic 'ping' for the app-opening sounds.

What is that example brand saying about itself?

Is it an energetic or aspirational brand? A classical and delicate brand? A pop-culture brand? A technological brand? Is it reliable? In other words, trustworthy?

Or is it a muddled, disoriented brand?

If the auditory selections don't relate to each other in the world of sound, you're wasting branding opportunities right and left. In fact, you are like our example: you are creating brand chaos and confusion.

In the visual sphere, your brand becomes more and more recognizable as people see its familiar colours, typefaces, shapes, logos, and other imagery used consistently, repeatedly, and frequently every time they encounter it. The Graphic Style Guide lays out a system and a point-of-view. The logo may be expressed a bit differently on a giant billboard than on a tiny business card but it will conform to the same standards. The logo at the end of a sales video will match the one in the commercials and on the website, and on the packaging. Colours and fonts remain the same too. Nobody would dare change IBM's sturdy blue to vibrant orange so they could 'infuse energy' into a sales meeting.

Why then, do some companies still use sounds from completely different universes for their meetings, retail environments, on-hold music, apps, videos, and other touchpoints? Why are they conscientious about branding their graphics and sloppy with branding their music? And, why do they think that advertising is the only medium that requires serious attention to the musical selection?

It's not hard to create a consistent but flexible audio universe that allows for both serious business situations and fun, high-energy occasions – as well as everything in between. It works like visual branding, but with some key differences. We'll explore the similarities and differences in the following pages and lay out a manageable process for developing, launching, and maintaining an audio brand for your products or services.

Audio branding: it's not just a sound – or a jingle – but a system

Welcome to the world of audio branding. Also referred to as sound branding, acoustic branding, and sonic branding, depending on the practitioner, it is the systematic creation of an entire audio language for the brand based on its essence, vision, values, promise, and personality – a language that gets expressed across every point at which your brand interacts with your key constituents, from the web and apps to trade shows and business meetings to TV to the retail environment and even the product itself.

And just as the verbal or visual brand expression is optimized at each point, the audio expressions are also sensitively adapted and optimized across the spectrum, so they're functionally and psychologically appropriate to the medium and the audience mindset.

Conversations about audio branding with marketers who are new to this idea, however, tend to get stuck down an advertising cul-de-sac. Often, they focus on jingles of yesteryear – those cute little slogans put to music that worked so well when commercials were 60 seconds long. And, while jingles technically fall within the audio-branding arena, as they do employ sound, people who focus on them are taking a very limited view of the discipline's opportunities and benefits. The music in an old-school jingle was typically composed to support the words rather than to build the brand. So the music doesn't create much brand equity and has limited applications beyond media advertising. And the lyrics are often merely a name and phone number or a feature of the product or service, so they too have limited ability to convey the brand character and extend the brand influence.

Other conversations tend to focus on the marketer's frustration with the fact that their ad agencies typically wait until the last minute and then present them with three choices of licensable music, some of which is, inevitably, too expensive. All of which is short-term, ad campaign-oriented rather than long-term, brand-building-focused.

These marketers – both in the business-to-business (B2B) and business-to-consumer (B2C) arenas – forget that customers, partners, and employees experience the brand at many auditory junctures.

In other words, audio branding is not just about the music in advertising and the sounds at the end of it. Rather, it is about thoughtful and inspired design, except instead of designing for sight, it requires designing for sound.

A few marketers might define audio branding as the distinctive sounds that are 'owned' by the brand that are used in mostly non-advertising situations.

Some examples.

Samsung Galaxy plays an elegant bespoke ringtone; Nokia uses a now-familiar snippet of a classical composition, Francisco Tárrega's *Grand Valse*; Harley roars with a branded 'po-ta-to, po-ta-to, po-ta-to' sound; Snapple opens with a gratifying pop; and the Apple operating system comes to life with a glowing start-up sound. These trademark sounds do exemplify the brands but only represent the tip of the audio-branding iceberg.

While these sounds are within the realm of audio branding and capture the analogy of 'design', the practice is actually more sophisticated than the use of an isolated sound for packaging, the singular reliance of a quaint jingle at the end of a TV or radio spot, or the choice of a simple and discrete audio logo such as the notes attached to the 'Intel Inside' button. Parallel to visual brand-building through visual design, the purposeful integration, design, and usage of all the brand's sounds are what makes the use of audio branding so compelling. And like visual branding, the brand sounds and music should be strategically employed across the entire experience, whenever possible, becoming a valuable asset of it. In fact, these sounds should be so strong that listeners recall the brand and its emotional impressions when they hear them, even without visual cues or words.

A UK example in which a consistent use of tailored music played a key role was demonstrated by Barclaycard from 1991 to 1997 (Roberts, 2005). According to the Barclay archives, their then-new agency (Barclays, 2016), BMP DDB Needham, was responsible for spoof spy commercials played by Rowan Atkinson. These spots featured an overconfident and supercilious character that, much like James Bond, had his own music, a very recognizable theme tune. Unlike Bond, this accident-prone character, 'Richard Latham', created havoc: burning rugs, breaking teapots, mistaking a senior MI5 official for a plumber. But his sidekick 'Bough', wielding a Barclaycard, always got him out of trouble.

The series of mini-movie-like commercials became extremely popular. The TV campaign was so long-running as to create a clear and recognizable earprint.

'During the 90s, people would hear the music and they'd run to the television,' said Angela Johnson, then business director overseeing the Barclaycard business at the agency. Eventually, the popular character found his way into the entertainment world with a film called *Johnny English* (Fahey, 2016).

A US brand that has gone further with their brand sound, and is often cited by marketers, is United Airlines. The airline has used *Rhapsody in Blue* since 1987 when they licensed George Gershwin's famous piece for $300,000 per year (Shales, 1987). Not only is the composition used in advertising; it graces a long moving walkway to the play of multicoloured lights in their Chicago terminal. Of course, travellers also hear the melody on their airplanes, call centres, and even adapted to their pre-take-off safety videos. *Rhapsody in Blue* is linked to the brand to such an extent that the famous melody survived a merger with Continental Airlines, although the United Airlines visual logo changed completely.

There will be an interesting crossroads when the music goes in to public domain in the US in 2019 (AudioSparx, 2014). At that point it will become freely available to any brand that covets it. That situation illustrates one of the dangers of using licensed music rather than investing in the creation of one's own core audio DNA.

As in the case of United Airlines, branded music and sounds can play both aesthetic and functional roles in most places where customers and employees meet the brand. They can make a wait feel shorter, make a corridor feel less interminable, add a sense of calm to an airport or train station, give employees a feeling of belonging, bring excitement to an event, take away the foreboding feeling of an unfamiliar parking lot (and providing a cue for remembering where you had parked), clarify a story or idea in the media advertising, all while subtly transmitting the essence and values of the brand.

In other words, audio branding is equally important to environments as to communication elements.

Walk into the admissions area of a university hospital and you'll hear the clatter of carts, the chatter of announcements, the buzz of phones… everything that says, 'You're in an institutional environment'. Nothing to say, 'Welcome, friend'. No sounds to help convey the experience you wish for the patient, family, or even staff, such as confidence, caring, optimism, teamwork, or scientific rigour.

Enter the equally large Unibail-Rodamco shopping centre in Lyon, France, and you get a different experience entirely. The music has been designed to suggest that a *magical* experience is in store for you. All along the route there are moments of auditory surprise, humour, and humanity. Plant walls carrying the sounds of birdsong and waterfalls, chairs whispering calming meditations, soothing music, or children's stories, corridors scored at a relaxed walking pace – all threaded with the sound of the brand.

And at a Lancôme Beauty Institute in Kuala Lumpur, Malaysia, a blogger reports on the treatment rooms, 'The music is original and specifically made for Lancôme, designed to be in harmony with the motions used in the treatment.' It's not the same old spa music. It supports both the experience and the brand (Zatashah, 2010).

So you may wonder what links the hospital, the mall, and the beauty institute. The answer is simple: all of them have the chance to use sounds and music to change the way people view the setting, the brand, and their experience. But while the shopping mall and beauty institute are using auditory elements to their full potential, the hospital is missing a valuable opportunity to use sound to create a positive connection with any of its various target audiences.

The take-away: if your organization is like the hospital, you are probably overlooking the power of audio to convey important messages and build relationships.

But while the practice of comprehensive audio branding is still essentially in its infancy – giving smart, visionary brands a unique opportunity to stand out – there are places on the globe that are more advanced than others in the use of audio branding. So if you are an international brand (or are not from those countries, which we'll identify in subsequent chapters), your competitors may be one step ahead of you.

To start, note that Huggies and Baby Bell deployed new global audio brands in 2016. L'Oréal's brand for sensitive skincare, LaRoche-Posay, debuted theirs in 2015. Peugeot added a new global audio identity as part of its rebranding effort in 2014. AXA has used one since 2008 and Michelin put one in place in 2010 (see Chapter 4 for a case study on their powerful audio brand).

The healthcare sector is now paying attention too. Dengvaxia, the world's first licensed vaccine against dengue fever, is using a distinctive audio identity to carry its message to the tropical parts of the globe where the disease is rampant.

A large US teaching hospital that competes for medical tourism patients began to subtly introduce an audio vocabulary into their new commercials with the vision that it would establish a base for the audio design of their new building that's now under construction.

Audio branding is also showing up in the business-to-business space. Areva, the world's largest provider of nuclear energy, uses an audio brand

and so does the city of Atlanta, which competes mightily for convention business with larger and like-sized cities around the United States and the world.

Welcome to your worldwide language

Why are international brands going to the trouble of framing their audio identities?

Because music is a language that people all around the world can understand. It carries universal meaning, which works at a symbolic rather than an explicit level. No matter the culture where they grew up or the country they're from, people are similar in the way they decode the intention of music and other sounds.

People around the world know if music feels optimistic or melancholy; they can tell if it's soothing or stressful; they can feel if it's authoritative or modest; they can identify if it's fun and light-hearted or powerful and serious. That transcultural understanding is of real value to brands that operate in multiple countries (or even in multilingual, multicultural countries).

There are both learned and innate reasons for this.

On the cultural side, people in every corner of the globe have been exposed to the many movies and TV shows that share a musical vocabulary for setting up the tense situations, heightening joyful ones, underscoring melancholy scenes, and announcing triumph. The language of movie music has been well learned by people across the globe, regardless of geographies and cultures.

Beyond movies, Western popular music has zipped around the globe at increasing speed. And not just Western music originating in the West. In 2012 'Gangnam Style' became the first music video to reach one billion YouTube views and had topped the charts of more than 30 countries, including Australia, Germany, Russia, Spain, and France.

Though it is becoming increasingly difficult to find cultures that haven't been exposed to Western music, field studies indicate that music communicates similar meanings even among people who haven't previously been exposed to it. In fact, people previously unexposed to Western music are able to recognize 'happiness', 'fear' and 'sadness' in it.

Researcher Thomas Fritz, from the Max Planck Institute for Human Cognitive and Brand Sciences in Germany believes this may help explain the universal popularity of Western music (Sprey, 2009).

Fritz and his team conducted two experiments with a group of 21 Mafa, remote farmers in Cameroon, Africa, who said they'd had no previous exposure to Western music. They were exposed to 42 instrumental excerpts of Western music with different tempos, pitch ranges, and rhythms including classical, jazz, rock, and pop. A group of 20 Germans was used as a control.

They were then asked whether they thought each piece of music expressed the emotions of 'happiness,' 'sadness' or 'fear' and to point to photos of faces showing the relevant expressions. The Mafa's ability to correctly identify the Western music's expression of the emotions was far greater than chance, picking the 'happy' music, on average, 60 per cent of the time. Meanwhile, the German control group, in contrast, scored 100 per cent with 'happy' music. As such, pieces with higher tempos were more likely to be classified as 'happy' and songs with lower tempos as 'fearful' or 'scary'.

'Most likely the Mafa were picking up on the same "tone of voice" cues used in human speech,' said study team member Stefan Koelsch, also from the Max Planck Institute. 'Western music mimics the emotional features of human speech, using the same melodic and rhythmic structures' (Sprey, 2009).

The music that Peugeot adopted in 2014 has shown that meaning delivered by an audio-brand identity has border-crossing abilities, too. A quantitative test in five countries – France, Spain, UK, Russia and Brazil – has shown that people hear the same connotations in the music. The sum of the parts added up to a more modern, stylish, and emotional image for the brand in all the countries, though the effect was stronger in countries in which the brand was a more recent arrival than in countries where it had a long-established image.

On the horizon: the sound of the lifestyle gains on the sound of the product

As did Peugeot, which sought to bring more emotion and style into its brand image, more and more brands are beginning to re-think their approach to audio and, recently, there has been an evolution from sounds based in function or product attributes, to sounds based in emotion and lifestyle. Nowhere is this more apparent than in the automotive sector.

The sector once expressed itself only in metallic and engine-like sounds. The old BMW audio logo was a double-note that sounded like a hammer hitting metal. It reflected the power, security, and boldness of the brand. It was very recognizable and on-brand. But by 2014 the brand's position changed, and the metallic sound no longer reflected its new stance.

BMW moved to a more emotional audio universe that carries the idea of power and conquest (BMW, 2013).

In the same category, a very different brand, Renault, was going through a very similar evolution. The audio logo that accompanied its previous tagline, 'Drive the Change', was punctuated by a metallic sound (Posada, 2012). But the new audio logo features a haunting tune and is carried by a woman's airy voice, which seems to contain a sigh, to convey the essence of its new tagline, 'Passion for Life' (Sixième Son, 2015a).

As illustrated by the automotive category above, when it comes to audio, sectors tend to get stuck in their traditional approaches and will default to specific sound styles. These can be thought of as category codes.

One category may use big orchestral musical arrangements while another category might use chimes. We've discovered that it's often the category leaders who break the mould and lead the way to new, more expansive audio territories.

For a specific example, the transportation sector often employed bells, chimes, or beeps that originated in the historical ringing to signal a train approaching or leaving a station. Now rail lines, subways, and airlines are using music that suggests the anticipation of the journey, the feeling of fluid movement, or the magic of the city. For instance, in Spain, France, Austria, Switzerland and Japan, you can find public transportation authorities adding evocative sounds and music rather than beeps and bells. France's national railway, SNCF, implemented their recognizable audio identity in 2004, a case study that we'll explore at the end of this chapter (Sixième Son, 2015b); Spain's RENFE launched their audio brand in 2006 (Audio Branding Academy, 2012a); and the public transportation in Vienna introduced theirs in 2012 (Audio Branding Academy, 2012b).

The same trend can be seen in the financial sector. To show stability and deep resources, the financial sector tended toward classical music with large orchestras. Then came the market slump in 2008 and 2009 and they had to be less bombastic, a bit more humble. In banking, there has been a movement toward lighter orchestral sounds and catchy pop tunes in an attempt to convey less distance from their audience. An exception, however, is ING Direct, France, which through a spacious composition containing few notes and played on a glockenspiel expresses a friendly, uncomplicated brand that promises ease-of-use.

And in the telecoms world, the audio identities tended to have been connected to sounds of landline telephones. But with the advent of smartphones, led by Apple's focus on lifestyle, the sounds have become more human, featuring more glittering, luxurious sounds.

The easiest big thing a company can do for a brand

An audio identity can lend a coherent voice across touchpoints, geographies, and product lifecycle. It captures the mind when the audience isn't directly paying attention. It allows a brand to stand out and be distinctive. It creates brand value that grows over the years.

On the operational side, it can simplify the job of global and local marketing departments both in decision-making and in reduction of the complexity. When the engineering department wants to know what sound to add to a device, they have a framework; when the social media group needs to score a video, they have a library to turn to; when a local agency needs to run a promotional ad, they don't have to negotiate a separate licence for the music.

Given today's omnichannel, audio-enabled, interconnected marketing environment, as a brand leader you must ask yourself, 'Can my customers identify my brand with their eyes closed?'

If the answer is no, then you need this book. Just as the earliest visual logos and branding programmes are iconic today, a wide variety of audio brands will become truly iconic tomorrow. So, if you do not have an audio brand, the time to get started is now. After all, done right, your efforts can provide rewards for years to come.

In the following pages, we're going to describe the process for creating a powerful audio brand. We'll start with a brief overview of where it fits in the branding universe and go through maintaining and updating your audio brand. It needn't be scary. After all, there is much overlap with processes and theories of traditional visual branding (but with a few key differences).

You should find *Audio Branding: Using sound to build your brand* to be a practical guide for developing your audio brand, making it perfect for chief marketing officers (CMOs) and their brand marketing teams in both B2C and B2B environments as well as agencies specializing in branding, digital, social media, advertising, mobile, event marketing, and more. Plus, with our focus on the practical over the theoretical, marketing, advertising, branding, and, yes, music composition students should find *Audio Branding: Using sound to build your brand* an approachable entry into this emerging discipline – a discipline filled with a quickly growing range of career opportunities.

So sit back and please enjoy whilst we immerse you in the power of audio branding and the process of creating one.

GUEST PERSPECTIVE   Michaël Boumendil

Music to your brand: the story of the first official audio-branding firm and the birth of audio branding

Michaël Boumendil founded Sixième Son, the first sound design firm solely dedicated to audio branding, in 1995.

Before Sixième Son, there were jingle houses that created songs for the end of television and radio spots; there were companies that distributed canned, easy, non-objectionable music into elevators, retail outlets, shopping centres, and more (the most historically famous company being Muzak); and there were sound designers for movies, plays, and television shows (as well as some events). And, yes, some brand-associated soundscapes, such as the NBC chimes here in the United States, became audio icons.

But Boumendil and his team were the first to treat sound design as an intentional branding mechanism, 'creating unique and coherent musical universes', the same way graphic and experiential designers create visual branding.

Join us as we explore how Boumendil got the idea for Sixième Son and the founding of his agency, told in his own words. Please note that his comments were edited for clarity.

It's been 20 plus years since I created Sixième Son. Did I have a precise idea in mind at that time? Both yes and no. I had the idea for Sixième Son (as a loose concept), at the end of high school.

At the time, I was experiencing what might be called a fairly tough separation. I'd been creating and performing a lot of music in those days and a record company had offered me a contract. Though it was tempting, I said no, because I did not want to become an artist with a big ego and all the other encumbrances of that profession. And since I primarily find inspiration in collaborating with others, a career as a performing artist didn't feel natural to me.

The idea of Sixième Son was actually imposed upon me. To be concrete, I had a dream in which I saw myself selling brand identity. Instead of coming up with a logo, I arrived at the client with something else: the *sound*.

Beyond that, when I watched commercials, the way brands used music made no sense to me. The use of music was tactical, ad hoc. It was chosen to accompany or illustrate a message, but it was not created to *be* the message. This seemed to be a waste because musical memory is extremely strong. And for this reason, the musical memory that we provide people with must be rewarding. In short, I liked the idea of exploring a new approach to the use of music for brands.

At the time, I set this idea aside, but it continued to ripen in a corner of my mind.

In those days, brands' musical messages were not sufficiently distinctive or differentiating. I came to realize that the challenge of a musical message is not merely to create impact. It is essential that the music also contain meaning. The challenge for a brand is not only to get noticed but to get noticed for the right reasons. So I quickly discerned this distinction in my mind.

I often draw a parallel with the way we dress. A strong sense of personal identity goes into the clothing choices that we make.

When we get dressed in the morning, we encounter a double challenge. First, we want to be comfortable with how we see ourselves in the mirror, but we also want to know that the impression made on others, and conversely reflected back to us through their eyes, will be positive and rewarding.

We also seek the quirk or 'trademark' if you will. I think of it this way: If we were all uniform, no one would stand out. But these personal touches help us differentiate ourselves. So it is for branding, too.

Every aspect of a brand contains both functional and emotional dimensions. The basic idea of design is to ally the useful with the beautiful. The challenge in brand design is to find a way to respond to the functional aspects but not to let them dominate the thinking that leads to the brand's creative expression. That's because, if we create a response to the function without taking the emotional dimension into account, it often crashes. Realizing the importance of that duality was a key to my approach when I created Sixième Son.

After some years, I had reached the stage where I was convinced that the idea of audio identities for brands had merit. But what I didn't know was how to bring it to life.

I quickly realized it was all well and good to have an idea, but that would not suffice. I decided to spend about three or four months getting in touch with people from whom I could get feedback and recommendations.

All these interviews helped me to mature. I began to understand several things.

First, I put my finger on what was to become our key 'deliverable' – a change in people's perceptions of the brand. I also realized that the value of our work would not be music itself. The value of our work is in enriching the link between the brand and its audience through the sound identity we would create. The challenge would be to make beneficial and meaningful music, so that it represents the brand values.

There was also the fundamental question of how work would be created and delivered. Pretty soon, I realized I had to bring everything in-house. That would be essential to the development of a sustainable and comprehensive expertise. It sounds ambitious, but the surest way to produce extraordinary results is to assemble a team of in-house creatives paired with brand strategy consultants.

In those days in France, you were required to have 50,000 francs before you could start a company. I didn't have anywhere near that amount, so I lived a double life. I carried out business meetings by day and, by night, I played music in bars and at house parties to earn the money I needed to open the company.

I gradually managed to raise the money for the creation of Sixième Son. And in parallel, through my many meetings, I met two people who were to become important to the launch of the agency. The first one was a creative person who had a musical expertise that was complementary to my own. The second person was very enthusiastic about the concept of audio branding and made it plain that he really wanted to help bring it to market. This was also the basis for the organization as I had imagined it: a creative part, together with a consultancy.

In fact, as our way of working evolved, we realized it would be impossible to dissociate these two portions of the task. My role as a creator is to say, 'This is what I hear in my mind, these are my convictions.' That's how it works with everyone in the creative team. From there, we dialogue, we exchange, and we experiment.

At the end of the day, we at Sixième Son work like a laboratory in the sense that no one works alone. It is extremely important to keep this bond among the participants in the process. The intelligence of the solutions comes from making sure there are no breaks in the cables uniting the strategic and creative teams.

Being extremely short of money, we started the business in a shared office space in a distant and decidedly not chic area south-east of Paris, Saint-Maur-des-Fosses. We were offered three months' free rent. It was so far from the centre that we could only book one meeting in the entire day.

Despite all our client acquisition strategies, our first client resulted from a night in a bar in which far too much alcohol had been consumed. My colleague met a marketing person from MATIF, a futures exchange, who was equally tipsy and, together, they decided his business needed audio branding. The next day, we showed up at his offices sober to explain our approach to music and sound design for brands.

We told him that, if the company didn't feel happy with the work, they wouldn't have to pay a penny. Luckily, they did pay their bill in the end. And, with that, we were on our way. And our first major client was Alstom, which had been born from the merger of two previous companies and was planning to launch its new brand name.

The idea of a different approach to music was brought to them by their branding agency, CBA, who recommended us. The client had her suspicions, but said that we would be granted one meeting. If they weren't persuaded then and there, we'd never be back.

We managed to convince her that our approach to music would embody the philosophy, values, and personality of her brand. This, in turn, would speed awareness, acceptance and understanding of the company itself. With that formative project, we encountered obstacles that pushed us to grow and become more professional. It was extremely hard and very rewarding at the same time. It left a special imprint on our memories because the project had all the traits of a difficult challenge: a very big company, short deadlines, and a tough customer, because she, herself, was under pressure, and, consequently, that engagement became the crucible in which we clarified and refined our business approach.

At the end of the project, the client had begun to see us as a strategic resource and as a sounding board for her ideas; she doubled our budget and, more importantly, became our biggest advocate.

In the early days of Sixième Son, we primarily sought to nurture referrals rather than to focus on making money. But when we began to work with such a world-class enterprise as Alstom, inventors of the high-speed train and the largest energy provider in France, we realized we would have the opportunity to become who we imagined we would be.

But we would have to operationalize our vision, and fast.

To achieve our goal, we would have to invest in people, infrastructure, technology, and knowledge. And we would have to put in place an organization dedicated to continuous improvement and constant learning both musically and strategically.

We soon realized that our charging practices must also support our aspirations, because we couldn't sustain a vision of this size on piecework projects. This led us to define our pricing strategy, which is a combination of short- and long-term charges in the form of project and licensing fees. This has allowed us to keep a team intact and, together as an organization, add layers of knowledge and ever-growing perspective on business and branding. This knowledge only builds as we work with more sectors, more countries, more points of brand contact, and more technologies.

Finally, if I often repeat my conviction that what nourishes expertise is the constant urge to learn, it is because the Sixième Son story proves this to be true. There's so much to learn from contact with others. Their thoughts and reactions can us help work our way through to new methods and solutions. At Sixième Son, the more we advance, the more we are able to live up to the ideals we talk about. Conversely, the more experience we gather, the better we learn how to talk about what we do.

Guest biography

Michaël Boumendil is Founder, President and Chief Creative Officer of Sixieme Son. A musician, composer, producer and branding expert, Michaël founded Sixième Son in 1995 and, with it, invented the concept of branded audio identities and musical design for companies. At the age of 23, he foresaw a new horizon in the application of music to serve brand communications. Today, Sixieme Son has become the leader in audio branding with clients spanning the globe. The agency's unique expertise is widely recognized in the world of branding and communication. And Michaël, who speaks French, English, Spanish, and Italian, spends a lot of his time on airplanes nurturing his ever-growing company.

CASE SNCF

Sound study: a case study of a 'moving' audio brand

Now that we have met the founder of modern audio branding, let's look at one of their well-known audio-branding projects – the French national railway, SNCF.

In conjunction with Sixième Son, SNCF launched an audio-branding initiative in 2005 for two key reasons. First, already in competition with airlines, they were also beginning to compete with German and Italian railroads. Second, consumers, when asked, associated SNCF with 'strikes and delays'.

They started their initiative by conducting a study of all the audio in their competitive set, revealing a lack of distinctiveness. They then created an audio DNA with the goal of communicating their leadership along with the comfort and caring that distinguished the brand.

It was introduced with a film that drew the connection between the company's heritage and its new position.

To bring the audio DNA to life, the music was interpreted in various ways. The station messages, for example, took into account travellers' anxiety. For those, the music was calm and reassuring.

Though the TV end frame uses the same tune, it has a more authoritative sound with more emphasis on rhythm.

The customer service line draws from the same audio DNA, but provides surprises and variety to make the wait feel shorter. And the now-familiar music was also adapted to the needs of meetings, corporate messages, brand advertising, and communications needs all throughout the company.

While the audio DNA has remained intact, the expression has evolved since its launch, in keeping with the developing brand. The first appearance in 2005, for instance, had to capture the idea of *leadership*, which led to a dynamic and authoritative musical universe, employing a rhythmic approach and a distinctive sound. Then in 2008, to emphasize the brand's *eco-mobility*, the instrumentation became more natural and acoustic.

And finally, in 2012, the brand needed to impart its new vision of simple, direct, and easy *mobility*, so sounds were simplified and a whoosh of speed was introduced. SNCF made a bold decision to give up the usual codes of the category and create something to which no link to the past existed, but that underscored its then current leadership and brand values. As a result, the audio brand has turned into a significant asset for SNCF. For instance, they found that they are correctly identified in testing by 92 per cent of the listeners – and that

88 per cent of these listeners correctly identified the brand upon hearing just two notes. Perhaps more significantly, 71 per cent of them now see the brand as being 'attractive' or 'very attractive', and SNCF has experienced an 18 per cent increase in the perception of leadership.

The SNCF audio logo then caught the attention of the legendary David Gilmour of Pink Floyd and became the inspiration for the title track of his first album in a decade, *Rattle that Lock*. 'I recorded it on my smartphone at the TGV Aix station… Every time I travel in France by train, which happens quite often on holiday or with my profession, when I hear that little music "papalala" in the Gare du Nord or Gare de Lyon, it makes me want to sing and dance,' he recalled (Samuel, 2015).

After Gilmour heard the four-note SNCF tune over a public-address system, he called Sixième Son and asked to talk with Michaël Boumendil, who was so convinced it was his friends playing a prank on him that he didn't return the call. After getting a second message, Boumendil did call the number and was so startled to hear his rock hero's voice on the other end of the line that he immediately hung up.

Gilmour was calling to obtain permission to integrate the tune of the station signal into his song and to offer Boumendil the opportunity to co-author the piece. Together with SNCF, they reached an agreement and within a couple of years, the song 'Rattle that Lock' broke at number one in France and the UK and as of 2016 the music video has received well over four million views (Gilmour, 2015).

In an interview by Jack Marshall in the *Wall Street Journal*, Christophe Fanichet, Head of Communications and Information for SNCF said, 'David Gilmour is a bit of a living legend. Like everywhere, there are a lot of David Gilmour and Pink Floyd fans within SNCF. The song is a kind of tribute to our jingle and we are touched that it has inspired such a musician' (Marshall, 2015).

References

Audio Branding Academy (2012a) *RENFE Sound Branding* [online] Audio-branding-academy.org, http://audio-branding-academy.org/aba/congress/2012-2/case-submissions/renfe/ [accessed 30 December 2015]

Audio Branding Academy (2012b) *Wiener Linien Sound Branding* [online] Audio-branding-academy.org, http://audio-branding-academy.org/aba/wiener-linien/ [accessed 30 December 2015]

AudioSparx (2014) *Knowledge Base Article: KB2421* [online] AudioSparx.com, https://www.audiosparx.com/sa/faq_article.cfm/kbarticle_iid.2421 [accessed 9 April 2016]

Barclays (2016) *Stories* [online] archive.barclays.com, https://www.archive.barclays.com/items/show/5404 [accessed 28 September 2016]

BMW (2013) CarPark: BMW New Sound Logo [online] https://www.youtube.com/watch?v=74UVjXOyvWM [accessed 29 December 2015]

Fahey, C (2016) Interview with Angela Johnson

Gilmour, D (2015) David Gilmour: *Rattle that Lock* (official music video) [online] https://www.youtube.com/watch?v=L1v7hXEQhsQ [accessed 28 March 2016]

Marshall, J (2015) Pink Floyd's David Gilmour Samples Brand Jingle for New Single [blog] *The Wall Street Journal – CMO Today*, http://blogs.wsj.com/cmo/2015/08/03/pink-floyds-david-gilmour-samples-brand-jingle-for-new-single/ [accessed 3 August 2015]

Posada, Nestor Daniel (2012) Jingle Renault [online] https://www.youtube.com/watch?v=2eeJjhaZdVw [accessed 30 December 2015]

Roberts, T (2005) My Favorite Campaign: Barclaycard series was a credit to advertising, *Campaign* [online] http://www.campaignlive.co.uk/article/510006/favourite-campaign—barclaycard-series-credit-advertising# [accessed 1 October 2016]

Samuel, H (2015) French national rail jingle inspiration behind Pink Floyd legend David Gilmour's new single [online] http://www.telegraph.co.uk/news/worldnews/europe/france/11747453/French-national-rail-jingle-inspiration-behind-Pink-Floyd-legend-David-Gilmours-new-single.html [accessed 14 October 2016]

Shales, T (1987) Gershwin's Rhapsody Perfect Pitch? Commercializing a classic to sell United's friendly skies, *The Washington Post* [online] https://www.washingtonpost.com/archive/lifestyle/1987/11/25/gershwins-rhapsody-perfect-pitch-commercializing-a-classic-to-sell-uniteds-friendly-skies/fff855e7-4a7f-4d40-80d6-260c06c59147/ [accessed 9 April 2016]

Sixième Son (2015a) Renault-Signature Sonore / Audio Logo [online] https://www.youtube.com/watch?v=sqVtN4OFY3k [accessed 30 December 2015]

Sixième Son (2015b) *SNCF: An audio identity that has become the sound of France itself*, Client Cases [online] Sixième Son.com, http://www.sixiemeson.com/en/audio-identity-sncf.html [accessed 30 December 2015]

Sprey, K (2009) *Music really is a universal language*, New Atlas [online] http://newatlas.com/western-music-universal-language/11246/ [accessed 1 October 2009]

Zatashah, P (2010) LANCÔME Beauty Institute, Frog + Princess Blog [online] https://frogandprincess.wordpress.com/tag/lancome-beauty-institute/ [accessed 23 January 2017]

Audio branding in the digital age 02

In the first chapter, we saw how the use of sound is a powerful but underutilized branding tool. But is branding even important today and, if so, what do you need as the foundation of a strong brand?

We raise these two questions because with today's nearly pure transparency powered by online search and the accessibility of consumer reviews, some argue that branding has lost its importance and that the pulling power of brands is now over (Lee, 2015). They argue that search and content marketing is the way to market and point to some select examples of organizations that built their company by online sales using these marketing approaches. It's easy to fall into the trap of claiming they are universal.

However, these businesses are building brand images whether they like it or not or have decided to consciously shape them.

Yes, people research and shop online. But that doesn't mean they suspend their prior knowledge and impressions and make decisions based on hard facts.

And, yes, for some shoppers, a brand image isn't important. For example, audiences who are more knowledgeable about a particular area are more likely to discount the power of brands in those areas and look at functionality – such as doctors, who are more likely to use generic medicines than are general consumers of over-the-counter medicines, or professional chefs who are more comfortable using unbranded ingredients than are home cooks (Bronnenberg *et al*, 2015).

But these customers are able to take a very functional approach to their shopping (Bronnenberg *et al*, 2015). For the rest, brands provide a powerful shortcut. As Julia Tang Peters, one of our former colleagues, leadership expert, psychologist (she's a licensed family therapist), business advisor, and author of *Pivot Points: Five decisions every leader must make*, likes to point out, branding creates cognitive bias (Minsky, 2016).

Also, people buy more than functionality or features. We're truly emotional animals and, when in doubt, select the stronger brand (Hollis, 2007). What's more, consumers also select and adopt brands because they help them convey a statement about themselves (Wellington, 2016).

So it's no wonder that branding is one of the top concerns of CEOs and CMOs, and smart firms are investing as much as ever on their branding initiatives – especially online. In the digital area alone, US advertisers are spending approximately '$17.46 billion on branding, or 41.6 per cent of total digital spend and by 2017, [the online] branding spend is expected to grow to $29.33 billion, or a 48.5 per cent share' (eMarketer, 2013).

In other words, as the marketplace becomes ever more crowded, branding is now playing an even more important strategic role. The rules have changed. But so has branding (a reason, perhaps, why the aforementioned marketing pundits got it wrong). And, perhaps another reason the pundits got it wrong is that most B2B and B2C organizations have not evolved their branding tools, so they're arguably seeing less advantage as a result of their efforts – if they're realizing any advantage at all (Rodgers, 2008).

Meanwhile, Laurence's recent book with William Rosen, *The Activation Imperative*, detailed how CMOs are requiring better short-term results and accountability, but also showed marketers how to build their brands while building businesses, reminding readers that marketers need 'to create a programme that so clearly and uniquely embodies the brand that even without a logo, audiences would know that it was an effort from the brand and not one of its competitors' (Rosen and Minsky, 2017).

The book also cautions marketers that 'while today's consumers are playing a larger and more active role in defining brand meaning (a role many would say consumers have always played, albeit less visibly), marketers cannot abdicate their responsibility for communicating with intention and providing consumers with the tools, cues, and information they need to understand and value the brand' (Rosen and Minsky, 2017).

Welcome to the new marketing landscape

So how else has the overall marketing landscape changed? And what does it mean for the use of audio branding? Consider these small and not-so-small ways.

The landscape goes digital

First, the landscape is going digital and, with digital, comes sound. Today, people are conditioned to take in sight and sound together. The media experience is seldom a printed page; audiences are accustomed to audio-enabled devices (even though brands continue to spend fortunes on their visual identities and leave their audio identities to the various agencies and suppliers who create their videos, telephone hold music, commercials, and events).

New promotional avenues open up

Second, as mentioned in Chapter 1, marketers now have more avenues than ever to promote your brand message and convey what you are about, creating more ways where customers can connect with you – and others – and making your job harder.

While we have already explored the growth of marketing touchpoints in the first chapter, what we failed to mention is that with this growth came the growth of various marketing specialists – both as agencies and as independent contractors. As every marketer is aware, gone are the days of managing three suppliers: a mainline advertising agency primarily focused on the big-budget media and generating the big idea; the public relations firm that helped build connections with the media, investors, internal audiences, and others; and the promotions firm that helped drive immediate sales through the use of incentives along the distribution channels and with consumers – replaced today by an overbooked calendar of managing an ever-growing list of marketing sub-specialties.

Yes, some marketers are still keeping their mainline advertising agency, public relations firm, and promotions firm on retainers, but they're also retaining a wide number of other marketing specialists, depending on their needs and marketing strategy.

They might also retain a firm for the targeted markets. In the United States, it can include the African–American or urban market, Hispanic, Asian, even smaller populations such as people from Russia or Poland, as well as other groups, including GLBTQ (gay, lesbian, bisexual, transgender and queer or questioning), as well as the visual brand design firm, social media company, website or online agency, the pay-per-click firm, and more – up to 12 or more agencies in all. Count in the regional agencies for national brands or suppliers spread across countries or continents for international brands and some firms can have as many as 30, 40, or even 50 different agencies.

Plus, there are the data scientists, customer relationship management experts, and others, either as in-house employees, part of the many agencies, or independent contractors. All with their own agendas and ways of driving business. But whatever the situation, they all need coordination.

Whew. Marketing has certainly become more complicated and dispersed.

And every brand experience from the website to the app to the store or sales call to the trade show to the packaging to the product or service itself as well as every touchpoint in between needs to seamlessly convey the same promise, personality, values, and experience. (Yet, the PR agency chooses music for the video news releases that's completely different from the event agency's selection and that is again significantly different from your digital agency's choice for the YouTube videos.)

But like using a splattering of layout formats, fonts, and colours in the visual expression, this haphazard use of sound is clearly not optimal. Julie Winther of the Copenhagen Business School, in her deeply researched thesis, 'Sound Brand Fit', reminds readers that, 'Repeated repetitions improve recognition while having (positive) impact on affect judgements (Peretz *et al*, 1998). The repeated exposure of a stimulus leads to increased ease of processing, which in turn is attributed to pleasantness and liking' (Griffith and Mitchell, 2008). This underscores the advantages of orchestrating your touchpoints, both visual and verbal, to work in harmony with each other to emphasize the good intentions of your brand.

Continuous partial attention

Third, our attention span has been shrinking since 2000, and is now shorter than the attention span of a goldfish, going from 12 seconds then to 8 seconds now (Weinreich *et al*, 2008).

According to writer and speaker Linda Stone, most people are now living in a state of 'continuous partial attention' (Stone, nd) – paying attention to a range of sources of information all at the same time, but only at a superficial level. With both Apple and Microsoft on her resumé, she describes the state as being 'always-on, anywhere, anytime, anyplace' and 'involves an artificial sense of constant crisis' (Stone, nd).

Consider how one 'watches' content these days. The TV or video may be rolling along but the temptation to avert your eyes comes from every direction. You might get a ping from your social media app, a bleep indicating an appointment is approaching, a ding from an e-mail that needs an answer, the triple-beep signalling popcorn in the microwave is ready, the melodious tone of the dryer saying the laundry's done, or the buzz of your phone, all guiding your attention.

Molly James-Lundak, a marketing executive at a leading pharmaceutical company, once described a moment in which she was vaguely aware of a commercial in the background while doing other things (Fahey, 2016a).

It was only when she heard the tagline at the spot's end that she realized that it was a commercial she had directly been involved in. And it was for one of her company's key products.

How often are you actually looking at what you are hearing? If you are like most today, you're always multitasking. Then consider which sense is more involved in causing the urge to act or react; is it sight or is it hearing?

If you suspect it's hearing, then you have noticed that people have been busy teaching themselves to understand multiple audio cues that come in at an almost subconscious level, cues that may be quite subtle but are present and helpful, nonetheless. (Again, a reason for creating an audio brand; sorry, but we can't stop talking about its benefits.)

Differentiation through sound

Finally, related to continuous partial attention, today's consumers are visually assaulted on every front, so, consequently, much of it gets tuned out.

Meanwhile, marketers intuitively understand the need to provide a consistent experience. They know that customers don't differentiate the brand offline and online. So, of course, branding is even more important because it ties everything together. And, not wanting to sound like an old-school broken record, there's one very powerful branding tool to help marketers achieve this goal and gain advantage on this levelled playing field: sound. It is fast and memorable. It conveys meaning and underscores your brand's distinction. And it helps you overcome the gauntlet of your audience's multiple, everyday distractions.

So, with our ever increasingly audio-enabled-environment (Snathanam *et al*, 2012) the strategic use of sound can play an important role in positively differentiating your product or service, enhancing recall, creating preference, building trust, and even increasing sales.

One way to be recognizable is to make sure your sound territory is consistent across all your places of customer interaction. Does your on-hold music define your brand? Does your sampling booth? Does your app? When someone crosses your threshold or even opens a piece of your content, do they experience a transition from the outside world to your unique world? A sound that subtly conveys your meaning?

Why do microwaves, ATMs, and refuse trucks emit the harsh 'beep, beep, beep?' Yes, ATMs want to remind us not to leave our cash or our card and refuse trucks need to warn us when they're backing up, but couldn't your appliance have its own family of unique, branded sounds? Couldn't your ATM have a sound reflecting back to your audio DNA (trustworthy?

friendly and accessible? Deeply experienced and global?). After all, what you decide to say through music and other sounds can be easily comprehended by customers.

But the sounds, just like the overall marketing programmes we mentioned, need to support your brand and convey where it's from with or without the visual logo. So what do you need for a strong audio brand? The requirements are actually the same as for a strong visual brand – and the descriptions and underlying foundation must be the same.

Defining the brand

When we begin working with clients to develop their audio brands, we encounter many different approaches to brand definition and varied levels of brand understanding. This range doesn't need to be an obstacle. The audio-branding process itself helps the client teams define what their brands represent, especially in terms of values, aspirations and personality. This occurs not only through competitive benchmarking but by the very nature of the medium.

By exploring a brand through a symbolic language, like music, rather than a literal one, like words, we can tease out surprisingly subtle distinctions in broad language like 'leadership', 'advancement', 'precision', 'hospitality', 'mobility' or 'performance'.

Branding best practice

Though Sixième Son works flexibly with brands at every level of development, Laurence Minsky has helped many companies define and activate their brand's foundations. In case your brand is at that early stage, has lost some of its energy, or was developed over time without the benefit of a strategic process, here is some of the best practice you should consider implementing for your brand.

Start with the brand essence or promise. (Some marketers use brand essence and others use brand promise. Either works.) It's the core or centre of the brand. Everything else in the brand foundation must ladder out from the essence.

A useful exercise is to try to arrive at a two-word brand essence. The two words define the outer boundaries of the brand and are often bordering on the oxymoronic, defining the range of the brand's personality. It's been said that Walmart's brand essence is 'Servant Leader'. As you can see, one part is about serving and the other is about the opposite end of the spectrum, leading, which creates tension. In their communications, they focus on serving customers (such as their product range or the famed greeter) or on leadership (including lowest prices) or on leading through serving.

On the other hand, it's been said that the brand for the US discount store Target is 'Affordable Style', again seemingly at odds with each other, which ladders to their consumer-facing tagline, 'Expect more. Pay less'. And it is translated in-store to their wider aisles and more fashionable items, which is not traditionally expected in a discount store.

Any given piece of communication might focus on the idea behind one of the words and another communication might be more focused on the interplay of the two words. Like a human personality, a brand essence or promise gives play to the brand actions and range to the brand behaviours, enabling it to appropriately adjust to the situation.

The two words of the essence should convey robust, intuitive meaning to stakeholders within the organization, serving as a guide for judging the branding elements, any piece of communication, and even product and service choices, but they should not be used in the messaging as a tag or campaign theme. That is because campaigns change, but the essence should be enduring.

If the essence is used as a tagline and, later, the campaign runs its due course, the essence could lose its power and energy and company can flounder. For instance, McDonald's long ago reportedly used the guide of 'Food, Folks, and Fun' as the core focus of their messaging strategy. But then they adopted 'Food, Folks, and Fun' as their campaign tagline. And when the campaign came to an end, they couldn't use these words anymore as the guideline and the company had to search for new ones (Elliot, 1991).

Rather, the brand essence or promise should solely work as an internal guide – and can even guide product development. Susan Hoffman, a Wieden & Kennedy creative legend who has worked on Nike since shortly after the shoe's beginning, has a story that sheds light on that usage of a brand essence.

To start, Hoffman considers Nike's brand essence to be 'Performance Sports' (Minsky, 2007).

Since you probably already know Nike's long-term tagline, 'Just Do It', you know that performance sport was never used as their brand signifier.

Most of their messaging either focuses on an athletic performance (or the athlete within you), on sports (or, more likely a specific sport and/or an athlete associated with the sport), or something combining the two. Says Hoffman:

> When they started doing sunglasses, I wondered how that fit the brand. But if you think about it, you need good equipment – shoes, glasses, hat, or gloves – whether you are a runner or a skier. On the other hand, Nike lost their focus when they had a jewellery line. That was years ago, and it was a total mistake. Some guy had designed all this jewellery, and Nike got all excited. But if you define the brand as 'performance sports', whether it's in their communication or in their product, it's clear what works and what doesn't: jewellery doesn't, sunglasses do.
>
> Source: Minsky, 2007

Other firms embrace a short declarative sentence of what the brand offers as their brand essence. And a few organizations use a longer essence statement. Each method has merit, as long as it works for the organization as a way to guide the development of the communications and other brand decision-making.

Whichever format you use, it should provide both direction and clarity as well as enable overall consistency within situational flexibility, so the brand will properly 'behave' within the environment.

The next needed areas of a brand foundation include the mission (also called 'purpose') and vision, the shorter and clearer, the better. Think of mission as your internal motivation beyond money, just as a missionary is set on some goal – wipe out disease; empower humanity in some new way; create happiness or some other emotion – and the vision as where you want to go or what you want to be as a brand.

Again, there are other models and we are open to them just so long as they provide a compass to your stakeholders and the people charged with bringing your brand to life.

We also need to determine its positioning – where does it sit compared to alternatives? This is key. Even if the brand features a new-to-the-world concept, it needs to take sales from somewhere – except, perhaps, media, which seems to be ever expanding (eMarketer, 2015). So what will people eliminate to buy the new brand, why is it better, and how does it deliver on its overall promise? The statement should identify its audience, competitive set, promise or benefit, and the 'proof points' that enable people to believe the brand will deliver on the promise.

> Finally, the brand needs to determine the personality or brand character, tenor, tonality, manner, and range of expression, so the team can get a sense of how the brand should behave.
>
> We call this part the building blocks for the brand's DNA.
>
> From these come the creative implications. For the visual branding elements, it means the logo design and usage, branded colours, font choices, photography or illustration style, the signifier or tagline, and more – even the language and grammar choices should be determined (formal or informal, contractions or no contractions).
>
> For the audio part of branding, it's the instrumentation options, range of the rhythm and tempo, the use of harmonies or layers, the textures and the type of melody. We call the short composition that defines all of this *the Audio DNA*.
>
> But you should note that the brand foundation works across all the senses, even taste, smell, touch. Just how they're brought to life through the creative implications changes across the various senses.

The brand foundation acts as the starting point for creating your branding elements – whether it's visual, auditory, tactile, or olfactory.

As branding professionals, we're frequently called in when it comes time to rebrand a company or to refresh an older brand.

For many firms, the competitive situation has changed, the product mix has changed, or the brand execution was not well maintained. Or, more drastically, the company has been bought, sold or merged with another company (and the value of the brand was not part of the equation for the acquisition).

So totally rebranding might be a consideration point. But we recommend you approach this deliberation cautiously and hesitantly. The first instinct should be to extend, revive, update, or fix your current branding. (Either way – starting a new one or extending your old one, the audio-branding process can help.)

In case you're considering rebranding, here are seven key reasons companies rebrand and three ways to tell if the effort was successful (note that the success criteria can work with existing brands as well):

1 You might not need to rebrand or refresh. It all depends on how you want your audience to view you. So the first question is: how is your brand being perceived? If you like the current perception, keep going. But if you have never formally defined its DNA, you might need to identify your key messaging to ensure that the brand is consistently conveyed in the future. If you don't like the way your brand is being perceived, however, then you might need to change it (or better define it). In other words, you will need to rebrand and create the tools, cues, and other information to enable your audience to correctly understand you and emotionally connect with your brand.

One client's marketing, according to their research, was seen as being disorganized, dated, and generic, and their sales presentation as less than professional. If they had been okay with maintaining this not-so-positive image, then a rebranding or refresh effort wouldn't have been required. But, not surprisingly, this organization didn't like to be seen in those terms. So they looked at the underlying brand foundation and created a new foundation and strategy, one that helped make them seem current, unique, organized, and professional in all aspects of their business. And they used it to bring consistency across their marketing and sales efforts.

2 If you're growing, but not as fast as your competitors, then you are losing share. And if it's not your product or service that's causing the lag, then it could be your brand or the way you are activating your brand. First, look at all the channels you're using. Are they the right ones and are they driving prospects closer to the transaction? Second, look at the value you're creating with your marketing. Can you find it? If you answered yes to both and it is still not enough, then it might be time to rebrand, better define your brand and/or make sure you execute it consistently across all your touchpoints (an area where having an audio brand can help). After all, changing your story or telling it better is the first step toward changing the outcomes.

3 All things being equal, a stronger brand will win a 'coin toss' between seemingly identical products or services – and, perhaps just as importantly, a strong brand can keep others with better financial positions from entering the category. So a good place to look if your brand is effective and strong is at those times when there is a coin toss. All other things being equal, are you winning more than your share?

4 People use brand cues to develop impressions and make decisions. If your brand imagery or messaging is dated and/or inconsistent, they will determine that your processes and/or your solutions are dated or lacking quality. So if you're seen as being behind the times, but your solutions are up-to-date or even innovative, then you need to change the impressions so they're in line with reality. (On the other hand, if your solutions or products are dated or lacking, then you should stay the course with your brand – at least until you fix the problems.)

5   If your people are not in alignment, prospects will be get a different 'vibe' from different people. Branding aligns goals and objectives across your business units. And it helps bring the messaging together. By developing communications and marketing tactics that align with an appropriate brand platform, you can do more with less, because they will all work with each other instead of against each other.

6   If your goal is to expand and be a leader, the company would need to attract more world-class talent, which is harder without a strong brand. In fact, branding has been shown to help business create an appealing culture that attracts and retains world-class talent (Hall, 2014).

7   If the company is ever to be sold, the owner would want to get the most for it and branding has been shown to help increase market cap – ie it will help you get more money. In fact, according to the *Harvard Business Review*, the 'branding' typically contributes between 0.5 per cent for an unmanaged B2B brand to over 20 per cent for a well-managed B2B brand to the value of the company. And the average is around 7 per cent of the company's value. In other words, on average for all B2B companies, if your brand is contributing 7 per cent to the value of your company, you're ahead of the pack; if your brand is contributing below 7 per cent to the value of the company, you're below the pack (Gregory and Sexton, 2007).

The HBR article also pointed out that 'a fraction of a percentage of brand equity can mean hundreds of millions of dollars in value'.

All of these reasons are indications that a marketer might want to focus on the branding of his or her product or service.

Can we tell how much more in the event of a sale? No. As we know, marketing is fluid. Other issues and new competitive actions can come into play.

Can we tell if it would turn around the loss of market share or stop lagging sales? No, again marketing is fluid. Because competitors are reacting in real time, the end result might be that the company doesn't slide as much.

Can we tell you how much a company will make as a result of rebranding? No, but we can assure you that in many instances, the cost of not acting could be greater.

Which brings us to the next point: possible metrics.

The big question is which metric to use? Please note that most of the research on metrics and the development of them have been within the consumer area, although many translate to B2B.

The value of branding: some initial ways to determine it for your brand

In selecting the key metrics, you'll also need to keep in mind that branding refresh efforts tend to take between three and five years before results become truly noticeable, but some metrics can give clues earlier. So here are what we consider to be three of the top options to consider:

1 **Company valuation.** We already talked about brand valuation when discussing the reasons for rebranding (see point 7 on p 29). This would take the longest time to get data after the refresh, but you might be able to identify where your brand stands today against its competitors.
2 **Close rate.** For this to be a successful metric, sales must truly adopt the new brand messaging and the experience from one salesperson to the next must be consistent (as well as from the rest of the representatives from the company).
3 **Perceived price/value.** Through either qualitative and quantitative research, you can determine the price/value perception. One way to do this is to ask people what they'd pay for a generic version of your product and then ask what they'd pay for one under your company's brand; calculate the difference and multiply by the size of the potential audience. (While the actual process is a little more sophisticated than described here, you get the idea.) This is one of the most prevalent metrics for measuring the strength of consumer brands, but is also used for B2B brands. Since it can be researched using projective techniques, evidence can be gathered earlier.

Other metrics could be unsolicited enquiries (although this also depends on the success of marketing communication programmes that reinforce the branding as well as taking into account activation programmes that can help generate leads even without strong branding); attitude toward the company; and more.

Consistent execution of all elements, when contemporary and appropriate, of the brand contributes to its valuation, from the logo and colours to the imagery and sounds. So while audio branding is still an emerging area, we bet the sound of your brand, if appropriate, will contribute to the metrics we suggested (as well as others).

So now that we have briefly explored the broader state of overall branding today as well as when you might want to rebrand, let's now explore where audio branding fits into the broader field of sensory marketing. We think you'll like what you will hear. So come along and join us in the next chapter, where we will provide a brief overview of sensory marketing.

> **GUEST PERSPECTIVE** Ben DiSanti and Ken Hicks
>
> **The emotional shopper: building the brand image through an emotional connection along the shopper's journey**
>
> *Branding is all about consistency and emotionality, an area that many numbers-driven marketers find hard to approach. And, ultimately, a brand's marketing activities need to result in a transaction. So we asked our colleagues at DiSanti Hicks + Partners, Ben DiSanti and Ken Hicks, to talk about their insights into how branding and emotionality influence the shopping experience, an obvious benefit of employing an audio strategy as part of your branding toolbox. Here is what our colleagues had to say.*
>
> Let's start with a basic, but powerful, statistic: shoppers tend to spend 9 per cent more when they are happy. This has been reported by BrainJuicer in past shopper research (Johnson, 2012) as well as more recent shopper research by TNS (Tolboom, 2013).
>
> This is a very simple and straightforward piece of data, but it is one that is overlooked time and again by retailers. BrainJuicer has shown that within several retail channels – from grocery stores, to DIY outlets, to electronics purveyors – there are multiple instances where initial interactions upon entering these environments have been negative.
>
> In a UK grocery setting, one observed example was when shoppers reached the trolley (shopping cart) area and discovered they didn't have the proper change, which created a hold-up right as they entered the store.
>
> This led to a moment of frustration, and happened to be followed by additional negative encounters within the first few departments inside the store such as produce that was out of stock or did not look fresh, or displays that were shoddily organized. This set the tone for a negative shopping experience, in many instances causing shoppers to approach their visit as a chore which they had to force their way through to completion. Further evidence of this is that shoppers are significantly more likely to be happy at the end of their shopping trip than at the beginning (Allchin, 2010).
>
> Compare this to a shopping experience at a store like Target, where in many cases the entry is clean, trolleys are easily accessible, the

Dollar Spot, full of impulse-purchase items, is right there as you walk in, encouraging a quick look, to be followed by wide lanes and well-displayed merchandise. This approach has helped Target connect with their shoppers on a deeper, more emotional level, building shopper appeal over the years. The mere design of the store says to the shoppers, 'I understand you', which is all about creating emotional connections.

During recent research we conducted for a local dry-cleaning chain, our team discovered customers faced a negative emotional engagement. Not surprisingly, most people do not like to clean laundry and see it as a chore, much like other household chores.

Currently dry-cleaners only address a portion of this problem, but it involves customers having to make two trips to the store. So in essence, this became an additional chore to cleaning clothes at home. Our qualitative and quantitative research highlighted negative emotions related to interactions with this brand – even though the service at the store was very positive.

In an effort to change this, we worked with the client to position their operation in a much broader way. The charge was to eliminate the chore of clothes cleaning. We found there is a certain segment of the population that expressed a high degree of emotional interest in and intent for this offering.

In addition, there was evidence that this opportunity has even greater potential once early adopters are aboard. There is a high degree of likelihood that this initiative will grow beyond current expectations – similar to how the bottled water category grew. Bottled water was once thought to be unnecessary; however, it is estimated to reach US $279.65 billion by 2020 (Transparency Market Research, 2015).

Another example of how retailers can better connect with their shoppers, leading to happier engagements, is the work by The Hershey Company for Publix. Within this supermarket chain located in the southeast United States, Hershey created a confectionery section where you are greeted by huge visuals of your favourite confection icons (M&Ms, Reese Cups, Hershey Kisses). These very icons engage the shopper's emotions and turn what could be a functional 'search and find' exercise into an interaction with characters, all the while guiding them to their preferred choice. Even if just for a brief moment, this experience provides an enjoyable lift (although it could have been further improved by introducing the sound footprint for these brands).

This effort shows how we can bring emotion into what is typically viewed as an impulse category at the store. However, it is important to note that emotional bonds with brands must be formed outside the store in order to have them pay off in-store. Conversations with marketing executives from the confectionery category as well as current campaigns by both Wrigley and The Hershey Company prove this:

- Extra Gum exhibits success by forming a bond with the consumers/ shoppers early on – long before they ever enter the store. One recent campaign shows a boy and girl meeting in school, and every time they see each other, the boy captures the moment by drawing on an Extra Gum wrapper. Eventually, he reveals the history of their relationship through the series of drawings presented to the girl, all leading up to him on bended knee asking for her hand in marriage. As she lowers the drawing, she sees her beau right there in front of her with ring in hand. This, along with other ads in the overall campaign, significantly improved sales for Extra.
- For Hershey, their S'mores programme is a successful effort at the store to bring together three brands (Hershey's Chocolate Bars, Honey Maid Graham Crackers, Jet Puff Marshmallows) into a display that evokes sitting-around-the-campfire memories of creating these sandwiches of melted chocolate and marshmallows, and anticipated memories among shoppers. The lifestyle visuals in-store act as emotional triggers to activate purchase in the moment. This programme continues to show returns year-after-year for all brands involved.

Christopher Brace, Founder and CEO of Syntegrate Consulting, states there are two ways to move a shopper to act within a retail setting – manipulate them or inspire them (Shopper Intelligence, 2015).

Brand marketers typically default to manipulation tactics – think about all the coupons and discount offers that continue to pervade contact points. Moving to inspiration is a more challenging space; however, it has been proven to produce a longer bond with the brand. Think about the Apple Store which most refer to as a great example where sales per square foot is not the main determinant of what is displayed where.

Building inspiration into grocery, mass, drug, or convenience store settings can certainly be more challenging. However, according to Geert Van Aelst (Head of Marketing for the Südzucker Group, Belgium) this effort can be guided by one simple screen: 'What would you tell your mother?' His point: we tend to be very emotional, demonstrative, and authentic when conversing with mum. This can lead to many new and different ideas for in-store connections with shoppers.

For Geert, storytelling is key. Given the short interaction time at retail, the story has to be created earlier in the shopper journey – prior to entering the store. Geert, in his marketing for the brand T-Sugars, employs a character (T-man) as a way to serve up a common baking ingredient in an unexpected and memorable way. The joy experienced watching these ads creates a stamp that can then be carried into retail settings – again acting as an emotional trigger for the brand at shelf. According to Geert, 'people recognize and identify with this' (the T-man character). (But just think how an audio brand could have further aided this connection from pre-shop to shop.)

Drew Iddings (former Marketing Director for The Hershey Company) echoes the point about engaging shoppers prior to entering the store. In fact, he states, 'the emotional connections before and after shopping are necessary to help your brand/product stand out from the others (at shelf) when that quick impulse decision is made'.

Thus, activation at store becomes more of a spark, or reminder, of a bond built prior to entering and reinforced through product usage after purchase.

One emotional area where this really comes to life is through seasonal sets. According to Drew, the goal is to 'become an expert of the seasons'.

Confectionery is, in many cases, an anchor of seasonal sets. Hershey embraces this and acts as an advisor for retailer seasonal sets based on their knowledge of the shopper and how they approach shopping differently from one season to the next. Displays become extremely important for overcoming holiday distractions, and using strong emotional ties to a season can almost instantaneously engage and draw shoppers in – eg the use of iconic visuals like Kisses Christmas Bells which many people have fond memories of from holiday ads.

Beyond seasonal in-store marketing, brands can work with retailers to draw upon heartstrings in other ways as well. Extra Gum is about connections. Working with Kroger, Wrigley was able to leverage this along with their retail partner's passion for supporting US troops, to bring the two together and create an emotional bond with shoppers. The 'Honouring Our Heroes' programme allows people to share messages with those in the military. At store, visuals of positive interactions – eg a wife hugging her military husband, along with a message inviting customers to buy one pack in order to share a pack with a hero – resonated with Kroger and its shoppers. Lena Lewis (Senior Manager, Shopper Marketing at Wrigley) stated that this programme was 'very successful at evoking emotion in an impulse category, and ultimately driving sales'.

Infusing shopper inspiration into the engagement

Success for retailers in building connections to their brands will be tied to utilizing a combination of both manipulation and inspiration.

Interestingly, both of these ways can be associated with emotional engagements; only one can be associated with a functional engagement. Yet, most current activity by brands or retailers focuses on the functional area (coupons, discounts etc), as these are direct and tangible approaches.

Emotional engagement entails more thought, and many times more collaboration, and it often leads to more long-term results. Just think about most loved brands and retailers today, and what you are likely to find is that there is a passion for each brand among the shoppers and buyers – eg iPhone, Google, Netflix, Amazon, Apple Store, the Disney store, even Trader Joe's or a local chain like Chicago-based Mariano's.

Establishing this emotional link during the shopping experience requires deciding which functional interactions can be converted to emotional engagements to drive more fulfilling actions within the store environment.

As a roadmap for satisfying shopper interactions, the thinking process must begin with Occasions, which drive all retailer visits.

Occasions can be broken down into functional and emotional groupings. Functional occasions are dominated by rational thought as shown in Figure 2.1 (overleaf) under the 'How Shoppers Think' heading. Emotional interactions are underscored by feelings – as exhibited with the questions under 'How Shoppers Feel'.

When the shopper is in functional mode, they can be susceptible to manipulative tactics. We've all experienced these – eg price discounts, promotions, coupons etc. Their purpose is to entice shoppers at that last moment to consider and/or choose one brand over another. There is extensive evidence across many brands and categories that these marketing tactics accomplish their task. However, we have found through a vast number of discussions with shoppers over the years that they do little more than perpetuate switching behaviour without significantly building a brand bond. Although this can move volume at points in time, it has a short-term effect, and shoppers revert back to rote behaviours when the incentive is no longer available.

Figure 2.1 Functional and emotional groupings of the Occasion

SOPHISTICATION →

How Shoppers Think
Does the benefit meet my needs?
How much do I need?
How much does it cost?
Will it last?
How many calories?

How Shoppers Feel
Is the category important in my life?
Can I relate to the message? Is it me?
Does it fit my occasion?
Is it a brand I trust?
Does it please my senses?

SOURCE DHP, 2016 (used with permission)

Those brands/products that create emotional engagements with shoppers have been shown to develop deeper, more profitable relationships. A Gallup study revealed that fully engaged customers represent an average 23 per cent premium in terms of share of wallet, profitability, revenue, and relationship growth compared to the average customer (Sorenson and Adkins, 2014).

By providing sensory cues and storytelling around brands and their categories, brand marketers can stimulate memories, which tend to lead to deeper interactions. This moves shoppers beyond just a price focus. This was shown in research conducted by TMS and BrainJuicer in 2013 where a visual sensory cue (bee mascot) on Honey Nut Cheerios packaging drew attention to the brand in the aisle even though it was displayed on the bottom shelf, and the emotional uplift was linked with an increase in sales (Path-to-Purchase Institute, 2013).

Multisensory triggers within the retail space act as a magnet to attract one brand over another. Developing more of these multisensory engagements – especially audio, one of the most powerful senses in retail – across the retail environment leads to a more positive shopping experience overall. Additional examples of the power of the senses to attract shoppers and build brand/product image include:

- The store perimeter. This area of grocery retail typically includes departments like produce, deli, meats, bakery, etc. Historically, this section contributed 30 per cent of store profits. It continues to gain favour and sales while the centre-of-store struggles. It is no surprise that this is happening as the perimeter provides a more multisensory shopping experience – appealing to sound, smell, and touch in addition to sight. One major US grocery retailer utilizes sight, sound, and touch to provide freshness cues in their produce section. Lightning and thunder warn shoppers that water misters will turn on shortly. They serve as a warning sign, but more importantly, they engage shoppers by heightening the image of freshness which creates a positive emotional interaction. This in-store experience directly lifts the image of this retail brand. When asking shoppers about their impressions of retailers, they will typically respond by describing these types of interactions with products from perimeter departments.
- Asian Paints. The challenge here was to move the Indian culture to embrace colour within their homes. Interestingly, this culture incorporates colour in clothing, but homes tend to be very stark. In fact, a key insight that drove a change in the company's retail strategy was that in India consumers are afraid of colour when decorating their homes. To change this, Asian Paints, along with their agency Fitch, created a 'walk-in home décor magazine' where shoppers could interact with colours in a multisensory environment – rooms immersed in the colour of the shopper's choice; displays where shoppers could touch and feel blocks in almost any imaginable colour etc. The showroom was structured to be an ultimate colour playground. The twist here was that shoppers could not purchase paint tins from this store – they simply interacted with colour on a new level. The power of this sensory engagement led to a 35 per cent increase in sales of paint tins from adjacent dealer stores (Fitch, nd).
- Cinnabon. The power of smell can create both positive and negative experiences that affect brand image and retail sales. Baked goods company Cinnabon knows this all too well. Many of their locations are in open-air mall settings, and the aroma of their cinnamon rolls acts as a magnet, drawing shoppers in. A test in which the company moved their ovens to the back of the store led to a significant decrease in sales (Nassauer, 2014).

- Starbucks. Around a decade ago, Starbucks offered breakfast sandwiches, and when they were introduced, the company soon learned that the aroma of these items overwhelmed the very item that put them on the map – coffee. Founder Howard Schultz initially vowed to remove these items from the menu, but the product development team was able to mitigate the smell of the breakfast sandwiches to the point where coffee remained the pre-eminent aroma that greeted customers upon entering the Starbucks store. This small operational change preserved the emotional brand connection with customers while still providing a logical complement to their core product (Nocera, 2008).
- Burberry. This prominent clothing retailer built much of its image on weather elements – specifically rain. They have incorporated this throughout all brand touchpoints, including fashion shows, and have successfully taken a negative (dark, gloomy, rainy weather) and transformed it into a positive sensory interaction. Rain is a major part of their fashion shows. The key here is that rain engages the senses of sight, smell, touch and sound. In addition, it stimulates memories within shoppers. The end result is a brand whose image is constantly reinforced through impactful sensory engagements that form new memories – all leading to an evergreen brand (Lamb, 2012).
- Abercrombie & Fitch. When we think of loud club music, each of us holds a distinct image, although they differ from person to person. Retailers like US clothing company Abercrombie & Fitch have learned to leverage this to their advantage. Based on the observation that younger people can withstand loud music for longer periods of time than adults, they use loud club music to ensure that younger shoppers spend more time in stores like A&F, or other similar retailers like Hollister, and, in so doing, reinforce the image that these retailers appeal to a younger target (Kahn, 2016).

Thus, one clear link to building or fortifying a brand bond is through establishing strong emotionally-driven interactions in a retail setting – whether online or in-store.

One proven way to establish these types of engagements is by focusing on providing displays, programmes, or communication efforts that are multisensory in nature. These engagements move shoppers from functional mode into more of an emotional space.

Lena Lewis indicates it is also important to take into account a shopper's approach to different retail environments. The example here is Costco. 'Shoppers are on the hunt here – looking for new things', says Ms Lewis. As a result, working with a retailer like Costco to introduce new products via a multisensory sampling experience can increase trial and purchase. 'This is where shoppers are most open to an experience of this type.'

These multisensory exchanges stimulate the emotional centres of the brain, stirring up memories, resulting in a deeper, enduring impression of the brand during the shopping experience and amplifying the brand bond beyond what is available through behavioural analysis alone. Current efforts around emotional engagements relate to testing how well this additive component improves predictive modelling and thus developing a system that provides both emotional and behavioural learning aspects to drive shopper interaction.

In the end, the benefits of building emotional connections along the path-to-purchase can be summed up with a short poem:

Give people a nudge and their choices will budge

Smell, sound, and vision can shift a decision

How prices are laid out affects what gets paid out

So frame offers right for shopper delight.

Source: John Kearon, BrainJuicer, *The Future of Insights*, 2016

In other words, the brand image can be built effectively by establishing the emotional connections with consumers. Leveraging human senses at retail is a powerful way to accomplish this – especially where shoppers' time and attention are limited.

Guest biographies

Ben DiSanti is Co-Founder, Managing Partner and Chief Curiosity Seeker, DiSanti Hicks + Partners, where he leads the data analytics and segmentation practice. As a senior-level strategic planner, he launched the planning departments at four different agencies, where he has worked with such clients as Coca-Cola, Walmart, Bank of America, Facebook, and many others. His pioneering work for McDonald's Restaurants created a zone marketing communications strategy that has been adopted by other quick service restaurants (QSRs) and has influenced many consumer packaged goods (CPGs) and service brands around the world. Ben holds a master's degree in Integrated Marketing Communications from Northwestern University's Medill School of Journalism. During down-time, he loves to hop on his road bike and ride through the countryside.

Ken Hicks is Co-Founder, Managing Partner and Client Solutions Partner, DiSanti Hicks + Partners. He has held senior-level positions at several agencies including Arc/Burnett and The Marketing Store, serving such clients as Coca-Cola, MillerCoors, McDonald's, Brown-Forman, General Mills, Redbox, United, AT&T, Whirlpool, and Ford Motor Company. Ken is a graduate of the University of Michigan and holds a master's degree in Integrated Marketing Communications from Northwestern University's Medill School of Journalism. He is also frequently to be found lecturing up-and-coming students at many different US universities including Exeter, Northwestern, DePaul, and St Joseph.

CASE Huggies

The sound of the bond between a mother and her baby

How does audio branding contribute to an overall branding effort? We got a glimpse into the answer in our case study for SNCF, but let's dig a little deeper by looking at a recent case study for Huggies. This extensively global Kimberly-Clark brand, Huggies, had recently introduced a new positioning, one that put greater emphasis on the emotional connection between mother and baby.

Their advertising agency, Ogilvy, was working to bring consistency to their client's messaging as well as to their far-flung logos and colours. The markets had largely embraced the idea of a charming logo animation, internally called 'Hugging Gs', but there was a lack of consistency about its use.

In the end frames, the graphic appeared in different colours with different backgrounds. Every time a logo animated onto the screen, it was accompanied by different music: whistling, guitar or just background music fading away as the logo appeared. No branded earprint was left to accompany the warmth of the visual.

An audio audit of the category revealed that the whole sector was overusing innocuous acoustic guitar. To some extent, Huggies TV commercials and branded content shared this trend, but the brand didn't use any sound consistently from place to place. And they use many audio approaches; for example, strings and piano in the USA, energetic guitar in Latin America, licensed pop music in Israel, harpsichord in Russia, soft feminine voice in Australia. Much of the music lacked energy or narrative intent.

The issue was: how to provide a flexible system that could work in many countries and deliver a touching message about the connection between mother and child, but give the markets flexibility to adapt it to suit a range of purchasers from mothers of newborns to mums of toddlers as well as a range of content from highly emotional stories to very functional messaging about absorption and fit.

Enter Ogilvy's Managing Director for the Huggies account, Angela Johnson, who felt that audio branding would provide a previously untapped solution. One that had the potential to underscore the connection message, unify the global markets, amplify people's emotions, and create coherence among the communications to a wide variety of targets.

The clients and agency formed a Listening Committee that included people from design and marketing, represented both diapers and baby-wipes brands, and was populated by two Europeans (UK and Spain), a Latin American, and US marketing staff. On the central Sixième Son team were a Canadian, a Frenchman (father of five young children), and an American who had grown up in Spain. Together, the combined teams worked through the musical yesses and nos that would capture the values and character of the brand to inform the composers/sound designers who would take on the challenge of creating the concepts for the audio DNA.

Of the five alternatives that were created and presented to the listening committee, one stood out as more distinctive and specific to the meaning the team sought to convey. It began with a mother humming to her newborn in very gentle tones and the unformed sound of a newborn responding. Then, during the course of this 40-second recording, the voice of the child became clearer and at the end of it, the mother is singing and the child is responding with the same tune.

The goal was to develop an audio identity that would work as a system, appropriate for all target audiences. The audio identity features the interplay between the voices of mother and child and reflects the duality of the brand; a reassuring quality for newborns and an active quality for toddlers.

The audio identity was quickly embraced by the markets and, within the first six months, had been adapted to new campaigns in many countries throughout the globe in ways that demonstrate the system's immense flexibility:

- Russia used both music and the voices of mother and child, even adding some baby sounds of their own to score a commercial featuring highly active and vocal babies.

- Brazil sought to use only the end frame in which the visual logo animates onto the screen accompanied by the brand's music and laughter.
- Ogilvy Argentina, on behalf of several Latin American markets, scored a series of 30-second commercials as well short-form digital ads. In one, the dramatic moment that unified the campaign was the instant in which the mother lets go of the baby's hand and the baby takes steps to explore the world on his or her own. This moment was intensified by adding musical tension to the score followed by a blooming of energy and confidence.

Given that their spots carried a good deal of copy, Argentina left out the mum and baby voices and simply had an instrumental version of branded music scored to emphasize the mother's ambivalence and subsequent relief, leading into the child's joyful exploration. These commercials have been eagerly adopted by neighbouring countries and may also be used in Central America and the Caribbean.

Says Johnson:

> The Huggies audio brand brings an immediate smile to everyone who hears it. At first the creatives were sceptical of the idea of a global brand sound, but the music itself and the flexibility with which it can be applied won them over fast. Sixième Son brought a rigorous process to the creation, which helped align the stakeholders and arrive at an audio identity that will build brand's power for years to come.

Source: Fahey, 2016b

References

Allchin, J (2010) The emotional shopper, *Marketing Week*, 14 October, https://www.marketingweek.com/2010/10/14/the-emotional-shopper/ [accessed 12 December 2016]

Bronnenberg, BJ, Dube, JP, Gentzkow, M and Shapiro, JM (2015) *Do Pharmacists Buy Bayer? Informed shoppers and the brand premium* [online] http://www.brown.edu/Research/Shapiro/pdfs/generics.pdf [accessed 19 September 2016]

Elliot, S (1991) The Media Business: Advertising; Full-price brands fighting off assault by cheaper rivals, *The New York Times* [online] http://www.nytimes.com/1991/12/06/business/media-business-advertising-full-price-brands-fighting-off-assault-cheaper-rivals.html [accessed 19 September 2016]

eMarketer (2013) Brand marketers put more emphasis on social, mobile, video [online] *eMarketer*, http://www.emarketer.com/Article/Brand-Marketers-Put-More-Emphasis-on-Social-Mobile-Video/1010144#V2vMUfoqwWGyVL8G.99 [accessed 6 June 2016] eMarketer (2015) US adults spend 5.5 hours with video content each day: digital video viewing adds significant time to the average US consumer's media day, https//www.emarketer.com/Article/US-Adults-Spend-55-Hours-with-Video-Content-Each-Day/1012362 [accessed 6 December 2016]

Fahey, C (2016a) Personal interview with Molly James-Lundak

Fahey, C (2016b) Personal interview with Angela Johnson

Fitch (nd) *Asian Paints,* FITCH, case study [online] http://insights.retailenvironments.org/wp-content/uploads/2015/01/13.pdf [accessed 4 May 2016]

Gregory, JR and Sexton, DE (2007) Hidden Wealth in B2B Brands, *Harvard Business Review* [online] https://hbr.org/2007/03/hidden-wealth-in-b2b-brands [accessed 19 September 2016]

Griffith, O and Mitchell, CJ (2008) Negative priming reduces affective ratings, *Cognition and Emotion*, vol 22(6), pp 1119–129

Hall, J (2014) Caterpillar's Stellar Move To Attract High-Quality Employees, *Forbes* [online] http://www.forbes.com/sites/johnhall/2014/07/24/caterpillars-stellar-move-to-attract-high-quality-employees/#403ef5f36fcb [accessed 19 September 2016]

Hollis, N (2007) *What Price a Strong Brand?* Millward Brown's POV [online] http://www.wpp.com/wpp/marketing/reportsstudies/whatpriceastrongbrand/ [accessed 19 September 2016]

Johnson, AJ (2012) Understanding the consumer in the moment and tapping their emotions and instinctive decision-making process, April, http://www.slideshare.net/rencosch/understanding-the-consumer-in-the-moment-aj-johnsonpdf [accessed 12 December 2016]

Kahn, H (2016) *How Retailers Manipulate Sight, Smell, and Sound to Trigger Purchase Behaviour in Consumers* [blog] Shopify blogs, https://www.shopify.com/retail/119926083-how-retailers-manipulate-sight-smell-and-sound-to-trigger-purchase-behavior-in-consumers?utm_campaign=buffer&utm_content=buffer0b32c&utm_medium=social&utm_source=twitter.com [accessed 4 May 2016]

Kearon, J (2016) *WFAMarketers* (video) https://www.youtube.com/watch?v=Hqh2A9zzGP4 [accessed 4 May 2016]

Lamb, R (2012) Burberry solidifies brand image via weather-focused mobile, social efforts, *Luxury Daily* [online] https://www.luxurydaily.com/burberry-masters-brand-image-via-weather-based-campaign/ [accessed 4 May 2016]

Lee, L (2015) *Itamar Simonson: Do brands still matter for online shoppers?* [online] Stanford Graduate School of Business, https://www.gsb.stanford.edu/insights/itamar-simonson-do-brands-still-matter-online-shoppers [accessed 19 September 2016]

Minsky, L (2007) *How to Succeed in Advertising When All You Have Is Talent* 2nd edn, p 317, The Copy Workshop, Chicago, IL

Minsky, L (2016) Private interview with Julia Tang Peters

Nassauer, S (2014) Using scent as a marketing tool, stores hope it – and shoppers – will linger, *The Wall Street Journal* [online] http://www.wsj.com/articles/SB10001424052702303468704579573953132979382 [accessed 4 May 2016]

Nocera, J (2008) The Starbucks Egg Sandwich Double Cross, *The New York Times*, http://executivesuite.blogs.nytimes.com/2008/09/05/the-starbucks-egg-sandwich-double-cross/?_r=0; [accessed 4 May 2016]

Path-to-Purchase Institute (2013) Shopper Marketing Summit Presentation, April

Peretz, I, Gaudreau, D and Bonnel, AM (1998) Exposure effects on music preference and recognition, *Memory and Cognition*, vol 26 (5), pp 884–902; quoted in Winther, J (2012) Sound Brand Fit: A cross-modal study on perception of fit between sound logos, visual logos and brands (thesis)

Rodgers, Z (2008) *As big brands embrace digital, digital's branding power wanes* [online] ClickZ, https://www.clickz.com/as-big-brands-embrace-digital-digitals-branding-power-wanes/76397/ [accessed 21 July 2016]

Rosen, W and Minsky, L (2017) *The Activation Imperative Need: How to build brands and business by inspiring action*, Rowman & Littlefield, Lanham, MA

Shopper Intelligence (2015) *The Reality Of In-store Communications* [online] http://www.slideshare.net/ShopperIntelligence/reality-of-in-store-communications [accessed 19 September 2016]

Snathanam, LH, Mitchell, A and Rosenstiel, T (2012) *Audio: how far will digital go?* [online] State of the Media, http://www.stateofthemedia.org/2012/audio-how-far-will-digital-go/ [accessed 29 July 2016]

Sorenson, S and Adkins, A (2014) Why customer engagement matters so much now, *Gallup Business Journal* [online] http://www.gallup.com/businessjournal/172637/why-customer-engagement-matters.aspx [accessed 19 September 2016]

Stone, L (nd) *Continuous partial attention* [blog] https://lindastone.net/qa/continuous-partial-attention/ [accessed 29 July 2016]

Tolboom, N (2013) *Finding Faster Growth: Happy shoppers spend more*, TNS NIPO [online] http:www.slideshare.net/TNSLT/tns-happyshoppersspendmore [accessed 7 December 2016]

Transparency Market Research (2015) Global bottled water market, Globenewswire [online] https://globenewswire.com/news-release/2015/01/16/697945/10115836/en/Global-Bottled-Water-Market-is-Expected-to-Reach-USD-279-65-billion-in-2020-By-Volume-Global-Bottled-Water-Market-is-Expected-to-Reach-465-12-Billion-Liters-in-2020-Transparency-Ma.html [accessed 28 April 2016]

Weinreich, H, Obendorf, H, Herder, E and Mayer, M (2008) *Not quite the average: an empirical study of web use*, ACM Transactions on the Web, vol 2(1), https://ccit.college.columbia.edu/sites/ccit/files/weinreich-web-use-study.pdf [accessed 29 July 2016]

Wellington, R (2016) We Brands – They make us feel good by reflecting our personality – They make a statement about us – They make shopping easy! 'I don't buy brands, I buy Marks & Spencer's' [online] Academia.edu. http://www.academia.edu/5968900/WE_BRANDS_They_make_us_feel_good_by_reflecting_our_personality_They_make_a_statement_about_us_They_make_shopping_easy_I_DONT_BUY_BRANDS_I_BUY_MARKS_and_SPENCERS_ [accessed 19 September 2016]

It's time we came to our sensory marketing

03

Sight. Sound. Smell. Touch. And taste. That's it. The five senses – our simple inputs for knowing and interpreting the world. The combination of them, married with our memories, is all we have for interpreting our experiences. All these senses can be used for branding and marketing to some degree. But some are more powerful for that than others.

We already discussed in the previous two chapters the power of audio branding as well as the overriding prevalence of visual branding in the marketing world today.

But given the richness of today's media environment and the truly fierce competition for attention and transactions, brands need to deploy all their tools to truly stand out from the pack. As a result of this changing environment, there seems to be a growing interest in sensory branding and marketing (Hulten, 2015).

Of course, you, our readers, should agree; otherwise, you wouldn't be engrossed in this book – one that explores one of the most powerful, yet currently underutilized, sensory branding opportunities: sound and music.

But before we go too far, what is the broader area of sensory branding and where does the use of sound fit into this bigger picture? Also, can the other senses be used for branding – and, if so, how? While we can't answer these questions deeply – some of the other forms of sensory marketing and branding require long books to themselves – we can provide some direction and considerations.

Let's start with a definition. In *Sensory Marketing: Theoretical and empirical grounds*, Hulten defines sensory marketing as 'a service process that focuses on sensory strategies and stimuli with the goal of creating a multi-sensory brand experience, in supporting the individual's identity creation through the mind and the five senses to generate consumer value, consumer experiences, and the brand as an image' (Hulten, 2015, p 106).

Most of his points conform to the generally accepted view of branding – that branding as an exercise helps people express their self-image and values while building the individual brand's image and values as well.

But as we unpack Hulten's definition, we want to point out that he also states that the marketer should also consider that branding is a service that creates consumer value, a point often overlooked.

In addition, the use of sensory stimuli is as experiential as using the actual product or service and it is ultimately the coming together of the sensory inputs that provides the message. As Neil Gains (whom you'll meet more fully in Chapter 7) pointed out in his book *Brand esSense*, 'Most senses comprise multiple feedback systems and are ultimately integrated in the brain' (Gains, 2013).

Now to answer the other questions in our list above, let's take a brief look at the different areas of branding, starting with the most popular one – visual branding.

Marketers have already set their sights on visual branding

At the last count, there were nearly 1,000 books under 'branding' on Amazon.com. Most are either on strategy, which we covered in the previous chapter, or on logo design and identity systems.

In fact, visual branding is a well-understood area and we bet that you are well-versed in the strategic and executional thinking behind it. After all, 'sight is the sense that is most used by humans to get an understanding of the surrounding environment' (Hulten, 2015). As a result, sight is 'the most used sense in branding' (Gains, 2013).

The issue: visual inputs need to be processed to be fully understood (Hulten, 2015) and, thus, could be filtered out by the individual. Additionally, as we have already explained, by being used to death, the visual landscape is truly cluttered, so it becomes harder to set your brand apart.

Of course, we're not arguing that marketers should stop developing and maintaining their visual branding elements. Rather, we believe marketers should make the most of every brand touchpoint and every form of sensory input, placing the use of the taste, touch, smell, and sounds in their brand toolbox as well.

Needless to say, some senses provide more branding opportunities than others. Let's now move to one that is rather limited, although powerful – taste.

What does taste mean in the world of sensory branding?

Unless it's a food product, physical taste typically isn't a consideration for any marketer's branding effort. After all, what marketer would want people licking the walls of the retail environment? (We should, of course, remind marketers that taste as an aesthetic concept should always be considered, but that is a different discussion.)

Physical taste is a result of chemical reactions being initiated at receptors in the mouth, and are limited to sweet, sour, salt, and bitter, though others add the taste of 'umami' (savoury) as well. While the individual taste sensations might have specific meanings – such as 'sweet' for energy and 'bitter' for poison (Gains, 2013, pp 37–39) – the actual understanding of a taste is the combination of the chemical reactions as well as the scent, the tactile inputs (such as the temperature and texture), memory, context (which is why people can enjoy the 'warning' taste of sour in candy), expectations, and more – including, as we will see in Charles Spence's guest contribution later in this chapter, sound. In other words, the perception of taste is really a multisensory experience.

Because of this combination, 'name, presentation, environment, scent, sound and texture must all be considered when branding with taste' (Olfactory Evangelist, 2014).

What's more, taste can be a strong component in creating multisensory experiences. For instance, look at the personal clothing stylist company Trunk Club whose Chicago 'Clubhouse' (ie retail location) offers 'complimentary beer, wine, and spirits' to shoppers (Trunk Club, 2016), as well as other retailers who serve food or drinks during the shopping experience. And even beyond the retail setting, Kia Motors invites consumers to experience it through taste by posting appropriate recipes on its website (Kia Motors, 2016).

Why are these important? Because as a marketing blogger points out, 'Taste is linked to emotional states, and so it can alter mood and brand perception' (Olfactory Evangelist, 2014).

Let's keep it in mind as we touch briefly on the next of the five sensory 'inputs' – touch.

Let's get in touch with the key idea behind tactile branding

Another sense that's great for marketers to consider engaging is that of touch, particularly for retail environments – including the packaging and product – as well as in restaurants, hotels, and other physical locations, enabling people to gain key sensory information such as shape, texture, temperature, firmness, and other qualities that could help the individual interpret the merits of the brand and the experience.

But engaging the tactile sense can also be used in conveying experiences as well. How? Easy. Take Marriott Hotels for instance. Through Oculus Rift technology, they enabled guests to experience selected travel destinations, adding heaters to simulate the sun and water sprayers to convey being near an attractive body of water (Marriott Hotels, 2014; Brown, 2016) as well as, of course, sound.

However, for the tactile input to happen, the consumer must take the action. The brand, on the other hand, can only make the experience available.

As a result, we suspect the strategic use of this sense for mass branding purposes is more limited, like taste, and is perhaps more powerful as a branding tool once the consumer is aware of the product or service and is now intrigued enough to test his or her hypothesis about it, reinforcing what the individual first learned through the senses of sound, smell, and sight.

Therefore, of course, the tactile branding elements should be consistent with the overall brand essence and values, bringing them to life while reinforcing the qualities conveyed first through visual, sound, and even olfactory branding.

Time to sniff out the status of olfactory branding

As we just discussed, for an individual to experience the physical taste of a brand, they must act and put the food item in their mouth. Likewise, for a person to experience the physical textures of a brand – touch branding – they must actually touch the item or thing. In other words, for both of these forms of branding, an action is required by the individual to experience taste and touch forms of branding. On the other hand, an individual can smell the scent of a brand without needing to take any action. In other words, the individual can be passive and still experience the brand. And, like sound, marketers can tap into the sense of smell even when the customer is staring at something else or they have their eyes closed. Additionally, unlike touch and taste, many people can experience the scent at the same time.

And the sense of smell is important to humanity's survival, affecting everything from our perceived taste in food – it serves as a warning against consuming rotten things and sets the stage for enjoyable meals – to our sexual selection. The sense of smell plays this key role, because, as Gains explains, it's 'the only sense with a straight line to our emotions, as the olfactory bulb is directly connected to the limbic system (the centre of the brain's emotions)' (Gains, 2013). And, it's the one that is considered to be highly connected to our memory.

What's more, the use of scenting can work to influence behaviour. In fact, 'customers tend to stay an average of 15 minutes longer in locations using a scent' (Mood Media, 2016). This is important because marketers have long recognized that the longer a person stays in a store, the more likely he or she is to purchase something. Citing another study, Mood Media also reported that people underestimate the time they spend in a scented store as well as the number of individual departments they visit (Mood Media, 2016). And, drawing from a test at a popular London nightclub, one could assume that scenting can help boost sales. In a test, a nightclub doubled the sales of a coconut rum when they scented the place with the smell of coconut scent (Mood Media, 2016).

With these types of results – and the increasing recognition that emotion is often stronger than reason as a driver of decision-making – olfactory branding, like the use of sound and music, is increasing in popularity as a marketing strategy (Fahey, 2016), although we should point out the available touchpoints for scenting are obviously more limited than those for sound.

Some examples include the scent implying fresh laundry in Thomas Pink stores (Gains, 2013), a floral infused rainforest for the Equarius Hotel at Resorts World Sentosa (Faure-Field, 2012) as well as the use of scenting by many other hotel chains (Clark, 2015), and an exclusive branded fragrance for Kia that car owners could purchase (Kia Motors, 2016).

About the power of scent branding, Caroline Fabrigas, Chief Executive Officer of Scent Marketing, Inc, said, 'You don't viscerally experience a logo the way you experience a scent' (Clark, 2015).

Fabrigas also commented in an interview that a scent may be conceived as a chord: with a top note, a middle note, and a bass note. For a simplified example, the scent for a brand might lead with a top note of lively, dynamic citrus scent, a middle note of green grass to evoke the brand's ecological nature, and a bass note of wood and a comforting and grounded musk to anchor the chord. Notice the similarity to the use of audio? After knowing what the brand wanted to achieve, she said she would pick the scents with the help of a global database that tracks people's associations with a wide variety of scents from all over the planet (Fahey, 2016).

Based on Fabrigas' description of scenting, one can see how it can support a brand when the elements are consistent with the brand essence and convey the brand values, DNA, and personality. So now that we've covered olfactory branding, we are almost done – just one more sensory input. And it should be music to your ears.

And now for some sound thoughts on auditory branding

As Colleen wrote for CMO.com, 'One of the most effective tools to unify a customer's experience is the often-neglected branding element that works on-screen or off-screen, in-store or on-hold, whether or not you're looking. That's a brand's music' (Fahey, 2014).

When considering sound, one thing to remember is that it's actually multisensory. That is because the ear picks up vibrations, so, in a sense, we 'feel' sound.

In other words, 'we hear even when we are not listening' (Arning and Gordon, 2006) – perhaps a survival mechanism out in the wild to warn us of predators. And the use of sound and music can shape and direct other perceptual abilities. For instance, congruent sound cues can increase the speed of a visual search for products, a key for success in both online and retail settings (Knöferle, 2012), as well as improve the perceived taste of food (Hui, 2013) and wine (North, 2012).

And, yes, some marketers have long employed sound and music as part of their branding efforts, including, as we have already mentioned, the familiar launch chime of an Apple computer, the pop of the Snapple lid, and the aggressive howl of a Harley in rev mode.

While these examples are within the realm of audio branding, the true practices are more sophisticated than an isolated packaging or product sound, such as those listed above or the Microsoft start-up 'Windows Sound', which Brian Eno, perhaps ironically, composed on a Mac (Higgins, 2013); the use of a now quaint jingle at the end of a radio spot; or a discrete audio logo such as the one attached to the Intel Inside button.

One caveat: don't fall into the trap of thinking that audio branding is about music. Rather, it's about the branding. To create an audio universe, you have to adapt your audio DNA to internal and external audiences in both digital and environmental platforms, across all of your touchpoints, optimizing the tonality of the sound and music in light of the context of each one.

Best yet, like taste, texture, and scent, you can brand with sounds and music, reinforcing your promise and values, without obstructing understanding of words. And it's even more effective when brands bring them together and use a multisensory approach. For a perfect example, just think of the car showrooms on the Champs-Élysées as they offer up music, concept cars and their distinctive scents, restaurants, small affordable licensed products, and more.

Finally, audio branding helps marketers address our new omnichannel world, where one needs to create the truly seamless experience that customers expect across the offline and online worlds (Rosen and Minsky, 2017).

So who should consider audio branding and why?

As we just mentioned, thinking of sound and music as mere filler or background music is a huge missed opportunity. But when used correctly, sound and music have the ability to deliver a distinct branding message – and make it stick once it gets there. So you should consider developing an audio brand if:

- you are in a highly regulated industry, and there are many claims you can't make but you still need to create a bond with your audiences;
- you are launching or repositioning a company or product and want to give it a boost;
- your competitors can outspend you, and you have to outsmart them, be sharper and use your branding opportunities more wisely;
- you are a B2B company with sales films, instructional videos, sales events, a trade show booth, a customer service centre where clients could be put on hold, a presentation app or dashboard for clients to use, or other places where your clients might interact with you, and you need to tie them together with audio branding;

- you have long corridors, big parking lots, hundreds of videos, or messages over PA systems, where you can create a better experience with audio branding;
- you have branches, stores, outlets, or other forms of multiple locations and want to bring them together to convey the same experience through the use of audio branding;
- you have virtual environments and want to suggest the taste, texture, or scent of your product;
- you want to position and emphasize the role of the brand in the customer's life to people who have learned to tune out the excess stimulation delivered through the multitude of media channels;
- you develop tools or technology that provide a feedback loop or warning sounds and want to make people love you, creating a kinder world, rather than providing the annoying 'beep, Beep, BEEPs', then invest in a sound identity – in other words, it is time to rethink train doors, ATMs, microwaves, ovens, alarm clocks, washer, dryers, airport people movers, and more.

Now that you see the urgency of making the most of each consumer touchpoint and know where audio branding fits into the bigger world of sensory marketing, let's learn about the rigorous process of developing an audio brand, so you'll know how to start your brand on the right way by discovering its consistent, unique, value-building sound. So be sure to stay tuned for more in the coming pages.

GUEST PERSPECTIVE Charles Spence

Sonic seasoning

The topic of sensory marketing may seem too touchy-feely for some marketers' executive committees (it is, after all, about stimulating feelings by finding ways to touch the senses and emotions).

So we invited Professor Charles Spence, the world-famous cognitive neuroscientist, who specializes in researching multisensory marketing, to share some of his findings from his Crossmodal Research Laboratory at the Department of Experimental Psychology, Oxford University. In addition, he is a consultant for brands across the world.

Prof Spence's studies span the mapping of the musical notes most people associate with different scents, the measurement of the remarkable effect that different musical tones have on perceptions of the same flavour, the speed with which someone can see an object with a coherent sound vs a non-related sound.

What's presented here is the intriguing tip of the crossmodal iceberg, which gives a scientific solidity to phenomena that many experienced artists and designers intuitively sense.

Sonic seasoning: this evocative term captures the growing realization that what we hear influences what we taste, and does so in ways that are predictable. Culinary artists, chefs, food and beverage brands, and even an airline have taken these findings on board (quite literally in the last case) to enhance the multisensory offering that they provide to their customers (Spence, 2014).

Crossing of the senses is, of course, nothing new in the fields of design and creative endeavour (Haverkamp, 2014). However, the problem is that all too often innovative cross-sensory connections, and unusual combinations of stimuli, have been based on the intuitions of the synaesthete – these are the rare individuals, though no one can agree quite how rare, who experience unusual sensory concurrents (like colour) on perceiving, or thinking about, a particular inducer (such as a letter, a number, or a unit of time). While the synaesthete's experiences are undoubtedly interesting, the problem for design and marketing is that their concurrents are, by definition, idiosyncratic (Spence, 2012).

Thus, while one synaesthete might experience a low-pitched sound while tasting something sweet, another might experience a bubbling sound. Just take the famous Russian mnemonist (that's someone with a very, very large memory) and synaesthete studied by Luria back in the 1960s (Luria, 1968). This individual experienced an especially wide range of different taste/flavour sensations in response to sound. When, for example, presented with a 50Hz tone (for musicians, this corresponds approximately to G1), he experienced a taste that he likened to sweet and sour borscht: 'a sensation that gripped his entire tongue'. Meanwhile, when presented with a 3,000 Hz tone (close to a G7), he reported 'an ugly taste – rather like that of a briny pickle' instead.

Are such observations interesting? Yes! Are they meaningful, when it comes to designing music and soundscapes to complement our tasting experiences, I doubt it – though it doesn't, of course, stop people from trying (Knapton, 2015; Spence and Wang, 2015). I would argue that while any composition/creation based on the unique experiences of synaesthetes may be interesting, and will possibly have a slightly higher chance of being liked than some other random combination of stimuli (Ward et al, 2008), it is unlikely that it will have widespread appeal for consumers (Spence, 2012).

What has been so exciting about the developments that have taken place over the last few years is precisely that a new science of surprising cross-sensory matching has emerged. One that is based on the crossmodal correspondences (Spence, 2011). It turns out that most of us (no matter whether we are a synaesthetes or not) share many surprising associations between our senses.

To illustrate the point, just think for a moment about whether a lemon is fast or slow? It has to be fast, right! As to why that should be the case, it is hard to say.

But I can guarantee you that the majority of people respond to that question, and many others like it, in the same way. I should know, we have been conducting a huge amount of cross-cultural research on just such questions over the last few years (eg Woods et al, 2013). A large and growing body of empirical research now demonstrates that most of us will associate high-pitched sounds with stimuli that are light, bright, small, angular, and localized high up in space, whereas low-pitched sounds are darker, larger, and localized lower in space (see Spence, 2011, for a review).

Welcome to the world of the crossmodal correspondences.

The key point here is that tastes, aromas, and flavours also correspond crossmodally to sounds of different pitch, to different timbres (just think of the characteristic sounds of different classes of music instrument), roughness, tempo, etc (Knöferle and Spence, 2012; Knöferle et al, 2015).

Knowing this allows one to make musical recommendations, or even to generate novel music and/or soundscapes that, when played, can actually change the taste of food and drink. Yes, you read that right. Remarkable, no? But this is the all new science of sonic seasoning.

In one study, for instance, conducted together with The Fat Duck Research Kitchen and Condiment Junkie, a sound-design agency based in the UK, we demonstrated that a tinkling high-pitched soundscape would bring out the sweetness of a bittersweet food (cinder toffee) while playing a low-pitched soundscape brought out the toffee's bitterness instead (Crisinel et al, 2012).

Sadly, the results were not dramatic enough to make it onto the tasting menu at The Fat Duck (this the restaurant, remember, that is famous, in part, for the 'Sound of the Sea' seafood dish – a plate of seafood that is brought to the table together with a conch shell, out of which dribble some earbuds, playing, you guessed it, the sounds of the sea) (The Fat Duck, 2016).

Nevertheless, Caroline Hobkinson (a culinary artist) incorporated the two soundscapes into the sensory dining menu that she curated at The House of Wolf restaurant in Islington, North London (now, sadly, closed). Each of the courses on the tasting menu was devoted to a different one of the diner's senses. For the sound course, the diners were given a bittersweet chocolate lolly. There was a telephone number on the menu for diners to ring. They could then either choose to listen to the bitter or to the sweet soundscape.

We have the findings to show that ratings of sweetness-bitterness vary, on average, by 5–10 per cent depending on the soundscape that you happen to be listening to, and the food you are tasting. British Airways went on to introduce its 'Sound Bite' soundtrack on its long-haul flights, incorporating just this idea – making the food taste just that little bit better at 35,000 ft (Victor, 2014).

Now, before getting too excited about all these cross-sensory effects, it is worth noting a few things:

1 While you can use sound to draw people's attention to a taste/flavour in a food that they might not otherwise pay so much attention to (and, by so doing, accentuate it in the consumer's mind), you cannot use music to 'magic up' a taste out of nowhere – or at least we haven't succeeded in doing that yet.

2 And while many are interested in using such insights to perhaps provide musical accompaniments for meal times that will allow people to taste the sweetness they crave while reducing the actual sugar content of the food (by, you guessed it, playing those sweet tunes), we do not yet know how long-lasting such sonic seasoning effects are. Would they wear off after a week? Or will they last a lifetime? We simply do not know. More research is most definitely needed here.

3 I suspect that, given how many associations there are with the sounds we hear, it helps to prime the consumer to the connections that may be present in the music. Otherwise, there is a danger that it might just all pass them by. Or, then again, maybe not. Once again, more research needed!

Where the modernist chef and culinary artist lead (supported, of course, by the eager psychologist), bigger brands and companies will eventually follow. The year 2013, for instance, saw The Singleton Sensorium, where 500 people were invited to Soho in London for a multisensory tasting event.

They were given a glass of The Singleton whisky, a scorecard, and a pencil. They were then led through three rooms, each with a different soundscape, different visuals, and a different aroma. The sweet room, for example, had tinkling high-pitched music (sonic seasoning) coming from the ceiling. Changing the atmospherics led to a 10–20 per cent change in people's experience of the aroma, taste, and mouth-feel of the drink (Velasco *et al*, 2013). Since then, several drinks brands have been sponsoring versions of the Sensorium in countries around the world, including South Africa and Canada (see also Spence *et al*, 2014). The multisensory experiential angle is even being extended to the museum setting, with special soundscapes composed to accompany particular art works, eg at The Sensorium at Tate Britain over the summer of 2015 (Davis, 2015).

Looking forward, though, I see the biggest uptake of these emerging insights around sonic, or digital, seasoning evolving with the next generation of sensory apps (Spence, 2014). For instance, just take the Concerto app launched by Häagen-Dazs to help the consumer gauge how long they should wait after taking their ice-cream out of the freezer before serving. (The app, developed by Goodby, Silverstein & Partners Inc can be downloaded at https://itunes.apple.com/us/app/haagen-dazs-concerto-timer/id670015815?mt=8).

Customers simply have to get their mobile device out, scan the QR code (that black-and-white square) that can be found on the lid of special packs. The next thing they know, an apparition suddenly appears above the tub of ice-cream when viewed through the screen of their mobile device. The viewer is then treated to a short musical interlude, in which musicians can be seen (and heard) magically floating on top of the ice-cream. Each of the musical selections lasts for about two minutes – or, in other words, just long enough for the contents to soften slightly. Once the music draws to a close, or so the claim goes, the ice-cream should be ready to serve. What is more, the different flavours are associated with different pieces of music. Now, while different tunes can be heard after scanning different ice-cream lids, I believe that there is a whole art and science to the matching of music to taste/flavour that is yet to be capitalized on.

Krug also has an app that allows the discerning champagne drinker to scan the label of their bottle and get a selection of music (King, 2014a), just a part of their strategy of drawing a parallel between the art of composition in the case of music and wine (King, 2014b). And let me assure you, I know of a host of other food and beverage brands who have been thinking about offering their own version of this. Though, taking a closer look at the apps that have been released so far, one sees that the choice of music, or soundscape, has typically been based more on intuition, and the personal preferences of the creator of the product or perhaps a famous musician.

However, looking forward, I believe that there is scope to deliver musical selections, and soundscapes, that can bring out, or enhance, a particular taste, or flavour. Who, after all, wouldn't want music recommendations that could help to make their food sweeter? In fact, we now have musical recommendations not only for sweet, but also for sour and bitter music.

Furthermore, we are currently working on spicy music, and music that conveys notions of hot/cold. The two tastes that we are still struggling to define musically are salty, and the fifth taste, umami. And while the focus here is primarily on food and drink, it should be noted that a number of perfume makers are starting to sit up and take notice of the correspondences too. To give some ideas of what is possible here, the Nez de Courvoisier cognac app from a few years ago (Crisinel *et al*, 2013; Spence *et al*, 2014; Studioish, nd) involved soundscapes specifically composed to correspond to each of six key aroma notes in the cognac. In the future, the same could presumably be done for high-end perfumes.

I also see great potential for home food delivery services, where the take-away, or meal, is delivered together with a music selection designed to enhance, or modify, the consumer's taste experience. Just take the recent team-up between Munchery and Google Play Music (eg Roncero-Menendez, 2015), or our own work identifying the top tunes to go with different styles of take-away with Just Eat (Sanderson, 2015). Once they realize just how important the atmosphere is to the experience of eating and drinking (Spence and Piqueras-Fiszman, 2014), food and drinks brands will realize that they should be doing everything in their power to optimize the sonic backdrop when the consumer tastes their products. It really can make all the difference.

Finally, it is worth noting that the emergence of the Sensorium concept, and the growth of interest in sensory apps, also fits nicely, I think, into the emerging trend toward 'Sensploration' (Leow, 2015). The fact that many of these cross-sensory associations (or correspondences) are surprising, while at the same time being shared across groups of people, makes it all the more interesting for consumers to explore their own sensory worlds, and the surprising connections that might lie therein. Given all the above, I would expect to hear a lot more about sonic/digital seasoning in the years to come.

Guest biography

Charles Spence is Professor of Experimental Psychology and Head of the Crossmodal Research Laboratory based at Oxford University's Department of Experimental Psychology. An internationally recognized expert in consumer neuroscience, sensory marketing, product development and innovation, neurogastronomy, neuroscience-inspired marketing and design, and consumer psychology, Charles is interested in how people perceive the world around them: in particular, how our brains process the information from each of our different senses to form the extraordinarily rich multisensory experiences that fill our daily lives.

Charles has lectured and consulted extensively around the world on the topics of consumer neuroscience and sensory marketing to a very wide range of companies and industries, including PepsiCo, Unilever, Twinings, Nestlé, P&G, Mars, McDonald's, Starbucks, Givaudan, Firmenich, and Takasago. He is increasingly asked to work with top restaurants, such as Heston Blumenthal's The Fat Duck at Bray, Denis Martin's Restaurant Denis Martin, Vevey, Switzerland, and The Paul Bocuse cookery school and restaurant, Lyon, France.

Prof Spence has published more than 750 peer-reviewed articles over the last two decades on various aspects of neuroscience and design. 2014 saw the publication of his latest book with Betina Piqueras-Fiszman, *The perfect meal: The multisensory science of food and dining*, which won the 2015 Prose Prize for popular science.

Charles has won a number of awards for his work, including:

- the Ig Nobel award for nutrition: 'The role of auditory cues in modulating the perceived crispness and staleness of potato chips', co-authored with M Zampini and published in the *Journal of Sensory Science*;
- with Cristy Ho, the American Psychological Association's Division, Young Investigator Award for 'Assessing the effectiveness of various auditory cues in capturing a driver's visual attention' in the *Journal of Experimental Psychology*;
- the Friedrich Wilhelm Bessel Research Award from the Alexander von Humboldt Foundation, Germany;
- the Paul Bertelson Award of the European Society for Cognitive Psychology, which honours scientists in an early stage of their scientific careers who have made an outstanding contribution to cognitive psychology in Europe.

CASE Nestlé, La Roche-Posay and Louis XIII Cognac

Taste and touch: examples of using music's flavouring to focus emotions and heighten senses

Nestlé Extrême

Music has been proven to measurably affect the perceived flavour of a food or beverage, for instance, making it taste sweeter or more bitter, as Professor Charles Spence discusses in his commentary on sonic seasoning. It can also impart a powerful emotional effect on the eating or drinking experience.

From Charles Spence, we know that the brain allows one sense to influence another. Branded music that is deliberately designed to influence the awareness of sensations of smoothness, sweetness, or complexity or to enhance soothing, stimulating or adventurous emotions has the ability to create a rich, layered experience that can greatly enhance memories, associations and feelings about your brand.

An audio DNA composition created for Nestlé Extrême Ice Creams, demonstrates how that can happen. The women who were the target audience often used ice-cream to calm themselves during stressful moments. They experienced their ice-cream break as a calming and sensual ritual. To enhance this emotional state, the music had to convey the ritualized aspect of the experience. It needed to be soothing but still suggest enjoyment. The audio strategy was envisioned as an 'Adult Lullaby'.

When the audio DNA was designed, the main musical theme was carried by a breathy, sensual female voice singing a simple syllable over and over: 'Lu-lu-lu-lu-lu'. Similar to the way the music builds in Ravel's *Bolero*, the wavelike rhythm repeats and rises in intensity. The music sounds like a lullaby at first and then rises in intensity and ends with the catch of breath and a woman's mischievous laugh.

Commercials had already been running using other music (one used an instrumental version of *La Paloma* for instance). These television commercials had their scores replaced with compositions based on the new audio DNA. Millward Brown's research revealed remarkable quantitative results (see Table 3.1) in terms of changes in emotional response. Some emotional states were enhanced (eg pleasant, distinctive, gentle) while others were diminished (eg dull, boring).

Louis XIII mansion tastings

In 2007, Louis XIII Cognac, a legendary, ultra-premium cognac brand containing 1,200 eaux-de-vie from the Grande Champagne region of France and whose bottles, on average, retail for $2,100 to $3,100, sought to reaffirm its high quality and its prestigious status.

Table 3.1 Changes in emotional responses due to new audio DNA

What increased		What decreased	
Pleasant	+18%	Dull	−11%
Distinctive	+16%	Boring	−9%
Gentle	+13%	Weak	−8%
Interesting	+6%	Irritating	−4%
Soothing	+7%	Unpleasant	−4%

SOURCE Sixième Son

From the house of Rémy Martin, Louis XIII comes in a Baccarat decanter. So, to help achieve their objectives, a special run of individually numbered Baccarat dark crystal decanters was produced containing 'Louis XIII Black Pearl', a limited-edition cognac.

The company envisioned a series of events in grand mansions in the world's premier cities like Paris, New York, Shanghai, London, Beijing, Los Angeles, and Tokyo to help spotlight the ultimate extravagance and many sensual pleasures promised by the cognac. It aimed to draw attention to its refined and complex symphony of scents and flavours.

The strategy was to focus individually on the experiences the consumer could expect as they immersed themselves in the enjoyment of the product. The team of clients, agency, and audio-branding firm achieved this feat by having visitors enter separated rooms that immersed them in the various sensations they could expect from the total experience of consuming Louis XIII, isolating each sensation to draw attention to it. As visitors were led through each room, they experienced a sensation, heightening their senses to the key aspects of the brand.

One exemplified the Baccarat crystal, with crystalline music laced with far-off voices and oddly dissonant touches. The qualities of the crystal were also embodied in the lighting, furnishings, and other objects.

To convey the influence of the century-old Limousin oak casks in which the cognac had been aged, the next room gave the musky, deep, and mysterious idea of a forest at night with suggestions of frogs, crickets, and a fairy song.

Visitors were then taken into the last room, a vault where a warmed snifter was waiting for them. Now, as each person was led through the ritual of holding, sniffing, resting a drop on the tongue, and finally tasting the fine cognac, the music they heard in the previous rooms was combined to bring to life the fullness and richness of the overall experience.

On 14 November 2007 the only remaining bottle of the edition of 786 without an owner was auctioned in the Mandarin Oriental, Prague. ABC Prague reported,

'Louis XIII Black Pearl is not only a gourmet delicacy and a piece of art, but also a unique investment chance. The first bottle was sold for €12,000, the highest price for one bottle came in Japan €62,000' (ABC Prague, 2007).

The La Roche-Posay delicate touch

The effect of branded music can heighten senses beyond mouth-feel and taste. Consider its effect on the sensation of touch.

For La Roche-Posay, an iconic brand that is part of the L'Oréal Group, the product is a line of very pure skincare creams designed for the most delicate of skins including those that are allergic, post-chemotherapy, and very young. The audio identity needed to express the duality of the brand: both its gentleness and its efficacy.

The resulting audio identity suggests the sensation of the most delicate touch on skin. It expresses purity, authenticity, and humane values. Piano with distinctive, subtle aquatic tones and an airy voice carry the melody.

Rather than emphasize drumbeats, the percussion uses brushy sounds, snapping, and soft clapping to produce an effect that's uncannily tactile and yet carries a sense of precision and confidence.

With music that's slightly varied to support different product lines, the brand has been endowed with a meaningful auditory expression that unifies it across the globe. It can draw on a varied audio library all based in the audio DNA that connects such disparate communication opportunities as employee events and digital consumer communications.

And anyone who hears it, won't need the words to know the product is pure and gentle (Sixieme Son, 2016).

In short, just as a person's enjoyment of food and beverages isn't derived from the flavours and fragrances alone but from memories, associations, motions, and, as importantly, from what draws your attention, the same is true for tactile sensations.

References

ABC Prague (2007) *Louis XIII. Black Pearl auction in Prague*, 1 November 2007, http://www.abcprague.com/2007/11/01/louis-xiii-black-pearl-auction-in-prague [accessed 7 May 2016]

Arning, C and Gordon, A (2006) *Sonic Semiotics: The role of music in marketing communications*, ESOMAR, 2006

Brown, E (2016) *Paving The Way To Improve Brand Experiences: Sense and sensibility!*, dm|DesignMantic, August 16, 2016, https://www.designmantic.com/blog/sense-and-sensibility-in-branding/ [accessed 31 October 2016]

Clark, C (2015) *Why Do Fancy Hotels Pipe in Such Powerful Fragrances?*, Bloomberg Pursuits, September 18, 2015 http://www.bloomberg.com/news/articles/2015-09-18/scent-branding-101-why-do-fancy-hotels-use-such-powerful-fragances- [accessed 16 April 2016]

Crisinel, A-S, Cosser, S, King, S, Jones, R, Petrie, J and Spence, C (2012) A bittersweet symphony: Systematically modulating the taste of food by changing the sonic properties of the soundtrack playing in the background, *Food Quality and Preference*, 24, pp 201–04

Crisinel, A-S, Jacquier, C, Deroy, O and Spence, C (2013) Composing with cross-modal correspondences: Music and smells in concert, *Chemosensory Perception*, 6, pp 45–52

Davis, N (2015) Welcome to the Tate Sensorium, where the paintings come with chocolates, *The Guardian*, 22 August, http://www.theguardian.com/artanddesign/video/2015/aug/25/welcome-tate-sensorium-taste-touch-smell-art-video [accessed 13 September 2015]

Fahey, C (2014) *Audio Branding in an Omnichannel World,* CMO.com, October 6, 2014 http://www.cmo.com/opinion/articles/2014/9/30/audio_branding_in_an.html [accessed 2 November 2016]

Fahey, C (2016) Personal interview with Caroline Fabrigas, CEO, Scent Marketing, Inc, April 11 & 13, 2016

Faure-Field, S (2012) This is what sensory branding can do for your business, *Singapore Business,* September 25, 2012, http://sbr.com.sg/media-marketing/commentary/what-sensory-branding-can-do-your-business [accessed 2 November 2016]

Gains, N (2013) *Brand esSense: Using sense, symbol, and story to design brand identity*, Kogan Page, London

Haverkamp, M (2014) *Synesthetic Design: Handbook for a multisensory approach,* Birkhäuser, Basel

Higgins, C (2013) Creating the Windows 95 Startup Sound, *Mental Floss*, May 30, 2013, http://mentalfloss.com/article/50824/creating-windows-95-startup-sound [accessed 2 November 2016]

Hui, A (2013) The five senses of flavour: How colour and sound can make your dinner taste better, *The Globe and Mail,* 19 May 2013, http://www.theglobeandmail.com/life/food-and-wine/food-trends/the-5-senses-of-flavour-how-colour-and-sound-can-make-your-dinner-taste-better/article9957597/ [accessed 2 November 2016]

Hulten, B (2015) *Sensory Marketing: Theoretical and empirical grounds*, Routledge, New York

Kia Motors (2016) http://pr.kia.com/en/now/brand/multisensory-branding/taste.do [accessed 31 October 2016]

King, J (2014a) Krug ID app creates mobile reference network for Champagne lovers, April 18, http://www.luxurydaily.com/krug-id-app-creates-mobile-refeence-network-for-champagne-lovers/ [accessed 6 August 2014]

King, J (2014b) Krug heightens sensory experience with listening device, *Luxury Daily*, January 2, http://www.luxurydaily.com/krug-heightens-sensory-experience-with-listening-device/ [accessed 6 August 2014]

Knapton, S (2015) Why sparkling wine sounds like beans falling on a plastic tray, *The Daily Telegraph*, 2 May, p 7

Knöferle, K (2012) *Product-Related Sounds Speed Visual Search*, Audio-Branding Academy, http://audio-branding-academy.org/aba/congress/2012-2/program-2012/sounds-speed-visual-search/ [accessed 2 November 2016] and Bronner, K, Hirt, R and Ringe, C (2013) Audio Branding Academy Yearbook 2012/2013, Nomos Verlagsgesellschaft

Knöferle, KM and Spence, C (2012) Crossmodal correspondences between sounds and tastes, *Psychonomic Bulletin & Review*, **19**, pp 992–1006

Knöferle, KM, Woods, A, Käppler, F and Spence, C (2015) That sounds sweet: Using crossmodal correspondences to communicate gustatory attributes, *Psychology & Marketing*, **32**, pp 107–20

Leow, HC (2015) Never heard of Sensploration? Time to study up on epicure's biggest high-end pattern, *The Veox*, 22 December, http://www.theveox.com/never-heard-of-sensploration-time-to-study-up-on-epicures-biggest-high-end-pattern/ [accessed on 13 January 2016]

Luria, AR (1968) *The Mind of a Mnemonist*, Harvard University Press, Cambridge, MA

Marriott Hotels (2014) *Marriott Hotels' Virtual Travel Experience (Behind the Scenes)*, September 18, https://www.youtube.com/watch?v=a9725H0ls7c#t=115 [accessed 31 October 2016]

Mood Media (2016) Smell is an extremely powerful sensory branding tool and it is often overlooked and underutilized by businesses, 2016, Mood media us.moodmedia.com/wp-content/uploads/2016/07/wakeup-marketing.pdf [accessed 1 November 2016]

North, AC (2012) The effect of background music on the taste of wine, *British Journal of Psychology*, **103**, pp 293–301

Olfactory Evangelist (2014) Sensory branding 101: To see, hear, touch, taste and smell, Allsense, June 25, 2014, http://allsense.com.sg/sensory-branding-101-to-see-hear-touch-taste-smell/ [accessed 3 October 2016]

Roncero-Menendez, S (2015) *Eat your chocolate cake with the perfect soundtrack: Munchery and Google Play Music team up to turn a simple meal into a dining experience*, 18 August, http://www.psfk.com/2015/08/munchery-google-play-meal-food-pairing-soundtrack.html [accessed on 11 February 2016]

Rosen, W and Minsky, L (2017) *The Activation Imperative*, Rowman and Littlefield

Sanderson, D (2015) Chinese tastes better with Taylor Swift, *The Times*, 8 December, p 3, https://www.thetimes.co.uk/tto/science/article4635202.ece [accessed 11 February 2016]

Sixième Son (2016) La Roche-Posay voice is markedly distinguished and heard all over the world, http://www.sixiemeson.com/en/audio-branding-sound-identity-portfolio/la-roche-posay/ [accessed 7 May 2016]

Spence, C (2011) Crossmodal correspondences: A tutorial review, *Attention, Perception, & Psychophysics*, **73**, pp 971–95

Spence, C (2012) Synaesthetic Marketing: Cross-sensory selling that exploits unusual neural cues is finally coming of age, *The Wired World in 2013*, November, pp 104–07

Spence, C (2014) Multisensory advertising and design, in B Flath and E Klein (eds), *Advertising and Design: Interdisciplinary perspectives on a cultural field* (pp 15–27), Verlag, Bielefeld

Spence, C and Piqueras-Fiszman, B (2014) *The Perfect Meal: The multisensory science of food and dining*, Wiley-Blackwell, Oxford

Spence, C, Velasco, C and Knöferle, K (2014) A large sample study on the influence of the multisensory environment on the wine drinking experience, *Flavour*, 3:8

Spence, C and Wang, Q (J) (2015) Wine & music (III): So what if music influences taste? *Flavour*, **4**:35

Studioish (nd) http://studioish.com/?portfolio=le-nez-de-courvoisier

The Fat Duck (2016) http://www.thefatduck.co.uk/ [accessed 31 October 2016]

Trunk Club (2016) https://www.trunkclub.com/locations/chicago [accessed 31 October 2016]

Velasco, C, Jones, R, King, S and Spence, C (2013) Assessing the influence of the multisensory environment on the whisky drinking experience, *Flavour*, **2**:23

Victor, A (2014) Louis Armstrong for starters, Debussy with roast chicken and James Blunt for dessert: British Airways pairs music to meals to make in-flight food taste better, *DailyMail Online*, 15 October, http://www.dailymail.co.uk/travel/travel_news/article-2792286/british-airways-pairs-music-meals-make-flight-food-taste-better.html [accessed on 11 February 2016]

Ward, J, Moore, S, Thompson-Lake, D, Salih, S and Beck, B (2008) The aesthetic appeal of auditory-visual synaesthetic perceptions in people without synaesthesia, *Perception*, **13**, pp 1285–297

Woods, AT, Spence, C, Butcher, N and Deroy, O (2013) Fast lemons and sour boulders: Testing the semantic hypothesis of crossmodal correspondences using an internet-based testing methodology, *i-Perception*, **4**, pp 365–69

Welcome to the world of audio branding

04

As we saw in the previous chapters, marketing and branding have changed due to our new digitally connected world, giving marketers ever more opportunities to communicate the brand attributes through the seemingly ever-growing array of touchpoints, and similarly, more messaging and more touchpoints are creating more clutter in the marketplace, driving marketers to work harder just to stand out. Meanwhile, we also discovered the potential and power of sensory marketing and branding, particularly sound, because of our new digitally-enabled world. After all, as we just discussed in the previous chapter, prospects, purchasers, and consumers of a brand experience and understand it, especially emotionally, in more ways than just visually.

So by including the sense of hearing in your branding efforts, your company can switch on a whole new battery of branding tools – melody, rhythm, instrumentation, harmony, and texture – with which to create highly potent brand influence. And the ability to use these audio tools is equally true for B2B companies as it is for B2C brands.

Each of the elements will be considered carefully as to their fit with a given brand. Slow or fast? Simple or layered? Regular or syncopated? Voiced or instrumental? Acoustic or synthesized?

There are infinite potential combinations, which is why each custom-tailored audio brand is able to sound like no other.

These ingredients are woven into a short composition that defines your company's audio DNA. At Sixième Son, this audio DNA is considered the core, defining composition that conveys each brand's values and aspirations. This custom-designed piece of music isn't intended to be cut up, pasted in, or played repetitively but, instead, it is to serve as the guide for the melody and rhythm and instrumentation for future adaptations to fit your important employee and customer touchpoints.

The hardest-working piece that emerges from the audio DNA is the theme that weaves through the composition and becomes the basis for the audio logo. This two- or three-second audio logo embodies the heart of the brand. The audio logo reprises the core motif that runs throughout the brand's audio DNA and ends the composition, but it also can stand on its own, and it should accompany the visual logo at every single audiovisual opportunity. Together, the visual and audio logos amplify each other's power, bringing in emotion and additional meaning to the visual impression and leaving a powerful 'earprint' with the audience.

Resilience within a defined structure

A good audio brand isn't a straitjacket that forces people to use the same composition over and over. An audio brand endows a product or company with a flexible system, a unique vocabulary that can be adapted with sensitivity and customer empathy to the increasing number of brand engagement points. It allows a brand to stand out and be understood in different ways at different points of interaction with different audiences.

Licensed music is no longer enough for a brand with any long-term aspirations. Though popular tunes or classic pieces have their place, they carry too many associations with TV shows, movies and, often, other products to be pure carriers of the core brand values and message. In cases in which licensed music is used, responsible marketers must take care to end the commercial, event, video, or other application with the unique sound of their own recognizable audio logo, rather than the sound of someone else's music.

Over time, the brand builds up a deep library of varied but clearly related compositions that fit many specific occasions and touchpoints.

Identify your brand's touchpoints – especially where sound design can improve the experience

Besides advertising, how can a company use its audio brand to clarify and, even, improve the experience of a customer, employee, partner, or other key stakeholder?

Let's take a trip around your potential audio interactions. As we examine each of them, you can rank them as to which touchpoints would have the most impact on each of your particular audiences. A unique benefit of audio branding is that each touchpoint's sound impression builds upon the others, thereby building a recognizable audio universe without adding significant cost.

Give yourself a call

Our client experience tells us that one of the first places you would want to evaluate is the company's telephone on-hold music. Your customer service line may be one of the only live contact points you ever have with your audience. It's an occasion when they actively reach out to you. Would you want this valuable impression dressed in generic pop music, oft-heard classical music, or cheap needle-drop tunes?

The customer experience can be significantly enhanced with a specific adaptation of the music and voice. If the on-hold music presents your brand in a familiar, but fresh way, full of little musical variations and surprises, your customer can perceive a shorter wait-time and experience a happier interaction with the brand.

You will probably need pre-pickup music along with a welcoming message, the on-hold music, and, if you are likely to have callers who are experiencing emergencies (such as a gas company), you should provide different, more serious on-hold music for customers who choose that option.

Voice casting makes a difference, too. Is your brand young or old, British or American, cheerful or serious, friendly or authoritative, male or female, or both alternating? You may have spent hours anguishing over these questions for your corporate video but left the phone system to a third-party interactive voice-response supplier managed by your technology department. So call your service line. If you don't like what you hear, your audio-branding partner can help you cast and contract the voice talent and manage the recording sessions, as well as sensitively join the voice recordings to the music.

Evaluate the music used in your branded content

Today's companies have become mighty production studios pouring out oceans of how-to videos, customer or patient stories, product demonstrations, care instructions, recipes, staff tales, guided tours, flash-mob films, holiday tips, general interest stories, industry or product news, and more.

Kraft Recipes, alone, shares more than 450 videos of 'game day' recipes, kitchen basics, grilling suggestions, and how-to tips, Thanksgiving recipes, patriotic desserts, and an all-Spanish channel with its more than 43,000 subscribers (Kraft, 2016).

In the same city, a large pharmaceutical firm creates corporate social responsibility films, announcements of new initiatives, statements of purpose, method-of-action videos, and recruitment videos, among other audiovisual experiences.

The use of your own audio identity for the intros, interstitials, and outros can be enough to suggest the content is within the same family as both the ad and the sales presentations they may have heard. Or you can, alternatively, score the whole piece with your branded sound. Either way, each bit of tactical brand content works in an understated way to build equity for the long-term brand.

When you adapt your identifiable sound to your instructional and promotional content, you'll remind your audience who's behind the messaging without overwhelming the experience itself.

Raise the impact of meetings and conferences

As we mentioned in Chapter 1, when it comes to a corporate meeting, many companies default to standard fare that's been used over and over. How many times have you heard 'We Are the Champions' at a sales meeting? Does it feel contrived or manipulative to you? Don't you suspect your staff might respond better to a high-energy piece of music that felt more authentically their own?

Then there's the ongoing problem of letting executives choose their own walk-up music. As a result, each executive has his or her own brand rather than giving the impression of a team all working toward the same goals. Among the dangers of this approach are that often the executive's favourite music seems out-of-date to the younger staff and provokes titters of veiled laughter. Sometimes the results are worse. An executive who had joined a wireless carrier from a 'more glamorous' beverage company chose to remind the wireless carrier's executive audience of that fact by playing a piece of music used in the beverage company's commercials. This provoked much eye-rolling and not much team spirit.

It's no wonder that many companies now own packages of meeting and event sounds. These take into account physical and emotional aspects of the attendee's journey.

When attendees are coming into an auditorium, they may still be distracted by their ever-present e-mails and texts, they're probably looking for seats, they may be having awkward conversations with people they slightly recognize from last year but whose names they can't recall. Here the music stays in the background, its role is to cover up those awkward pauses and gradually shift their mood and attention to the matter at hand.

Once the audience is seated, music becomes more prominent. Its key role now is to build anticipation and give a taste of what's to come. Then as the opening speaker is announced, the music should build to a crescendo, which can lead to rousing applause.

Between speakers, there are the empty moments as one comes off the stage and another comes up to the podium. These transitions can be brightened – and even psychologically shortened – by the brief musical passages. And these snippets can be tailored to suggest the upcoming topic: more technical, more controversial, more inspirational, news – good or bad – all these can be implied through the treatment of the music.

The end of the meeting requires closure and also a way to send people out energized and inspired by what they've heard. Again, brand-oriented music has a role. It can put a bounce in people's steps and leave them with an emotional reminder of what they've just participated in. The earprint they carry will recall the message of the meeting.

Share tailored ringtones

As your sales team or target audience leaves your conference wouldn't it be great if they could take something with them to remind them of the emotional impact the meeting had had on them?

If so, then consider offering the audience its choice of ringtones, all of which carry a hint of your audio brand.

People are particular about their ringtones. Some people like them to start quietly and grow in volume, some want them to attract their immediate attention by starting strong, some prefer odd, unexpected, or synthesized sounds that stand out from the background, and others like a touch of humour.

Ringtones allow you to explore the range of your audio brand and allow your audiences some level of choice and control. You can offer a range of them to choose from for the attendees of your events and other situations where a reminder comes in handy. So you should offer no fewer than three and as many as a dozen. As a practical matter, you need a larger number if you intend to offer them to a large group of employees who work near each other. If you only offer a couple of them, people who hear the sound will constantly be checking to see if it's their phone that's ringing.

Offering ringtones also helps truly seed your audio brand in people's memories. In order to choose their favourites, people typically listen to all the different permutations, some more than once. This helps them gain familiarity with the sound and will lead to even quicker recognition.

So consider offering ringtones to sales teams after a big sales meeting, to employees just after you've launched your audio brand, to prospects at an expo booth, to partners and key suppliers as an e-gift during the holidays or a product launch.

Stand out at expos, trade shows and conferences

When you walk the floor at an exposition or industry conference, you will find an array of visual material clamouring for your attention: digital signage, banners, inflatables, multicoloured pennants, motion displays, product turntables, and more. You name it, you'll see it.

Now think: how common is the deliberate use of a recognizable sound?

What if the audience at a trade fair, who has recently heard your branded music at your presentation, were to catch a similar sound coming from your booth on the expo floor? Chances are, they would recognize the connection and they would probably have a warmer feeling about your booth than the one next door. Do you think that would increase the chances of their stopping in? Because that's what we've found.

Though they limited the number of people in the booth to 700 at a time, Renault's booth at the Paris Auto Show in 2013 was the most visited attraction at the event. Renault had commissioned a composition that took the audience through the life-stages of a driver, from their first barely affordable car, to the car for seduction, to the car for adventure, to the car for work and beyond. The music was accompanied by buoyant floating orbs that changed colour as each of the life-stage transitions occurred. Around the booth, screens showed glimpses of the lifestyles of which the cars were an integral part.

If you were standing near the oil-fuelled cars the music carried a more acoustic sound and included natural sounds of birds, water and laughter. If you stood closer to the electric cars, the sound became airier, electronic, and synthesized.

The audience was surrounded by music above and below, as a three-dimensional sound system employed subwoofers built into the floor and strategically placed speakers aimed from different heights to create an enveloping sound environment.

Sixième Son, who had created the composition and managed the audio design for Renault, wove the Renault audio vocabulary throughout the varied pieces so, even though each car model carried its own individual sound, together they all related to each other as a family.

Most brands don't require a full composition with six movements in order to use music effectively. Atlanta's booth at a convention for convention planners, for instance, made a big impact simply by bringing their print ads to life. By the adding of animated graphics and adapting their branded sound to the different topics (nature, nightlife, technology), they created compelling audiovisual attractions that felt like short movies.

With or without sound, your booth should strive to provide your audience with the sense of having crossed a clear threshold, one that truly divides your part of the world from the cacophonous expo centre floor. And branded music gives you a powerful tool to signal that the transition has occurred in a way that conveys the emotions you want attendees to feel.

Design product sounds and signals

Imagine you are a retail bank with ATMs all over the country and a mobile banking app. What if your ATM, instead of beeping loudly at your customers, played a three- or four-note tune that matched the sound in the end frame of your commercials? Or what if your app's signal also came from the same sound vocabulary to tell the customer, 'opening', 'password recognized' or 'your transaction was successful'. What an opportunity to create a pleasant brand experience during a routine transaction.

Unfortunately, right now, the world is too full of noisy beeps.

In the household, microwave ovens, coffee makers, conventional ovens, and washers and dryers could all be pleasant instruments instead of the alarming beeping like the rubbish trucks backing up the road.

In train stations, public transportation systems and airports it can be hard to catch travellers' attention over the din of conversation and the roar of vehicles. But some transportation systems use artful pre-announcement signals that tie back to their brands.

As proof that the sounds that alert travellers to incoming trains may be evocative rather than generic, one need look no further than SNCF, the French national railway, which we discussed in Chapter 1. As we mentioned, their four-note signal was noticed by Pink Floyd's famous guitarist, David Gilmour, in the south of France. Gilmour was inspired and he recorded it at the Aix-en-Provence station. In 2014, the song he created with it in collaboration with Michaël Boumendil became the title track of David Gilmour's first album in 10 years, *Rattle that Lock*, released in September 2015. 'Rattle that Lock' immediately climbed to the number one slot in both the UK and France. Just think of the positive PR SNCF receives each time the song is played publicly and the positive connections that are generated to the brand each time a David Gilmour fan listens to the song: opportunities that can't be generated through the use of generic bells, beeps, bleeps, and pings.

On the horizon are ever more electric cars, which don't necessarily have to sound like a vroom-vroom engine any more than David Gilmour's iPhone has to have a ringing sound.

Make TV and radio work to build brand's value

Watch TV commercials through the lens of audio branding and you'll see that, when the visual logo appears, the audio often goes wandering. Often, the music quits abruptly in mid-stanza and the logo appears silently; sometimes the volume is turned down, so the music doesn't get in the way of noticing the brand. On the other hand, a minuscule number of brands strive to leave a powerful audio memory.

One result that client research consistently demonstrates is that when you score the music in a commercial to support the spot's storyline, it's easier for audiences to comprehend what's occurring. This happens much more naturally than when the story is accompanied with some random, perhaps unrelated licensed music. Just think: the timing of licensed music could never be quite right because it was not written to the rhythm of the storyline or the values of the brand.

It makes sense, right? For example, a popular song playing over a film can direct your attention away from the rising tension, drown out the dramatic reveal, and obscure the satisfying resolution. In contrast, a musical score that is minutely timed to heighten the drama of the story focuses your attention on the right emotion at the right time. And the audio logo comes on simultaneously with the visual logo at the end of the piece. The audience could then understand the intent with multiple senses.

Now imagine this same score is related to your brand values and is subtly recognizable to your audience. Besides telling your story more effectively, you build, layer by layer, a brand relationship with your target audience without shoving your brand in their faces.

That's an ideal scenario from the audio-branding perspective.

However, many creative directors, comprehending the emotional power of music, want to capture the borrowed interest of people's associations with classic or contemporary songs. It's understandable. Just note, these music selections may change with each campaign, seldom building a lasting impression. If you use licensed music, all the more reason to be sure you give two-and-a-half seconds at the end to your audio logo to make sure you're building your brand, as Intel has done.

Dramatize press events and new product reveals

Appropriate musical staging can add heft to press events, building anticipation, giving subtle suggestions about the brand, and increasing the theatricality of the presentation. Automobile expositions, for instance, provide an ideal press communication opportunity. Reporters are looking for news and are apt to come to unveilings of new car concepts or models. This is equally true for other expos.

As Ramón Vives observes in his examination of auto shows, eventually the models and hardware begin to run together in the audience's overwhelmed mind. But the emotional experiences linger. Brand films give you the opportunity to connect the brand values and promise to the model and tie the strand of your company's history through to the current innovations. They work to build the brand and remind people of the consistency and trust that's bound you to the brand over the years.

Create a more welcoming environment

Even outside of retail, a brand's music can play a big role in enhancing an environment. The auditory brand experience can begin as early as the customer's arrival in the car park.

Car parks can be isolated and scary, even when the associated shopping mall, airport, hospital, theme park, or corporate headquarters feel welcoming and expertly designed. They are usually places of low sensory stimulation. Where better to create a sense of anticipation, a hint of what a visitor can expect? Why not foreshadow the upcoming enchantment or precision or adventure or magic or dynamism?

Because it's a transition point, the threshold between the outer environment and the space that your brand inhabits makes for a potent point of contact. Your music, woven with a message of welcome, can signal the delineation in a way that makes your employee or visitor feel wanted and gratified.

Corridors and passageways can feel less onerous if music provides a comfortable walking rhythm. This music, too, can be woven in an understated way with the melody, textures and instrumentation that defines your brand. You can even create the sounds of a walk through a village park, as does Place des Halles mall in Strasbourg, where within the music, the sound of the local storks' clapping beaks can be heard.

And because people often adjust their pace to music, it can be used functionally as well, to encourage browsing by slowing down the rhythm or, similarly, to discourage loitering by speeding it up.

To create surprising moments of unexpected delight, music and sound design can interact in a playful way with the environment and the décor. A simple plant wall might emit a surrounding three-dimensional sound that makes visitors feel they are in a jungle or a forest, near a waterfall, or in a bower. A window may whisper flirtatious compliments. A chair might offer you meditative music. The approach to a sink could trigger mermaids singing. These sounds dotted, now and then, with a brand's musical motif aren't imaginary. They have all been used in creative malls and shops.

Tiny sounds matter, especially in the Internet of Things

Let's go back to the urgent nudge provided by the ping from your social media app, the bleep indicating an appointment is approaching, a ding from an e-mail that needs an answer, the triple-beep signalling popcorn's readiness, the melodious tone of the dryer saying the laundry's done, or the buzz of your phone.

Consider which sense may be more involved in causing the urge to act or react; is it sight or is it hearing?

If you suspect it's hearing, then you have noticed that people have been busy teaching themselves to understand multiple, non-linguistic audio cues that come in at an almost subconscious level, cues that may be quite subtle but are present and helpful, nonetheless.

If these sounds are helpful, they are not seen as intrusions. Unlike the warning beeps and sirens, which penetrate the consciousness with piercing and shrill sounds to admonish you or alert you to trouble, these efficient little sounds can create the feelings of both anticipation and accomplishment.

In the Internet of Things, the design of the sound should help users clarify the function, including for instance, 'opening', 'searching', 'connecting', 'error', or 'disconnecting'. Your sound will never be a stand-alone signal but part of a sonic universe that includes the website, instructional videos, YouTube channel, even your advertising. Because you are reading a book about audio branding, you won't leave this subtly instructional and emotionally connective touchpoint up to whichever engineering team is working on a given function.

Brands need to think about these signals as important elements of their audio universes. They should create them with empathy for the audience and with a view to creating the brand experience you desire, so it supports its personality and conveys its values. The choice, no matter how small, should not be left to engineers.

Tip: save time with an audio library for videos and branded content

One of the handiest and most cost-efficient aspects of your audio brand is replacing your random collection of licensed music with a mix-and-match audio library for use with all kinds of videos that pour out from the various departments or units in your company.

Hospitals, for instance, create many hundreds of videos ranging from 'Nurses' Week' to patient stories, doctors' biographies, post-operative care instruction, health fair promotions, news of breakthroughs, treatments, and other video news releases. Some are used only once, eg for a particular meeting.

The typical array of videos can represent the 'wild west' of branding, as different brand managers, department heads, and practice leads use different voices, styles, and music, and have radically different production budgets. A library of approved audio tracks based in the unique audio identity of the brand can help bring order to the auditory chaos. Composed to communicate different moods (for instance *serious, tense, calm, steady, cheerful, playful, optimistic, celebratory,* and *rousing*) they are designed to work together. The library comes with transitional elements that help teams join one piece to another and to connect any piece to the audio logo at the beginning or end. As a result, people will still recognize the brand and the video sponsor will still be able to convey the desired and storyline-appropriate emotions.

One client has taken the idea of an audio library further. It has built its branded music collection into a musical collection to such a formidable strength that the library is able to power television commercials around the globe.

The musical library consists of compositions designed to fit a problem/solution structure, providing music that sets up a problem in the first half of the commercial and to indicate the resolution of the problem in the second half.

The selection of music for the problem set-up may be anxious, stressed, enigmatic, soft, unsettled, suspenseful, melancholic. The music for the second half can then convey such emotional states as confidence, dignity, hope, enthusiasm, strength, and serenity. These different emotions are joined together by a simple but consistent transitional sound. The audio logo completes the piece.

Over the years of brand management, more music can be added to the library, so it would eventually contain interpretations of the audio identity in various regional instrumentation styles as well as in music box and acoustic styles. When a new piece is added, it's always part of the family, and works in continuity with the others, so it removes the possibility of creating an incoherent brand.

Underscoring your brand at retail

Retailers use music as a matter of course, often streaming Pandora playlists or even using the music from their own iPods, although – important warning – the latter is not legal in the USA, unless your store is under 2,000 sq ft and it has fewer than six speakers (Lavine, 2013). In other words, unlike the descriptions from our colleagues Ben DiSanti and Ken Hicks in Chapter 2, not as many retailers use music strategically to create the clear recognition and understanding most would desire for their brands.

A group of high-end European menswear stores uses a deliberate approach that takes advantage of subliminal storytelling. Because the company's products are created by expert craftspeople who have honed their skills over many years, one of the audio strategies is to emphasize the rigour it takes to become an expert. Consequently, their in-store music is interspersed with the sounds of musicians practising their scales or rehearsing difficult arpeggios, even making mistakes and righting them.

When the Sixième Son audio brand strategists audited these menswear stores vs those of their competitors, they also noted that these particular stores stood out by creating an atmosphere that brought to mind a country estate. Taking that idea as a theme, the agency recommended a strategy of choosing licensed music that the customer might encounter as a guest on a visit to a country manor. A large classical orchestra, for instance, wouldn't fit. But an intimate chamber group, acoustic band, or solo virtuoso would. Thus, the music deepened the brand experience and immersed the customer in an aspirational brand story.

For another example, a global, classic upscale chain of jewellery stores sought to capture the glamour of the legendary movie and jazz stars of the 1940s and 50s without sounding as if their shops were meant for grandmothers.

Sixième Son created a signature six-note sound for them that resembled a glittering rainfall of diamonds. In the stores, this signal led into the little 20-second 'winks' of music sung by exceptional voices including Marilyn Monroe, Audrey Hepburn, Eartha Kitt, and Blossom Dearie. These were sprinkled throughout sophisticated playlists that contained timeless tunes, as well as contemporary and even avant-garde selections. The hand-picked music was designed to be cozy in the mornings and upbeat or unexpectedly capricious in the afternoons. It was instrumental. But when there were voices, it was sung by mostly female vocalists whose voices had an airy quality and whose style tended toward subtle delivery rather than showy or highly dramatic performances. In between, the afternoon tunes tended to be more rhythmic, but eschewed forceful percussion.

In contrast, Abercrombie & Fitch brings a strong musical point-of-view to their stores that has become a core asset of their brand and a well-known part of their brand experience. They claim their target audience is 18–22. Many of those customers and the younger ones who look up to them are too young to go to clubs. The store provides them with a club-like experience right at the mall. The din keeps mothers out too, giving teens a place to shop on their own.

Surround sound

Your brand has an audio identity, whether you manage it or not. It may be chaotic and fragmented or it may be recognizable and consistent. A deep, 360-degree audit of your potential audio touchpoints will tell you where you stand.

As the world becomes ever more distracting and the devices become continuously more audio-enabled, all wise companies will use a tailored, proprietary sound vocabulary that makes them as distinctive and recognizable, as does a person's voice.

So, it sounds like you are convinced about the power of audio branding, know the places you can use your audio library, and you are ready to find the unique sound for your brand. If so, you are probably thinking, how should I start? Easy. Just stay tuned and turn to the next chapter, because we will take you through the key steps for finding the unique sound system of your brand.

GUEST PERSPECTIVE Ramón Vives Xiol

Sound management at the Paris Auto Show

An experienced audio-branding professional, Ramón Vives Xiol is a lecturer on audio branding in Elisava, the Barcelona School of Design and Engineering, and is the Co-founder and Managing Director of Sixième Son Spain. When he had the opportunity to tour the Mondial de l'Automobile (Paris Auto Show) with Michaël Boumendil, the president of Sixième Son, and a client, here is what he had to say about the experience, which was originally published in PuroMarketing *and reprinted with his permission (Vives Xiol, 2014). Please note that while the piece below was edited for clarity, his observations are particularly pertinent.*

I visited the Paris Auto Show (Mondial de l'Automobile) with the president of Sixième Son and a car company's senior marketing team.

The Porte de Versailles is one of the most important expo centres in Europe; and the Paris Auto Show is a must for car enthusiasts. Some 250 brands from 17 countries occupied seven large pavilions over the course of two weeks. Among the new models presented were prototypes of spectacular super-sports cars, ultra-compact cars, and, of course, a wide range of electric vehicles. Brands invest heavily in presenting their new models and I witnessed an explosion of technology both in cars and in their staging. The clients were investigating how their exhibits could take better advantage of the use of sound.

As we moved from one brand to another, we discovered how much sound contributed to, didn't contribute to, or detracted from each exhibit space. Of all the brands we visited, there were two that stood out for their captivating presentation: Renault and Volvo.

Renault invited visitors to delve into an enchanted forest of lanterns hanging from the ceiling that were moving up and down to the rhythm of enticing and truly elegant music.

As a result, professional, delicate, and exquisite sound and lighting transitions set the brand experience apart as immersive, friendly and value-laden. Its staging reminded me of the memorable summer holiday in the Gracia district of Barcelona, where the streets are decorated and vying for a prized annual trophy. The French brand has repositioned itself in my mind!

Meanwhile, Volvo re-created the four different seasons by using a complex system of projections that wrapped completely around a single car.

The projections were accompanied by the sounds of the natural elements that often challenge the Swedish vehicles. There was also simulated rain provided by a water curtain surrounding the space. The rest of the models were presented virtually in life-size proportions on a large 3D screen.

Despite these exemplary experiences, through the lens of audio branding, the category presents an opportunity for huge improvement.

Most brands don't even speak
At a time when competition is fierce, how can brands that are sharing the same space with every one of their major rivals neglect

the terrific opportunity to truly differentiate themselves via sound? Could they differentiate themselves by using audio that's aligned with their graphic identities? It's possible to create an environment that's welcoming and comfortable and at the same time, unique, original, coherent, and consistent with the key values and aspirations of the brand.

A category expo is the ideal occasion to leave an imprint on a group that's segmented, actively looking, and very tuned in to the brands' propositions. Brands should keep in mind that their potential customers can compare their offers within a very few minutes of elapsed time.

Some of the brands limit themselves to showing a fan of products. Other brands show indistinguishably similar products from each other. At the same time, they fail to take advantage of the opportunities to establish emotional connections with their visitors.

> 'There are spaces in which nothing happens, spaces where things happen without sound, and other spaces where the sound is wrong.'
>
> Ramón Vives Xiol

In some zones on the exposition floor, there are other huge lost opportunities. For instance, some companies have paid large sums to rent valuable square yards in which nothing happens and, therefore, no one visits. If there were strategically developed sound environments, not only would they create greater attractiveness for visitors, but they could also express the brand more forcefully. In this way, the brand and its image would be subtly embedded in the mind of the customer, creating deeper recognition and better comprehension of the brand.

We passed booths with huge screens showing corporate videos and presentations in which the audio was simply nil or very soft. We saw great visual montages in which very professional and high-production-value images were accompanied by poor sound. Much of the desired effect was lost. It was like watching an action movie in silence, something that the audiovisual world considers a sacrilege but that surprisingly many brands treat very casually.

In the same way that a pleasant, relevant, and well-calibrated sound becomes a booth attraction, an ill-fitting sound, especially one that's too loud or stress-inducing, drives away the potential audience.

The biggest difference is in the experience, not the cars. After a few hours and miles of walking, I left the auto show feeling that, given so many similar models offering similar performance, it was hard to distinguish one brand from another.

As much an exhibition space as a sales environment, music should contribute to the attraction of the brand and create a stronger connection between the brand and its audiences. It should definitively reinforce the capacity of a brand to differentiate itself and stand out from the crowd.

In the past, it was enough for brands to focus on more rational elements like quality and price. Today, those elements are only the price of entry and the trend is to activate the emotions to turn brands into objects of desire. Emotion is the shortest route to the customer's heart.

The experiences in special spaces where automotive brands and drivers have a chance to meet in the real world transcend the models themselves. This is when the intangibles come into play. And in those intangibles, large differences were apparent at this show: some exhibits were designed through the prism of brand experience and others were simply displaying the new models.

And branding is precisely this: managing the difference.

After the visit, the car company's alert marketing team was convinced that, in terms of sound, much remains to be done. I'm sure their booth space and its visitors will benefit from the experience in the future.

Guest biography

Ramón Vives Xiol is the Barcelona-based Co-founder and Managing Director for Sixième Son, Spain. He's also a lecturer on audio branding at Universitat Pompeu Fabra and at Elisava, the Barcelona School of Design. He has a degree in Economics at the University of Barcelona (UB) and a masters in Communication at UAB, while at the same time pursuing a career as a performer. He plays guitar, sings, writes songs and manages the band Plou that's been together for a decade. Before that he led the indie band Clementines. Besides the language of music, he's fluent in Catalan, Spanish, English, and French and speaks Italian and German.

CASE MICHELIN

A brand now heard round the world

Over the years, Michelin has introduced countless innovations, from the radial tyre to their innovative use of content marketing through their guides.

And, though the company is dedicated to research and technology, the mere fact that the firm has been around since 1889 means Michelin needs to battle the perception that's it's an old-guard company.

In fact, Michelin is a modern and forward-thinking global entity.

In 2008 Michelin took steps to assert its progressiveness and leadership along with the idea of better, sustainable mobility. The company created the tagline 'A Better Way Forward' and reinforced the idea by commissioning Sixième Son to create a global audio identity for the brand.

Though the MICHELIN brand has maintained remarkable visual brand consistency in all of the 170 countries (Michelin, 2015) in which it has a marketing presence, its many different markets had been using all kinds of different music. While visually the iconic and constantly evolving Michelin Man brand mascot had been incorporated into the logo animation in all TV spots and almost every brand video, its audio brand was all over the place. Meanwhile, MICHELIN's audio communications needed to be equally powerful and effective.

As a global brand, its audio identity had to ensure consistency and effectiveness of its communications across borders. It needed to convey modernity, innovation, mobility, distinctiveness and driving pleasure.

In 2010, Michelin introduced its new audio identity: the assertive melody translates the concepts that are at the core of the brand.

Beginning with a global meeting and a brand film and proceeding to the rescoring of their exciting TV campaign, which presented the Michelin Man as a brawny superhero, the audio brand began to make its way around the world.

The first results came in soon after the music in the campaign began to air. The same commercials with the new music were more easily understood because the music emphasized the storyline. According to the results of a US advertising test, the brand climbed 18 per cent on the perception of leadership. The tyres were seen to be 12 per cent more innovative, as well as 5 per cent more friendly and 7 per cent more drivable.

In 2012, based on a new insight about the MICHELIN consumer, a new element was later introduced to the music to convey the further idea of 'sustainability'.

Today, the Michelin music presents a modern and progressive brand in the 170 countries around the world. Guided by an audiovisual 'Brandbook' and an Audio Style Guide, marketing teams around the world understand the multisensory nature of its brand expression. It has been adapted to countless commercials and brand videos for meetings, new product introductions and technical demonstrations.

Adaptations of the brand music are used for their customer service line, for ringtones, for the opening and closing of their meetings as well as musical transitions among speakers.

Even the videos for the MICHELIN Guide are grounded in the sound identity.

Here, the audio DNA has been adapted to create a carefree feeling using instrumentation and rhythms that suggest the joys of travel. For instance, an acoustic guitar carries the melody (you even can hear the intentional squeak of the instrumentalist's finger on the string), a shaker is introduced into the percussion and the rhythm is 'more bouncy'. But the audio logo lightly floats through the composition and ends the piece with a clear earprint.

Today, Sixième Son is the coordinator and international supervisor for all of Michelin's audio communication. And this memorable audio logo has become the seal of recognition and the carrier of the Michelin brand values worldwide. Adapted to all media and in all countries, this audio identity is also present on all Michelin advertising campaigns, no matter what country (Michelin, 2011; Michelin, 2013).

Summing up the success of the ongoing audio-branding initiative, Jean Douroux, MICHELIN Group Brands' Director of Communication, said:

> For several years now, the Michelin audio identity has successfully differentiated the brand. The music reflects the Michelin spirit of innovation and achievement while maintaining a feeling of closeness at the same time. It perfectly synthesizes the brand promise, offering each consumer a better way forward. Overall, the audio identity is an essential component in increasing the brand impact and ability to stand out.

Source: Sixième Son, nd

References

Kraft (2016) http://www.kraftrecipes.com/cooking-tips/cooking-videos/dinner-videos.aspx [accessed January 2016]

Lavine, L (2013) What you need to know about music licensing for your business, *Entrepreneur*, http://www.entrepreneur.com/article/226049 [accessed January 2016]

Michelin (2011) https://www.youtube.com/watch?v=F5rVqbS57uc [accessed January 2016]

Michelin (2013) https://www.youtube.com/watch?v=zblRqO5y7F0 [accessed January 2016]

Michelin (2015) http://m.michelin.com/eng/michelin-group/profile [accessed September 2016]

Sixième Son (nd) http://www.sixiemeson.com/en/audio-branding-sound-identity-portfolio/audio-identity-michelin/ [accessed 23 January, 2017]

Vives Xiol, R (2014) Environmental sound design: The unfinished business of brands, *PuroMarketing,* http://www.puromarketing.com/44/23271/sonorizacion-espacios-asignatura-pendiente-marcas.html [accessed May 2016]

The search for your sound   05

Of course, you want to go places. But what should you wear? In Chapter 4, we described all the places you could use your audio brand, but you want your sound to convey your values, essence, and personality. And you want it to stand out. So just as you sought your unique visual style, you need to find your one and only unique sound, which is what we'll explore here.

To start, as we are all aware, a brand's personality, like an individual's personality, comes with many facets. You may be shy, intelligent, and funny. You may be precise and scientific but outgoing. You may be take-charge, spontaneous, and family-oriented and, of course, you'll have a host of other traits and values.

If you think of a brand as a person (a technique that many branding people use), you will find the same to be true. Your brand will have many aspects. Consequently, your brand's sound will never convey just one part of your personality. There are countless ways these facets can be combined.

Your brand's audio identity will focus on just a few key areas, not on all your traits and values, but certainly not on just one. The winnowing and combining of these is part of the audio-branding process, which will be explored in Chapter 6.

Besides the need to communicate multiple traits, brand management teams have the need to convey the subtle differences between the way your brand interprets them and the way other brands interpret them.

Say your brand is a leader, but what kind of a leader are you? Do you bestride the world with your mighty powers or are you, perhaps, a quietly confident leader? Are you quick-witted, authoritative, collaborative, or mentoring?

Your audio-branding agency can work through recognizable audio 'symbols' to help you specify your approach to leadership. In music, for instance, authoritarian-style leadership can be carried by a bass drum with deep resonance and ringing finality; in sharp contrast, the quiet type of leadership may be communicated through a simple, steady beat carried by a much less thundering instrument, like a bass guitar. In these clearly different musical approaches, you can hear different styles of leadership.

Symbols, sounds, and structure

With sound, your brand message enters the mind, not in a literal way, but in a symbolic way (Arning and Gordon, 2006). And the brain comprehends its meaning without giving it much thought (Arning and Gordon, 2006).

Sometimes, music and sound convey meaning with a more direct approach. Say you have a product that supports lung function and you wish to convey the idea of air, breath, and airiness. These impressions can be made through a breathy quality in a singer's voice, a sigh, the sound of wind rustling leaves, or the ambient reverberation you hear when the music is recorded in a spacious environment like a cathedral. These 'descriptive' sounds work on a more explicit level to draw attention to breathing.

But music lets you add symbolic meaning in this example, too. Say you are also striving to have your brand convey the quality of 'reassurance'. That may lead you to choose the woman's voice, a sound that is often associated with calming. Alternatively, if you need to convey 'endless possibilities', perhaps the spacious room would help the message along.

Meaning can also be conveyed by the structure of the brand sounds or the music itself, which also carries associations to certain moods and emotions. Common associations include the feeling of mystery or melancholy conveyed by a minor key, or the sinister feeling conveyed by the dissonant-sounding interval called a tritone, commonly known as *diabolus in musica* (the devil in music). Your audio experts have many tools to work with beyond symbols, literal sounds, and musical codes. The time spent to get these tuned to your meanings is well worth it because it gives your audiences a new and non-intrusive way to understand you.

The recognition of music's ability to work through symbols is fairly recent. In 1997, for instance, a paper presented by Branthwaite and Ware at Esomar (the world association for market, social, and opinion research) proposed that music could only fill four roles. 'Music could work as a *magnet* (drawing people in), mood *magnifier* (intensifying the visuals) *mnemonic* (stimulating memory) or *mask* (brand identity), but not as a *messenger* (delivering information)' (Branthwaite and Ware, 1997).

But, by 2006 the view had advanced. In that year, a new paper took issue with the last point – that music is not good at delivering information – and, instead, made the case that music can indeed work as a truly effective messenger and can frequently stand for something beyond itself. In the paper, they used the example of the music in the movie *Jaws* becoming a stand-in for the shark that one barely ever saw (Arning and Gordon, 2006).

Much of design, whether it is visual or auditory, communicates through symbols rather than explicit words. The human mind can understand symbols very well. However, it understands the meaning of these symbols in an impressionistic way rather than in a linear one. And it remembers them (Heath, 2001).

In the visual realm, you could think of a rose quite literally: it has a stem, some thorns, petals, and leaves. But if the rose were handed from a besotted boy to the girl of his dreams, it's a different thing, right? The rose has become a symbol of his love and the rose's power as a symbol far outweighs its botanical make-up. Not too many people would have to think very hard about it.

In the audio realm, you could hear the sounds of a group clapping out a rhythm and make the literal association with percussion, but the brain could also interpret it as a symbol of teamwork or unity.

Some of these symbolic effects are very subtle. In music, one way to suggest 'luxury' is through slow tempos and unexpected silences (since luxury items are seen to be created thoughtfully with no detail left unexamined), 'human touch' can be heard via 'oohs' and vocal harmonies. And if you want to convey 'precision', you may want to consider very defined notes, more staccato than fluid.

The good news is that the brain is so skilled at detecting auditory symbols, it can process them when you're not consciously listening, when you're distracted, and even when your attention gets divided among many different tasks. However, the not-so-good news is that, because it is operating below the level of conscious engagement, it becomes harder for people to articulate the precise meanings they pull out from what they have heard. To quote Adrian North, a professor of cognitive psychology at the University of Leicester, 'People do not always necessarily know and cannot always report accurately how they are reacting to music. Sometimes some of those processes are not available cognitively' (North, 2006). We will, however, examine ways to measure music's meanings and behavioural effects in the next chapter.

Arning and Gordon provide a perspective originally from a social scientist, Philip Tagg of the University of Montreal, who believes you can extract people's interpretations of the meaning imparted by music. Tagg recommends 'inter-subjective testing', whereby one plays the same piece of music to different people and records their associations. For Tagg, the stunningly similar reactions to a piece of music from people with a similar cultural background indicate that music is not purely and necessarily polysemic (carrying multiple meanings) as some academics claim (Arning and Gordon, 2006). For this research:

…respondents are asked to jot down as quickly as possible (they should be given no time to 'think') what they envisage ('see', 'hear', or 'feel' in their mind's ear/eye) to be taking place on an imaginary screen along with the music they hear. Results collated so far show considerable statistic reliability and homogeneity of response.

Source: Tagg, quoted in Arning and Gordon, 2006

Along these lines, one question that often comes up is, 'How universal is the meaning in music?'

In our experience, the ability of music's meanings to transcend borders of geography, socioeconomics, age, or gender is its most astounding super power. A common global understanding has been created by music in movies and TV shows, music videos, brand films, homemade podcasts, and videos that blanket the world.

In Sixième Son's listening committee workshops, we often hear a diverse group agree on something as abstract as, 'What *colour* is suggested by the particular music selection?'

As we discovered with Peugeot, people in China, France, the UK, Russia, Spain, and Brazil derived similar meanings from the brand's new music and the respondents from the six countries were unanimous in rating the brand as both confident and confidence inspiring across the board.

But that doesn't mean that your brand's music can't be varied to fit local markets or to support storytelling that requires a sense of place.

Universal vs local. Consistent vs varied

As to whether a brand should communicate via music based in local culture or use a more international voice, there's no right or wrong answer. That decision will be made by your strategy. Local styles are perfect for some brands. Other brands, like MICHELIN, which we detailed in Chapter 5 as the featured case study, and AXA, whose case study will be provided in Chapter 9, benefit more from a less region-based, more universal sound.

Once your audio DNA has been designed and committed to, it's fairly easy to vary it to express different moods, incorporate touches of local culture, or suggest different musical genres. For instance, if you have an international-sounding audio brand, and you are telling a story of a man learning to ride an elephant on a crowded street in India, you would be wise to season your brand sound with a sitar and other Indian instrumentation.

However, if you are Royal Air Maroc, and you want to encourage tourism to Morocco, you'll benefit from an audio identity to reflect the particular tapestry of sounds that make up your country's traditional music to conjure an inviting image in your target's mind.

Marketers often wonder if their brand's music should be different in China than in Europe. The answer is, not necessarily. Again, it depends on whether it's positioned differently to the Chinese consumer than it is to the Western audience. If it's positioned similarly, then there's probably no need to change the brand music.

In some categories, Chinese consumers associate rigorous quality control with Western countries, so a westernized sound might have the effect of creating a halo for your brand and would be more appropriate for your product than would a traditional Chinese sound.

Let's say, however, that your product was infant formula and that you wanted to provide branded soundtracks for Chinese mothers to use for their baby videos. For that specific application, it would probably be a good idea to share musical options that contain your audio DNA, but that add local sounds and musical influences.

Like visual branding, audiences don't need utter consistency to recognize the main motif of the sound. You just have to make sure your audio designers know what proportion of the original audio DNA needs to be kept in the composition for a new application. As a general rule of thumb, the more time and exposure your sound has had in the market, the greater leeway you have for variance.

But always remember the test performed by Intel, in which they played the 'Intel Inside' sound on a violin and found that many people no longer recognized it (Intel Free Press, 2014). The instrumentation is part of brand identity, too. In other words, you can't stray too far from your sound. Instrumentation and timbre are part of the brand as much as the tune. The important part is to keep it bringing some part of the music home to the brand. For most brands, the 100 per cent consistent, untouchable part of the audio identity is the audio logo.

According to Uli Reese, the author of *Great Minds on Music*, 'Any brand is in the trust-building business because, without trust, there will be no sales'. Reese shares his trust-building formula in a compact phrase, 'Trust is built through consistency plus time' (Fahey, 2016).

Six audio-branding dos and don'ts for marketers

In the next chapter, we will dive deeply into the proprietary process Sixième Son uses for collaborating to create an audio brand, perhaps even revealing some trade secrets. In the meantime, however, here are a few guidelines to get your teams ready for the initiative. Please note that while the following six Dos and six Don'ts appeared in an article Colleen published in *Strategic Health Care Marketing* (Fahey, 2015), we are providing it here with some slight edits and additions, because it makes a handy overview.

Don'ts

1 Don't leave audio strategy until the last minute. Just like creating your visual brand foundational strategy and elements, plan your music and sound at the outset. (Of course, if you already have an ongoing visual brand, you are not prohibited from creating an auditory one. You just need to take the current equities into account.)

2 Don't confuse audio branding with entertainment. It has a strategic, trust-building job to do. Your goal is to completely define the audio universe for your brand, just as your graphic standards define your brand's complete visual universe, so that no matter where your audience encounters your product, service, or communications, they'll recognize your audio brand and know what it stands for.

3 Don't forget that impact without meaning can be distracting and counter-productive. Your audio footprint must convey the brand's essence, promise, and values. Even if your colleagues love nostalgic music, don't be tempted to use it if your brand stands for forward-thinking innovation.

4 Don't choose a piece of music just because you like it. Ask instead, 'What does it say?' Music is a universal language. Your audience can tell if it's warm and friendly, if it's optimistic, if it's powerful, if it's caring and approachable. Be deliberate in the way you select music for your tactical marketing. (Once you've established your audio DNA and audio logo, this becomes easy.)

5 Don't repeat the same music mindlessly. Adapt it to the context. Telephone on-hold music should have lots of variety and surprises to keep the caller interested and reduce hang-ups; music in car parks should be calming as the audience is often in an anxious state; music in cavernous areas should avoid low tones, which will get lost amid the reverberations; music for meetings should start calmly and then build a sense of anticipation; music for videos should support the storyline, not toddle merrily along on its own path.

6 Don't confuse music production houses with audio-branding experts, even if they claim to be able to create audio logos. Branding experts are focused on finding a way to make your brand distinctive in the category

and precise in its communication of brand essence, promise, and values. They will analyse the competitors, take you through a defined process, and offer an Audio Style Guide and other tools to help ensure buy-in and branding controls and consistency. They are also music experts but, specifically, they use it to create brand influence rather than using them for soundtracks to movies or TV shows or for the writing of commercial songs.

Dos

1 Do articulate what your brand ideally represents before addressing what the audio brand must do. Because your audio identity's role is to express the core of your brand essence, the first task is to fully define it. Only then can you design the music that expresses it.
2 Do think of your audio brand as a system of distinctive sounds and music, not as a jingle or even a stand-alone audio logo at the end of TV and pre-roll commercials.
3 Do investigate the audio approaches your direct and indirect competitors are using, so you can stand out – just like you would for your visual brand.
4 Do enumerate your key audio touchpoints, including your branded content, your on-hold music, your trade-show booth, your radio and TV spots, your app-opening sounds, your events, your car parks and corridors, and more.
5 Do make sure you use the right music to support those needs in various circumstances. In different situations the audience has different needs. Your identity system for your audio brand will be designed to be coherent within the overall brand but must be adaptable to fit each setting.
6 Do plan to **adjust** your audio logo whenever your visual logo animates onto the screen, at the same time. After all, the most powerful branding tool in your kit will be your multisensory end frame.

So now that we've set the groundwork for finding your sound, we will take you through two important considerations: 1) identifying your key performance indicators (KPIs) and how to track them through market research; because, after all, as we previously stated, but is worth repeating often, audio branding is ultimately a long-term, business-building endeavour, not merely an exercise in developing an entertainment enhancer at your various audio-enabled touchpoints; and 2) a proven process for creating a unique audio brand based on your brand's distinct essence, promise, values, and brand attributes. While you might be eager to jump into creating this sound, please take the time to study the next two chapters before you get started.

GUEST PERSPECTIVE Mickey Brazeal

Highlights of recent academic research: music effects in marketing communications

In Chapter 3, Charles Spence provided an overview of how music affects perceptions. But how is this translated into marketing communications? To find out, we asked a source close to us: Mickey Brazeal – former big agency creative leader, and an associate professor in the Graduate School of Integrated Marketing Communications at Roosevelt University in Chicago. Mickey has an academic researcher's eye toward the power of music use in marketing communications, so he conducted a review of the current research. Here is an overview of what he found (in his own words).

While audio branding is still considered a newer field, music indeed has become one of the most frequently used and heavily relied-upon communication devices in mass media marketing. A 2008 study, in fact, shows that 94 per cent of prime-time television commercials include music – often music that is custom-made for the brand or the message (Vermeulen and Baukeboom, 2016).

What's more, music in marketing has been studied for decades. A review of the results yields many common elements: demonstrations that music has the power to dramatically increase the effectiveness of media communications in several different ways; but also demonstrations that it can sometimes be not powerful at all – and it can have downright negative results, depending on how it is composed and how it is applied.

Following are some extremely brief descriptions of the findings in recent studies. All of them have been peer-reviewed and published. All of them are publicly available, most are online. Readers in search of more detail can find many entire articles in the end-of-chapter References.

To help you follow my write-up structure, my summary proceeds from those looking at the more limited, tactical effects of music to those exploring more sophisticated, strategic effects. No attempt was made to prioritize my description of these studies, as different effects will be important to different readers.

More music means more learning
A very recent study by AC Nielsen finds that commercials with some form of music outperform commercials without music across four of Nielsen's proprietary metrics: creative, empathy, emotive, and information (AC Nielsen, 2015). Much the biggest effect was in the commercial's ability to transfer information. People learned more, understood more from commercials whose communication was aided by music.

Change the music and you change the message
Mark Zander of Freiburg University studied music effects with testing approaches drawn from clinical psychology (Zander, 2006). He points to the use of music to attract attention, perhaps the earliest and most primitive of its applications, but critical to information transfer. He also finds cases where very explicit messages are delivered primarily by music. A car commercial with a hard-rock music track is interpreted by its audience as communicating power and forcefulness. The same video and words, with a classical music track, is perceived to communicate refinement and sophisticated design. Zander finds many more examples where music adds an implicit element to a visual–verbal message. In one example, a change in music makes a particular brand in the first instance energizing, and in the other instance, calming. He finds repeated evidence that music has helped with the retention of information.

A study by Anand and Sternthal (1990) points out that custom-made music makes it possible to repeat a phrase several times without annoyance to the audience. This repetition can be used to improve both information transfer and recall.

Information transfer in the environment of the website is a very different problem. In the website environment, the customer is simultaneously in the medium and in the outside world. The communicator's goal is to increase the level of attention paid and thus information transferred by the site. Mangini and Parker (2009) find a substantial difference in how this is accomplished when a website has music. They measure more interest in the content, more emotional arousal, and importantly, an increase in the 'flow state' of attention to the site that makes the reader almost oblivious to the outside world for a few minutes. An increase in the flow state is associated with much greater information retention and with a more positive perception of the reader's subjective experiences.

Music transfers the emotional message
Finally, a study by Morris and Boone (1998) suggests that the increase in information transfer is much more focused on the affective components of a message than on the cognitive component. This is interesting, because the affective component is often much harder to communicate with visuals and words.

Music that fits, forces recall
With a focus on recall, we introduce the concept of musical 'fit' or congruity – a subjective perception by the audience of the relevance or appropriateness of a particular musical composition to the message or the product characteristics or the essence of the brand. This book has returned again and again to issues of congruity. Research described below will offer some reasons why.

Reviewing the research of others, Oakes (2007) finds a clear causal connection in which higher congruity (as measured by the audience) produces higher brand recall. Studies by Yalch (1991), Tom (1990), and North *et al* (2004) find the same thing. 'Custom' music, successfully matched to the brand or message increases recall. Music that is merely well-known, or familiar, does not. Multiple studies report that music which 'fits' with product attributes will increase recall of visual images in a commercial, and will do so far more than verbal cues do (Stewart, Farmer and Stannard, 1990). A study by Kellaris, Cox, and Cox says music perceived as congruent with the visual images in a commercial will increase both message recall and brand recall. (Music not perceived as congruent reduces both; Kellaris *et al*, 1993.) The North *et al* (2004) study attempts to quantify the level of congruity, and says the better the fit, the higher the recall. Two other studies, one by Stewart, Farmer, and Stannard (1990) and another by Yalch (1991), echo this.

Mood modifies behaviour and music modifies mood
Many marketers believe that advertising changes the relationship with a brand by connecting the brand with an emotion that might not already have been there.

Some early research looked at Pavlovian conditioning as the mechanism by which music works. This produced dramatic results, but they were not always replicated in subsequent studies. Recent studies pay more attention to 'mood induction' as a way to explain the power of music (Janishevsky, 1988; also Oakes, 2007). A mood is perhaps less intense than an emotion, and might not be as recognizable to the individual. But there is a large volume of research which suggests that moods modify behaviour and especially that a positive mood enhances the likelihood of many behaviours, including all sorts of consumer behaviours, like finding out about a product, finding where to buy it, or deciding to try it. In this view, behaviour comes from an interaction between thought processes and mood, but does not happen without the presence of a positive mood. Mood induction is not well understood, but it has long been associated with music, and the study cited above links it directly to advertising response.

Music is most powerful with decisions you don't know you are making
Psychologists have long distinguished between the high-involvement situation – when a person is concentrating on a choice, and consciously evaluating the alternatives – and the low-involvement situation, in which information or ideas are offered that might be relevant to a future decision, but is not part of a current decision-making process. Obviously, most advertising effects happen in the low-involvement model. Several studies (Alpert and Alpert, 1981) suggest that music is far more powerful in the low-involvement environment. It is important to understand that decisions, many and important decisions, are still being made and influenced, even though instant, on-the-spot, high-involvement decision processes are not happening. Studies of musical congruence with visual and verbal messages say that, in high-congruence situations, music affects brand attitudes in both low- and high-involvement decision-making (North *et al*, 2004). And the congruence of lyrics with visual messages appears to influence decision-making in both high- and low-involvement (MacInnis and Whan Park, 1991).

Music tells us how to feel
When we look at an image on film, it is always somewhat ambiguous. We can eventually figure out how the source of the image wants us to feel, but it may take a bit of time. Music is the quickest way to an emotional connection; it is routinely accomplished in 30 seconds. When the marketer's goal is an emotional relationship with a brand, there is almost no tool or technique so powerful as music.

We measure emotional relationship as attitude. Again, congruity is critical. Many studies display a clear relationship: when music has high congruity with the brand or the message, it can create positive attitudes about the particular commercial, positive attitudes about the brand,

and even positive attitudes about the spokesperson, which presumably improves believability (Zander, 2006). The effect is routinely observed when music is customized for the brand or for the message. And again, the better the fit, the more salient are the positive attitudes. In situations where an emotional lift does not happen, one key study says it is almost always attributable to a problem with the fit – MacInnis and Whan Park, 1991.

Music creates purchase intent

Purchase intent is important, because it is much more predictive of behaviour. If you want to know whether someone will buy, you don't ask how much they like the product – you ask if they intend to buy. Again, the studies are plentiful and powerful: high congruity creates clear and consistent purchase intent. See North *et al* (2004), Oakes (2007), and Eckhardt and Bradshaw (2014) among others. Studies that use the mood induction model, here represented by Alpert and Alpert, find that fit between the mood of the music and the mood of the communication increases purchase intent (Alpert and Alpert, 1981).

Music builds brand authenticity, but only if it's the right music

The most strategically powerful effect scholars have traced to music in marketing communication revolves around brand authenticity. A brand is an expectation about the experience a customer will have with a product from a particular source. The brand is the vessel in which all a marketer's successes and effects over time are contained. That which can make the brand be, in the mind of the consumer, the vision that its makers and marketers had, is the ultimate communication tool.

One key to this phenomenon is non-verbal communication. Words will always be at the centre of marketing. But words create a cognitive response that always includes the counter-argument. If you say 'this is how it is', the human mind will always imagine that it might also be some other way. But non-verbal argument does not provoke the counter-argument. We do not summon up the alternative visual or the alternative music.

The second key is congruity. If the music experience is clearly relevant, appropriate and congruent with the brand idea, then it creates an argument that is never rebutted. It says that the values of the brand truly are what they say they are. And it is believed. Music that captures the essence of a brand consistently and measurably enhances the authenticity of the brand as perceived by its customer (see Hung, 2000; Holt, 2002 and many others).

Guest biography

Mickey Brazeal is Associate Professor of Marketing Communications at Roosevelt University. He spent 28+ years in the advertising business, the last 11 as Executive Creative Director at Grey Chicago, where he ran a department of 30 writers, art directors and production people, and helped to manage the agency. His work includes national TV campaigns for car waxes and corn herbicides, shampoos, spice blends, fuel additives, fruit juices and food stores, drugstores and deodorants, and dotcoms as well as internet, direct, and sales promotion. And, his creative awards include Addies, Tellies, Eagles, Towers, Windys, Louies, Mobius, NAMA Gold, and Effie. He is the author of *RFID: Improving the customer experience*. Mickey holds a BA in Journalism from the University of Nebraska, and an MS in Advertising from the University of Illinois.

CASE Roland Garros/The French Tennis Open

Expressing a mythic stature at the French Open

Sports venues and race events benefit from their audio identities in one way other brands don't get to enjoy. Because TV, radio and webcasters actively report at tournaments and matches, the venue's own audio brand gets plenty of extra airplay, which helps extend their brand's influence for free.

Music is not only played as fans enter the stadium; it also plays when the athletes parade in, when a match is about to commence, and when a trophy is awarded – all highly media-friendly moments.

The French Open is just one example. It is currently followed by 3 billion viewers around the world, so you can imagine the brand value being created each time viewers hear their sound.

In order to express the mythic stature of this tournament, the French Tennis Federation turned to Sixième Son. 'We analyse what the brand aims to accomplish,' said Laurent Cochini, Managing Director of Sixième Son, Paris. 'The musical creation becomes the brand's identity.'

'The French Tennis Federation wanted to use music as a custom tool to unify all its communications with a consistent and exclusive musical vocabulary,' recalls Cochini.

The French Open tennis tournament has set a high bar in creating a unique brand sound that can be adapted to various audiovisual montages and tributes, and can be used in lounges, walkways, shops and the player village in the famous Roland Garros stadium. Fans, players, and passers-by, as well as global media audiences, have begun to recognize the famous French Open tournament just by its *sound*.

The branding effort started in 2014 and today, the Roland Garros tournament has a musical identity that's also a hymn to the game. Oddly, it is still the only major tennis tournament that has built its own audio identity system.

How did the rousing music come to be what it is? Cochini explains the background and the process.

'We studied what happens in the world of sports and in particular the world of tennis to create an identity that was distinctive from a musical point-of-view. One thing we found inspiring was the idea that Roland Garros is the only major tennis tournament that isn't in an Anglo-Saxon country. Think about it: there's the Australian Open, Wimbledon, and US Open, all from English-speaking countries.

'Then there is the French Open with its Latin-based language. We were moved to go beyond France to encompass the entirety of the Latin world. This became a fundamental strategy behind the sound design.

'Another inspiration was the physical action of tennis that is so different from that of other sports. There is often an aspect of the motion that looks like dancing. For us this characteristic needed to find expression in the music.

'We also needed to bear in mind that Roland Garros *is* France, *is* Paris. This dimension particularly needed to be present in the sound identity of the tournament.

'The final creation also linked the French aspects with Latin dance; this is why it is the bandoneon, the instrument of the tango (closely related to the more typically French accordion) which was at the heart of creation.

'The idea that Roland Garros is the spring tournament for the players, which we learned through our discussions with the French Tennis Federation, suggested that lightness should be present in the composition. But the event offers an epic dimension that we wanted to capture in the sound identity, too.

'The fact that the Roland Garros tournament is played on clay also guided us. We decided to eschew any synthesized sounds and choose real instruments played in an organic way.

'Between the first meeting and the delivery for the 2014 tournament, it took us about two months. Two good months of work that included contributions from almost everyone on the 25-person Paris team. Beyond the client input and approvals we had to test the sound at the centre court and the Suzanne Lenglen court at the stadium to make sure it would have the desired effect on the fans in the stands.

'The music has already evolved. It is presented in different formats in terms of time but also in terms of intent. The way to address the audience, ready to experience emotions before, during and after games is not the same way it would be for internet users. And again, the music needs to be different for a TV commercial. The thundering and very epic vocabulary when the players enter for the final match is not the same as that in the corridors of Roland Garros stadium. The ultimate idea, of course, is to enrich the French Open brand.'

From the beginning, the finished product was a huge success, and its adaptation to the award ceremony created the longest standing ovation in the history of the event. As Rafael Nadal walked up to receive his ninth title, the stadium was filled with the usual and well-deserved roaring applause, but that year the emotional level was heightened as he received his trophy to the unique music of the French Open.

The tearful 2014 French Open champion, Rafael Nadal, said of his winning experience, 'To receive this trophy, with this magnificent audience who has supported me and with this incredible music was a powerful and emotional moment for me' (Sixième Son, 2014).

References

AC Nielsen Inc (2015) I second that emotion: the emotive power of music in advertising, http://www.nielsen.com/us/en/insights/news/2015/i-second-that-emotion-the-emotive-power... [accessed 1 September 2016]

Alpert, JI and Alpert, MI (1981) Background music as an influence in consumer mood and advertising responses, *Advances in Consumer Research*, vol 16, pp 485–91

Anand, P and Sternthal, B (1990) Ease of message processing as a moderator of repetition effects in advertising, *Journal of Marketing Research*, vol 27 (3), pp 345–53

Arning, C and Gordon, A (2006) *Sonic Semiotics*, Congress 2006, Esomar World Research Paper, https://www.esomar.org [accessed 14 May 2016]

Branthwaite, A and Ware, R (1997) *Music in Advertising*, Esomar Congress, pp 1, 10

Eckhardt, GM and Bradshaw, A (2014) The erasure of antagonisms between popular music and advertising, *Marketing Theory*, vol 14 (2), pp 167–83, Sage Publications, UK

Fahey, C (2015) Hear the Brand: A hospital marketer's field guide to the surprising world of sound, *Strategic Health Care Marketing*, 8 December 2015 [online], http://strategichcmarketing.com/lp-hear-brand-hospital-marketers-field-guide-surprising-world-sound-6175/ [accessed 5 October 2016]

Fahey, C (2016) Interview with Uli Reese, 14 March 2016

Heath, R (2001) *The Hidden Power of Advertising: How low-involvement processing influences the way we choose brands*, pp 44, 83, London Admap

Holt, DB (2002) Why do brands cause trouble: A dialectical theory of consumer culture and branding, *The Journal of Consumer Research*, vol 29, no 1 (June 2002), pp 70–90, University of Chicago Press

Hung, K (2000) Narrative music in congruent and incongruent TV advertising, *Journal of Advertising*, vol 29 (1), pp 25–34

Intel Free Press (2014) *Intel Bong Still Going Strong After 20 Years*, Intel Free Press, 6 August 2014, http://www.intelfreepress.com/news/intel-bong-chime-jingle-sound-mark-history/8390/ [accessed 9 October 2016]

Janishevsky, C (1988) Preconscious processing effects: The independence of attitude formation and conscious thought, *Journal of Consumer Research*, vol 15, September 1988, pp 199–209

Kellaris, JJ, Cox, A and Cox, D (1993) The effect of background music on ad processing: a contingency explanation, *Journal of Marketing*, vol 57 (4), pp 114–25

MacInnis, DJ and Whan Park, C (1991) The differential role of characteristics of music on high- and low-involvement consumers' processing of ads, *Journal of Consumer Research*, vol 18 (2), pp 161–73

Mangini, VP and Parker, EE (2009) The psychological effects of music: implications for hotel firms, *Journal of Vacation Marketing*, vol 15 (1), pp 53–61

Morris, JD. and Boone, MA (1998) The effects of music on emotional response, brand attitude, and purchase intent in an emotional advertising condition, *Advances in Consumer Research*, vol 25, pp 518–26

North, A (2006) quoted in C Arning and A Gordon (2006), '*Sonic Semiotics*', Congress 2006, Esomar World Research Paper, https://www.esomar.org [accessed 14 May 2016]

North, AC, Hargreaves, DJ, MacKenzie, LC and Law, RM (2004) The effects of musical and voice 'fit' on responses to advertisements, *Journal of Applied Social Psychology*, vol 34 (8), pp 1675–708

Oakes, S (2007) Evaluating empirical research into music in advertising: a congruity perspective, *Journal of Advertising Research*, vol 47 (1), March 2007, pp 38–50

Sixième Son (2014) (online) 21 November 2014, Identité sonore Roland-Garros / Grand Prix Stratégies du Design 2014, https://vimeo.com/112506086 [accessed 10 October 2016]

Stewart, DW, Farmer, KM and Stannard, CI (1990) Music as a recognition cue in advertising tracking studies, *Journal of Advertising Research*, vol 30 (4), Aug–Sep 1990, pp 39–48

Tom, G (1990) Marketing with music, *Journal of Consumer Marketing*, vol 7 (2), pp 49–53

Vermeulen, I and Baukeboom, CJ (2016) Effects of music in advertising: three experiments replicating single-exposure musical conditioning of consumer choice (Gorn 1982) in an individual setting, *Journal of Advertising*, vol 45(1), pp 53–61

Yalch, RF (1991) Memory in a jingle jungle: music as a mnemonic device in communicating advertising slogans, *Journal of Applied Psychology*, vol 76 (2), pp 268–75

Zander, MF (2006) Musical influences in advertising: how music modifies first impressions of product endorsers and brands, *Psychology of Music*, vol 34 (4), pp 465–80

What gets measured 06

If you're like most people in marketing, your head is already swimming with ideas. You see the possibilities and might already know what you want to express. But audio branding, just like visual branding, is a disciplined process. And it begins with research.

After we have collectively developed hundreds of brands, it is impossible to resist acquiring certain strongly held opinions about the role of research.

The first of these is that the time you take in expanding the learning you acquire before you start creating is the most valuable part of the research – at least to the creators. Among the important questions for audio-branding development that should be answered upfront are:

- What are the codes, clichés, and expectations of the category?
- What do the competitors communicate, even visually?
- What – if any – music or brand sounds do they use?
- Is anyone using sound exceptionally well inside the category?
- Is there a company outside the category who is close in positioning?
- If so, how are they using music?

Some investigation also goes into researching the auditory heritage of your own brand.

Also, because one of the main goals of audio branding is to appropriately stand out and be distinctive, one of the investigative disciplines you must pay attention to is to look for what's *not* there. Where are blank spots where your brand can be different from the crowd and fill an unmet set of needs?

One example of finding what's not there, comes from the analysis done for SNCF. As part of the research for the SNCF project, the agency went to airports and train stations in the UK, Spain, Italy, Germany, and Switzerland, among others, and found a pervasive similarity in their signals. All of the competitors used bells, clangs, and beeps to signal announcements. Also, the tones all tended to be authoritarian, as if to express, 'We are the transportation authorities. Now pay attention to what we have to say.'

The environments themselves also had many stressors: crowd noise, cart noise, obstacles created by bags and the crossing streams of rushing passengers that added to the normal travel tensions, including worries like, 'Did I remember to bring everything?', 'Do I have my ticket?', 'Am I at the right gate/track?' and 'Will I make it on time?'

Given these stresses, the audio-branding team realized that though travellers have a need for calm reassurance and a sense of safety, the tone taken by most transportation systems was clearly insensitive to the passengers' states of mind. Nobody was providing a sense of calm and positive anticipation. This gave SNCF a way to provide a true auditory point of difference, to demonstrate both kindness and approachability in their sound. Through the audio brand, they were able to refocus attention away from the dangers and difficulties of travel and turn it toward the pleasure of the journey ahead.

Likeable as the SNCF sound is, it leads to a second point about testing that may seem contradictory. There is grave danger in focusing the initial research on an audio design's likeability. Although 'likeability' is important, as Gene Topper points out in his guest perspective (p 111), too much focus on likeability at the initial stages of development can set a trap for a brand whose goal is to be noticed, because people initially tend to like music that's familiar.

We have found that if the audio identity is immediately likeable, it's probably because it sounds like a lot of music playing in the environment. If the music doesn't have any quirks or idiosyncrasies that raise eyebrows, it is likely to disappear into the world of familiar music and won't be interesting enough to break through the clutter. The brand music will be likely to lose in the important brand measure of 'salience'. A better question is, 'Can the sound be interpreted as recognizable, distinctive, and meaningful?' If the audio identity offers a good fit for the brand, likeability is likely to come as familiarity is established. As Mickey Brazeal demonstrated in his Chapter 5 guest perspective, brand congruity in the music leads to greater recall of both the message and the brand.

In general, it's not a good idea to ask directly for opinions about the music itself, or you will soon find yourself in a thicket of personal tastes and political posturing. Rather, we recommend sticking to exploring what's being communicated about the brand and see if the music conveys those attributes.

In other words, one good practice is to measure implied meaning. It is also important to measure fit with the brand including whether the audio supports or complements other branding elements such as the animated logo and the tagline. The goal, after all, is to extend the brand essence, promise, and values in all the modalities possible, creating the cohesive, seamless experience that creates trust in the brand.

We have found that the Sixième Son clients who use research – not all of them do – use it for many different purposes at several different stages. They employ both qualitative and quantitative techniques and conduct the research both in person and online. The agency usually helps guide the research professionals and makes sure the questionnaires aren't headed toward any landmines, but the ultimate instruments are left up to the client as well as research professionals.

Some companies use upfront research to help winnow out the options from among the front-runners; or to check an executional aspect (eg with voice or without voice?); to see if and how the branded music has changed the understanding of a TV commercial that, previously, had used licensed music; or to find out if the overall message is being interpreted similarly in different parts of the world. Later, after the brand has been in the marketplace for some time, companies can measure how well the audio logo has established itself vs the competitors. Sometimes brands look for very basic information like recognition, brand attribution, and attachment. In many ways, audio-branding research is analogous to the research questions and techniques used for judging the effectiveness of visual branding elements and efforts.

Deconstruction and layering

One technique that works for discerning the meaning derived from an audio brand is to deconstruct it and then layer on the audio and visual elements. Playing the animated visual logo without the music and exploring what it communicates, and then playing the same logo along with the music and asking the same questions can enable you to assess what messaging has been added by the audio brand. You can do the opposite too. First, play the visual and auditory elements together and then withdraw the music. The comparison of the two experiences can yield rich information about the meanings and emotions contained in the audio composition – even from something as short as a 2.5-second composition, comparable in length to the typical audio logo. Try it yourself to see how the meaning and impact is affected.

A car company used this deconstructed vs layered research approach in a third way. Using an online survey that lasted under 10 minutes and querying a few hundred French drivers on the company's proposed audio logo, their research firm played the music alone and then added the visual. Why?

They sought to measure the perception of the proposed audio logo alone and then to evaluate the music's harmony with and impact upon the brand's visual identity.

When they played the music alone, they looked for the perceived meaning: whether it felt modern or aggressive; whether it came across as annoying or agreeable to listen to; and if it conveyed a sense of momentum, uniqueness, or originality. When they explored these questions in the research, however, their order was randomized to ensure against one question continually creating the framework for the next. Secondly, they looked at the ratings on such measures as status, quality, passion, power, and generosity and compared them against each other.

Then they played the music simultaneously with the video and measured whether or not the audio composition imbued the visual with the feelings of enthusiasm, movement, modernity, and differentiation from other brands as well as 'brings strength', 'gives a strong personality', and 'evokes emotions'.

The car company's highly original audio identity now extends across the globe. And it's proven to convey the top three values in all of the markets. What is more, the research indicated that the newer markets showed a stronger effect, as they weren't carrying years of previous brand impressions – views formed from when the respondent's grandparents owned the company's cars.

Which creative execution?

Often clients use comparative research to help winnow their choices; often, for instance, to help make the choice between their two or three best options. Here it's useful to add a ranking system to the exploration of brand values. Respondents can listen to each choice individually and rate the different positive and negative qualities that each sound communicates to him or her.

Sometimes there is a need for help deciding between creative executions. What is the difference in what each one communicates? Which is more moving to the audience you seek to influence? Which is more appropriate to the environment? Then the questionnaire can ask listeners to compare which is stronger at delivering each of the core values. For instance, 'Which one felt the most welcoming?', 'Which conveyed the most optimism?', and 'Which one best communicated technological innovation?'

In the case of an airport, the team needed to decide which version of the audio identity would best achieve their goals: one that included a woman's voice, and another that was purely instrumental. One concern, as was already learned from the SNCF initiative, was how to use the music to help the travellers feel reassured, instead of the typical anxiety of travel. Further goals included:

- Which of them better translated the values that the client wished to highlight?
- Which would be most easily memorable and identifiable in the various brand touchpoint situations?
- Which would be the most adaptable to an international clientele from many regions and from varying sociodemographic strata?

Using both focus groups and one-on-one interviews with domestic and foreign travellers – research that included both occasional and frequent travellers – they tested similar pieces, one had a high but soft female voice as the lead instrument and another was carried by the other instruments, without a voice.

Among the choices, there were some similarities in the way both options were perceived (like the sensation of being within a serene and protective 'rounded' environment). But in the end, the results were conclusive. To the travellers, the music without the use of the voice felt heavier, emptier, and less refined. On the other hand, in the context of the Paris airports, the crystalline soprano voice carried the day. In addition, the verbatims from the research report were reassuring to the marketing team, too:

- brings joy, gaiety, and freshness: the voice-over makes people feel very welcome;
- gives dynamism, movement, enthusiasm, and energy: the voice arouses people's curiosity and maintains interest;
- protects them from the exterior world and its aggressions: the voice is comforting and reassuring;
- allows them to position themselves as witnesses of life: the voice is real and human;
- provides well-being and serenity: people are calm and relaxed.

In other words, the travellers could imagine a story that preceded the announcement: the voice made it feel as though they were part of a dialogue rather than the cold recipient of an announcement. Of course, these results don't mean that a truck tyre, medical device, or pipeline company would benefit by the same voice usage, but it turned out to be ideal for a *bienvenue* to or an *au revoir* from Paris.

We have also found that some organizations prefer to take a more quantitative approach to market research and many like the convenience and often cost-savings of conducting their research online. While this approach won't provide such poetic answers as 'I feel as if I'm in the middle of a story', you can get good guidance from it.

A simple online questionnaire

The following example of an excerpt from an online research questionnaire uses a slight variation. As mentioned earlier, one method that works well is to play the music and video together – let's say of an end frame featuring an animation of the logo – and then cutting the music and playing the video silently. People can often articulate what's missing for them. Conversely, you can play just the visual part, probe for what it communicated and then add the music and see what has changed. But in this methodology, you can play a video or the animated end frame silently for some respondents and *with* the music being tested for a different set of respondents. Then, it becomes simple enough to just compare between the adjectives each group chooses to describe the brand.

You don't need to ask them to describe the music itself, because if the music is truly adding meaning to the brand and the communications, the respondents who are exposed to the proposed audio identity will detect and describe different aspects of the brand.

At this point, the respondent will either be shown a video with music or without it and will then be given a questionnaire featuring a set of possible adjectives and will be asked to complete it. Table 6.1 provides an example, keeping in mind that, typically, the order of the choices is randomized, so each participant is offered a different list.

Does it work across borders?

For international brands, marketers should also test how well a brand is translating values across cultures and geographies. For one international brand, the company ran four one-hour focus groups, with eight participants each, with a mix of both customers and non-customers in their home country, and then they held two one-hour focus groups in each of five different countries, again with eight participants each and a mix of customers and non-customers.

Table 6.1 Example questionnaire

Questionnaire Form				
Q. People have said different things about the brand the way it is shown in the following video. Please let us know whether you agree or not.				
In this video, (brand) appears to be…	Totally agree	Somewhat agree	Tend to disagree	Do not agree at all
Friendly				
Creative				
Corny				
Wholesome				
Original				
Easy				
Fun				
Generous				
Premium				
Shareable				
Approachable				
Cheeky				
Simplistic				
Naive				
Childish				
Irritating				
Boring				
Distinctive				

In each of these groups, they measured:

- coherence with the brand identity (brand values, vision);
- coherence with the tagline;
- memorability; and
- the ability to differentiate, both in the marketing environment as a whole and from competition.

Their goal: to determine the global performance of the audio identity and its perception in each of the individual countries where they operate.

Ultimately, the research conclusions underscored the universality of music as a highly communicative language.

TV commercial comprehension and memory

When licensed music in a TV campaign is replaced with music that's scored to drive the action while reinforcing brand attributes, you can compare audience comprehension of the commercial, before and after. You are likely to see a jump in comprehension in the scored spot in part because, when you score a commercial to support the storyline, rather than to compete with it, people don't have to work as hard to get the message. Every aspect reinforces the other. And you can increase the tension in the moments where you want it, build greater excitement in the active moments and underscore a feeling of triumph in the resolution, as well as convey the other emotions you wish to evoke.

While brands can't immediately track whether this comprehension and enhanced emotion turn into long-term memory, there are strong indications that they help do just that. The research company Neuro-Insight, for instance, tracked brain responses while the study participants watched 150 ads, mapped the responses to their data on long-term memory encoding and found that ads that are driven by their soundtrack were 14 per cent more efficient in producing long memories than those that used 'background' music. This effect was produced both in memory of the big picture as well as memory of details (Heilpern, 2016).

Testing a known audio brand at grocery

It's also important to note that audio-branding research can work in physical locations as well. In a now classic audio-branding study, a test was run in a British wine shop, where they played German and French music on alternating days. On the German music days, the shop sold more wines from Germany – three bottles of German-branded wines, in fact, for each bottle of French wine. And on the French music days, the shop conversely sold more French-branded wines. This time, however, they sold four French-branded bottles for each German bottle (North, Hargreaves and McKendrick, 1999), perhaps speaking to the stronger overall branding of French wines.

In a similar way to the wine study, the audio consulting group took research into the retail environment to test the theory that audio branding could move sales of specific products at shelf. Working with the University of Applied Sciences, Kiel, in cooperation with 50 supermarkets in the same chain, the research firm ran their test on a brand in the sparkling wine category. The brand had been using the same music on air for two decades.

As a benchmark, they tracked sales for the brand and the category for two weeks. For another two weeks, 25 stores continued as normal and in another 25 a 7.5-second piece of the brand's music was played six times an hour embedded within the customary in-store music programme.

Sales rose during that period as it was the year-end holiday season, but the sales of the test brand in the stores that played the branded music far exceeded the seasonal sales boost, as proven by the difference in product sales between the test stores, which rose 45 per cent vs the control stores, which rose 15 per cent.

The music also appeared to raise the sales of the category itself. Every competitor in the store with the sparkling wine-related music saw higher sales than they did in the stores without the music. No words were used, no lyrics were sung, the work had all been done by the music alone (Langeslag, Santos and Schwieger, 2011).

So now that you know some of your research options, you need to solidify how you will eventually judge your audio brand, from the initial criteria for determining your music to your key performance indicators over time. We have provided some that have been used by other marketers (and our guest perspective will provide others). But ultimately, you need to select the key performance indicators important to your business and brand.

But once you have identified them, you are ready to progress to the next branding stage and go through the process of creating your audio brand. Stay tuned, because that's just what we'll explore in the next chapter.

GUEST PERSPECTIVE Gene Topper

Reflections on the value of brand-tracking importance and role of brand tracking

So if your audio-branding effort is effective, it should move the needle, which you should be able to see in your market research. But how should you best track the changes in your brand? What are the key considerations? And what are the key concerns? To help us answer those pressing questions, we asked market researcher extraordinaire, Dr Gene Topper, to provide us with his thoughts, drawing from his more than 30 years of experience. The following is what he sent us in response. We hope that it helps you as much as it has helped us.

Brand tracking represents the most important (other than sales) vehicle for assessing where a brand stands in the minds of a target audience. Yes, sales data are the ultimate measure of performance. But, sales, while providing a measure of how a product or service is doing in the critical metric of brand revenue, does not provide any diagnostics on the reasons for the level of a brand's performance. Sure, if a brand continuously outperforms budgeted sales there may be little need for diagnostics. The reality is, however, that most brands, at least temporarily, will not reach sales goals. Brand tracking is a critical tool for diagnosing brand health.

What makes brand tracking so useful is the ability it provides for assessing all aspects of the marketing funnel, eg awareness/saliency, imagery, consideration, motivation, trial, and loyalty. These measures are not in a vacuum as key competitors are also assessed at the same time.

When all of the marketing funnel metrics are being assessed for a brand we have the ability to diagnose why sales may not be reaching established goals.

At any given point in time a brand tracker can provide the following insights:

- What is the level of brand awareness of our brand?
- Is our brand salient (unaided brand awareness) or just recognized?
- What are the equities (positive and negative) of our brand?
- Is our brand proposition understood?
- Is our brand proposition considered relevant?
- Where does our brand stand in the consideration set?
- Why hasn't trial occurred and how likely is it to occur in the future?
- If trial has occurred, what is the likelihood of future usage?
- What is the overall satisfaction level for our brand among triers?

Not only does a brand tracker provide these insights at a given point in time but they are easily trended (assuming no changes in methodology) over time. And, by assessing the same metrics among competitors we can see if we are outperforming, underperforming or equally performing the competition in the category. Trackers also provide the ability to track the individual targets or segments to see how the brand is performing within its various audiences.

Brand-tracking design that best meets client needs

Over my more than 30 years designing brand-tracking studies for clients, I have recommended almost every variation on timing, method of data collection, and metrics to be incorporated in a tracking study. Here are a few basic principles on designing brand trackers and expectations for detecting brand movement:

1. The timing of tracking waves should be based primarily on the level of marketing investment in the brand during the tracker. For heavily advertised brands (usually consumer packaged goods, retailers, and financial services) tracking waves can be as frequent as every 3–6 months. For low-level marketed brands (including most B2B brands and durables) tracking can be more infrequent, with 1–2 years between waves.

2. Continuous tracking is very expensive and should only be reserved for heavily advertised brands with variations in their media schedules over time. Continuous tracking can be very valuable in identifying efficiencies in media plans, eg how long/short do media flights have to be to impact brand metrics or what is the duration of a lag in brand metric growth and decay for different media schedules and weights?

3. Can I afford a tracker? The answer is almost always 'Yes' as there are ways to reduce costs such as reducing sample size, broadening the target (if low incidence), and shortening the interview. For example, for budget considerations, I can get a tracker down to a five-minute interview by simplifying screening questions and limiting metrics to unaided and aided brand and advertising awareness, past trial, future interest, and reason for interest/lack of interest. Another way to reduce costs is to just look at open-ended verbatims instead of paying for coding.

4. Moving the needle in a tracker is not easy. The bigger the sample size and heavier the brand advertising, the greater the chance one will see significant changes wave to wave. If movement looks hopeless, have patience as most brand movement takes months, if not years.

5. Think about the big, longer-term picture for the brand. You must remember that in sampling, normal variation in responses is likely to happen wave to wave. The implication of this is to not overreact to a significant shift (either positive or negative) in one wave. The key is to see if these shifts are maintained or only temporary variations of sampling.

6 Can a tracker determine if our campaign is wearing out? This issue is one of my favourites as in almost all cases brand advertising will never wear out because spending levels are too low and competitive clutter reduces impact. As a colleague years ago explained, wear-out occurs when the spouse of the president of the company gets tired of the advertising. Wear-out, though, can be measured through tracking by observing metric increases that plateau and decline. If the decline cannot be explained by reduced spending or increased competitive activity, then wear-out may be occurring; however, this is rare.

7 Auditory (and visual) logos in advertising can also be tracked by evaluating aided awareness of the auditory/visual logo after playing/showing them and probing on-brand association (if buried among competitive brands and control logos).

Finally, I am frequently asked for my opinion on what one brand metric is the most important one to value. I feel strongly that unaided brand awareness is the most critical measure of a brand's health. Unaided brand awareness measures the saliency of a brand and how that compares to competitors. How can a marketer expect a brand to be considered if it is not salient, especially vs relevant competitors? There is ample evidence that unaided brand awareness is the highest correlated variable with brand usage/intent to use in the future. As an example of salience, I was especially impressed by the metric quoted in the SNCF case in Chapter 1 of this book: '88 per cent of these listeners correctly identified the brand upon hearing just two notes.'

Don't forget copy testing

When you get to the advertising stage, creative copy testing (one could make the argument) may be even more important than brand tracking. This step is especially important when you're starting a new strategy or approach. As in other elements of the campaign testing, the goal is to learn 'What does it say about the brand?' and 'Is it communicating what we think and hope it is?'

Copy testing, if done properly, can identify potential communication flaws in the eventual advertising. Most copy testing can be done on rough executions of the proposed advertising. If copy testing is conducted and identifies potential issues, there is then time to take corrective actions prior to the costly production of the advertising.

In almost all cases advertising can be tested in a rough form with only a few exceptions such as when a potential dramatic visual or representation of the brand may be needed in final form. Consumers readily understand that rough advertising is preliminary and they can project what will eventually be shown.

I have in fact evaluated several new ad campaigns in rough format and then later in finished form, and have actually had more positive comments on the brand in the rough form. The reason for this was that the final execution actually fell below what consumers responding to the rough form envisioned about the brand and its portrayal.

Researcher vs the creative perspective

During my agency days as a researcher, I was 'affectionately' called Dr Doom, someone who has killed more creative than any person on earth.

Let me summarize several confrontations that occur between creatives and researchers with regard to the role of the consumer in evaluating brand communications:

1. Researchers do not want consumers to be creative critics in evaluating the music used, how the copy was put together or the value of the visuals. But there is abundant evidence that the more consumers like what they see and hear from a brand, the more likely they are to be patrons of the brand. If consumers are the intended audience of the communication, it is important to determine how they feel about the communications… do they like what they hear about the brand, how do they feel about what was said and shown, does the communication fit the brand and do they like the brand based on what they viewed and listened to in the advertising.

2. It is important to listen to what the creatives would like to know from the consumer but do not let them design the instrument for getting the information. For example, suggesting that the consumer in a copy-test situation should be allowed to view the creative as many times or as long as they like is not a good test of reality. Consumers seeing a television commercial or listening to a radio commercial do not have the luxury of extended time to study the message, unless they record the advertising and review it. For measuring key metrics like brand recall and perceived main idea you do not want to allow more than two exposures to the advertising. It is OK to expose test advertising a second or even third time to evaluate brand imagery and tone of the communications but further extended exposure is not a realistic situation.

3. The use of auditory cues can be a very effective executional device for improving the recognition/association of a brand to a commercial

message. However, the marketer needs to ensure through tracking research that the auditory cues not only generate recognition of a familiar message but an association to the brand behind the advertising. Appreciation of the advertising and its messaging generates no benefit if the consumer has no idea what brand is being advertised. We are not talking about evaluating the melodic quality or appeal or technical aspects of the music but rather its message and fit with the advertised brand.

4 I heartily agree with the procedure of evaluating combined auditory and visual commercial elements in isolation, together, and then in the context of the advertising. It is important not to have the same respondents evaluating the auditory/visual logos both in isolation and then in context since their responses in isolation can influence their reactions to the same stimuli, now in context. The proper way to handle this is to have separate cells evaluating stimuli in isolation vs those seeing the stimuli in the advertising.

Guest biography

Gene Topper has applied his doctoral degree in Experimental Psychology and MBA in Marketing Management for over 30 years to assist clients in addressing critical marketing issues by designing marketing research studies that obtain target audience input for making better decisions.

Gene has been recognized for his leadership skills by having served as President of both Chicago's American Marketing Association and the Society of Consumer Psychology. He has lectured in Marketing Research at Northwestern's Kellogg Graduate School of Management and currently is an assistant professor at Colorado Technical University.

CASE Intel

Lessons learned from a fuzzy brief: the durable Intel bong

Let's take a moment to tip our hats to a brand that has brilliantly stuck to its sound for over 20 years. The ubiquitous Intel signature (aka 'bong') was born in 1994 and has remained largely unchanged since. Oh, yes, they've added some bass and made some updates to the sound but they've kept it recognizable through the years.

Imagine trying to create preference for a component that's inside a closed computer. We think it is rather like trying to sell a dress based on its brand of thread. Your customers can't see the product, hear it, taste it, or touch it. The very nature of the product makes it hard for people to imagine it or keep it in mind. And, yet, the Intel marketers worked strategically and creatively to create real brand preference, and, even more improbably, to build this invisible product into a global brand.

The Intel bong got its start when Intel was turning to television advertising in 1994 and had commissioned R/GA in Los Angeles to create the animated version of their logo, a spiralling, dynamic whirl that resolved into a still-familiar shape with the company slogan inside an open blue oval. It was R/GA who found the composer, young Austrian-born musician Walter Werzowa who was in the USA studying movie and TV music scoring at University of Southern California.

Werzowa composed the well-known melody that was featured in all Intel commercials and, in a brilliant Intel co-marketing strategy, was also included in most commercials for computer companies who used the chips inside their products.

By 1999, the audio signature was already catching attention. The *Los Angeles Times* devoted an article to its genesis (Kaufman, 1999). Here's an excerpt about its start: 'Intel… wanted tones that evoked innovation, trouble-shooting skills, and the inside of a computer, while also sounding corporate and inviting.'

To achieve these goals, Werzowa reportedly blended xylophone, marimba, and bells.

The client probably didn't know it at the time, but what Werzowa described as a 'fuzzy' brief was, no doubt, more helpful in inspiring the creation of a unique and tailored sound than are many music briefs. Why? Because the brief focused on the branding need, rather than on the music. Indeed, as a brief, it could have been deeper and more introspective about the brand. But it avoided the worst habits of audio briefs, in that it didn't specify a style of music or a recommend a song to be copied. That openness gave the composer room to intelligently explore how to bring the brand to life.

Which he did with a simple four-note melody – D flat, G flat, D flat, and A flat – announced by a brilliant introductory note that sits apart from the tune. He added smart touches to the rhythm, too, choosing the inspired cadence of the words in the slogan, 'In-tel In-side'. Another deft detail in the composition was the connection between the two uses of the syllable, 'In'. Each time 'In' is expressed, the same note, D flat, is used.

In an interview with Werzowa, Grant Robertson of *The Globe and Mail* added to an insight into the introductory note they call the 'sparkle' saying, 'The first note is a throwaway; just there to clear the mind of whatever noise came before, so the brain is ready to hear and, more importantly, to remember the jingle that follows.' He then quotes the composer as saying, 'There is this initial energy burst which closes off whatever sound was there before. It prepares you for the melody, then the melody comes in' (Robertson, 2009).

The audio logo travelled far beyond the Sherman Oaks studio and made its way around the world. The *Globe and Mail* article, published in 2009, reported that it was 'played in more than 130 countries, it's the most-heard commercial mnemonic going. On average, the bong appears somewhere on earth every five minutes, either in the company's own ads or in commercials for products using Intel's technology.'

In 2014, The Intel Free Press reported a finding that underscored a not-so-obvious insight that audio-branding professionals know well. Many people had a hard time recognizing the famous tune in the absence of the tone. 'Interestingly, Werzowa and Intel discovered that the sound of the notes was at least as important as the melody itself. Among a 60-person focus group, researchers found only 80 per cent of participants recognized the correct melody played on a violin, but 100 per cent recognized it with the proper sound – even when an incorrect note was added' (Intel Free Press, 2014).

The multisensory approach and, indeed, the audio signature have buoyed the awareness of the Intel company's innovations for many years, so much so Intel is now recognized as one of the world's top brands, neck-and-neck with giant consumer brands like Budweiser. In fact, in early 2016, *Forbes* named Intel as one of the world's most powerful brands and assessed its brand value at over $32 billion (*Forbes*, 2016). Though these brand rankings often shift around and the companies that rank brands aren't always in total agreement, Intel's rank is impressive.

It's hard to imagine achieving that impressive level of strength by using a silent visual logo showing the word 'Intel' within an open blue oval, no matter how dynamic the animation that surrounded it. As good as the graphic design is, it's the five-note audio signature that brings out the emotional connection. No wonder Intel has firmly stood by its significant sound for more than 20 years.

References

Forbes (2016) The World's Most Powerful Brands, *Forbes*, http://www.forbes.com/pictures/fell45elff/no-6-intel/ [accessed 4 October 2016]

Heilpern, W (2016) How to make the most memorable TV ad, according to neuroscience, *Business Insider*, 22 March 2016 http://www.businessinsider.

com/most-memorable-tv-ad-according-to-neuroscience-2016-3 [accessed 16 October 2016]

Intel Free Press (2014) Intel bong still going strong after 20 years, *Intel Free Press*, 6 August 2014, http://www.intelfreepress.com/news/intel-bong-chime-jingle-sound-mark-history/8390/ [accessed 4 October 2016]

Kaufman, L (1999) The Man Who Created Intel's Audio 'Signature', *LA Times*, 20 October 1999, http://articles.latimes.com/1999/oct/20/business/fi-24321 [accessed 8 May 2016]

Langeslag, P, Santos, R and Schwieger, J (2011) The effect of branded acoustic Stimuli and Purchase Behavior, Congress 2011, Audio Branding Academy

North, AC, Hargreaves, DJ, and McKendrick, J (1999) The influence of in-store music on wine selections, *Journal of Applied Psychology*, vol 84(2), April 1999, pp 271–76

Robertson, G (2009) The Mozart of Jingles, *The Globe and Mail,* 15 May 2009, http://www.theglobeandmail.com/report-on-business/the-mozart-of-jingles/article4211353/ [accessed 12 May 2016]

The audio-branding process 07

So, now that you are fortified by knowing all the benefits of having an audio brand and key steps for judging its success, it's time to take the plunge. But are you really ready to get started on the process of actually creating your audio brand?

But we have a warning: as you announce that you have decided that you are going down this road with your brand, you may ignite a confusing internal discussion. That is because, when people see audio branding in the plan, they often offer their opinions about music. 'We are more of a classical music company', one person typically might say. 'No, too highfalutin, I think we're rock 'n' roll but maybe softened with a touch of flute', another might offer. 'No slide whistles, please!' a third might say. You will also hear, 'I have always liked this piece of music, how close can we get to it without getting sued?' And, inevitably, someone will ask, 'Doesn't our ad agency handle the music?' (Probably, yes, at the campaign level but almost never at the brand level.)

Don't let it throw you. You can reassure them that you have a plan that provides a clear process that includes your ad agency (or agencies) along with an internal cross-functional team.

Then you'll select an audio-branding resource. Here, you will want to be very careful that you're not hiring a music house, but a branding expert that can build an intelligent *system* that can flex and build over time, maybe even over decades.

Here's another warning: some firms and music houses claim to do audio branding and then provide a long piece of music that is designed to be cut up and used in snippets. That is not a system. Go along with this approach and you'll find that your company will soon find itself suffering repetition fatigue. As a result, your efforts could fail and your investment would be wasted. All too often, as marketing consultants we hear that an approach, a platform, or an overriding strategy doesn't work for a company when in fact it was the execution of the approach, platform, or strategy that didn't work. Please, don't fall into that trap with audio branding. The upside is just too great for your brand to miss out on this unique opportunity to help your brand stand out and build emotional connections with your audiences.

Now that you have these warnings, and are prepared in advance, you are ready to begin. Expect any audio-branding process to take about two to four months. The process we describe is the one created by Sixième Son and has been used in creating more than 350 audio brands around the world. So we know that it works.

A familiar process but an exciting one

The audio-branding process will be reassuringly familiar to anyone who has gone through any strategic branding process (see Figure 7.1). The steps are the same, but the lens is different. The briefing, competitive research, category, and brand analysis must be part of the process but, in this case, the guiding perspective focuses on the behaviour of the sounds and music in the category and the musical heritage of the brand. The mood board explorations are critical but aren't done using collages or video montages; they employ purely auditory inputs. The concept presentation doesn't require visuals because your mind will create its own; instead, it includes short original compositions created specifically to communicate and differentiate your brand. At that point, a couple are chosen, refined, and, possibly, tested. In the end, your brand will possess a clear, coherent and audio universe that's as distinctive as your graphic universe and, of course, an Audio Style Guide.

Brand briefing and analysis

The goal in the briefing is to help your audio-branding agency understand the brand. You might be asked questions like: What is your brand promise?, What are your brand's values and aspirations?, Who is your key target audience?, What choices did you make when creating your visual logo and identity system?, Is there a brand in another category that could be a model for your brand?, How are you different from your competitors?, How are your competitors presenting themselves?

Of course, these questions are just the beginning. The point is, you should expect to be grilled. A good audio-branding firm, just like a visual-branding one, will want to know everything.

With the information as the basis, your audio-branding agency will conduct a benchmark study of your category. This audit will determine the

Figure 7.1 The audio-branding process

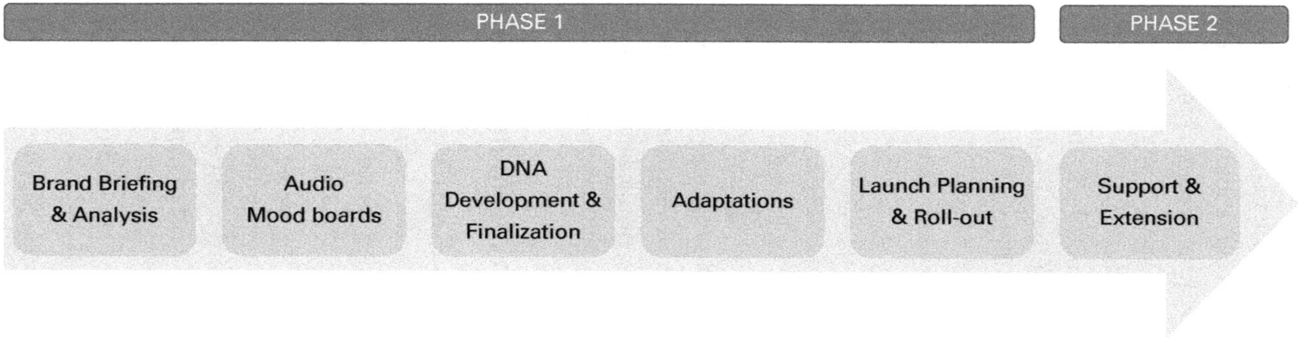

PHASE 1 | PHASE 2

Brand Briefing & Analysis → Audio Mood boards → DNA Development & Finalization → Adaptations → Launch Planning & Roll-out → Support & Extension

SOURCE Sixième Son, 2015 (used with permission)

key competitive positions in the category and their musical expressions. It will usually also reveal the audio defaults or 'codes' in your sector. It may uncover more fertile territory to help refine your position. And it will help you determine whether you want to create your own new and distinct musical path or bring a fresh take to a musical path that already exists.

We recommend you create a listening committee at the start of the process. Usually, this consists of 6–10 people who know your brand very well. These people do not have to be musicians or musical experts. It is key, however, that they know and care about the brand. They may be product managers, marketing communications professionals, product designers, agency people, management, or someone with a special perspective.

In the case of a hospital, we found it was helpful to include a nurse who carefully guided us away from any sounds used in the monitors and other medical devices.

It's worth noting that it's typical for the client to bring their most trusted agency (or two) into the process. It may be the ad agency but some clients also prefer to include their web design agency, their branding agency, or even their 'messaging strategy' agency, instead.

With your help, your audio-branding agency will do an audio touchpoint analysis of your company as we discussed in Chapter 4.

All this information is then distilled into a strategic proposal that includes a refined positioning, touchpoint recommendations, and roll-out plan.

Setting the tone with audio mood boards

Based on our experience, the next step is for audio-branding strategists to create a series of audio 'mood boards'. Each 'board' is a playlist that contains a carefully selected collection of musical clips that explore 6–10 different ways of conveying a particular meaning. Brands are rarely one-dimensional. Depending on the values of the brand, one mood board might look at ways of conveying 'innovation'. A second might look at the ways to say 'human touch'. And a third might explore the ideas and feelings of 'intimacy'. Another brand may wish to communicate 'effervescence' and 'fun' or 'rigorous precision' and 'high style' and they would receive an entirely different set of mood boards. The goal of the mood board session is to find a way to represent the most promising audio vocabulary for the brand.

It's important to keep in mind that these sets of boards are custom-created for each organization, infused by the content and benchmark findings and analysis in the briefing stage. After all, just as one 'fun' person is fun in a different way to the next one described that way, so is a brand.

The first meeting of the listening committee (LC1) allows for an evaluation of each piece of music in the mood boards keeping two main questions in mind: 1) Does it succeed in conveying the intended meaning?; and 2) Does it do so in a way that feels appropriate for the brand? These listening sessions are very dynamic and the listeners often evolve in their opinions as they hear the different interpretations unfold.

The results of these sessions set up the strategy team for a tight creative brief that guides the audio designers away from certain expressions of the brand and toward others that are more promising.

It's often true that, while a listening committee judging the musical excerpts never comes to 100 per cent agreement, the group shares certain unspoken feelings about their brand and find many things to agree upon. It's not a requirement that everyone be in perfect agreement.

For illustration, the box below provides an example of the raw meeting notes taken by one Sixième Son representative during a portion of a mood board listening session. These, combined with the observations of the other colleagues, helped guide the creative brief that began the exploration of the brand's audio DNA.

Mood board #2

Extract 1: YES
+ very classical, 'clumsy mobility'
+ very exploratory
+ physical comedy
+ through the eyes of the child
+ sense of humour
+ playful story
+ very catchy
− too treble

Extract 2: NO
− too old for toddlers, too educational, brand is not trying to teach kids anything
− a little too literal interaction between mum and baby
− felt like basic music you play for kids, too sing-songy
+ positive: mum/baby connection
+ end was pretty interesting

Extract 3: YES
+ last part is interesting, simple series of instruments
+ like the bridge and the guitar part
+ positive melody, playful
+ speed and energy feel like the brand
+ don't mind the soft whistling

Extract 4: NO
− too hyperactive
− too western culture
− too nursery rhymish
− nice rhythm, but not enough… too carried by the voice

Extract 5: YES!!
+ very unique, interesting, catchy
+ universal/global sound
+ complex
+ positive
+ a little too adult (voice)
− didn't feel baby enough
+ like the off-beat rhythm, and like the xylophone
+ 'Aah' and 'Ooh' feel more universal and interesting

Extract 6: NO
− too dramatic − like a warm-up for an HBO movie
− boring, not toddler
+ emotional and aspirational
+ progressive
− end is too abrupt… doesn't say 'thriving'
− too theatrical, too forced

As you can notice, even before these reactions and analyses are tightened into a final creative brief, directions are being suggested about the brand's rhythm, instrumentation, vocalizations, sophistication level, and natural vs dramatic tone. A whole new idea was revealed as well, that being the hope that the final music not sound too westernized, as it needed to appeal to a global audience.

DNA development and finalization

After the client approval of the creative brief, a creative team begins composing alternative approaches to an audio DNA of about 45 seconds in length, which is essentially mapping out the potential audio vocabulary of the brand as well as creating the all-important 2.5- to 4-second audio logo.

Though we have found that different audio designers will emphasize different aspects of the brand's character, all will strive to include each of the key brand dimensions.

Once approved internally (at Sixième Son, it is approved by the agency's artistic director and creative director) the three to five alternatives will be presented at the next listening committee meeting (LC2). While some agencies might come back with a recommendation at this point, we prefer to see it as further exploration. Sixième Son at this step will not take a strong position or try to hard sell a particular composition. We know each one will do the job, but we don't know which one will speak best for that particular company. So we listen intently. And we watch expressions and body language. We offer our perspective if it's requested but we find it often isn't asked for as teams navigate their way to their own unique brand expression.

During this stage, it's important that the client and the agency team stay focused on the brand, its essence, and its values. Secondly, the listening committee may attend to the question of how well the music might stand out in the category. We believe that one's own musical tastes and preferences have no place at the table. At that meeting usually, two concepts are chosen for further refinement.

This exercise often provides an inadvertent team-building exercise. As people begin to share their musical impressions, explore subtle dimensions of the brand, and even find themselves emotionally moved by the music, they get to know each other's human side. In the end, teams are unified by the fact that they've created something meaningful and valuable that represents all of them.

The refined concepts are presented again at the third listening committee meeting (LC3). By this time people have become familiar with the process and some even participate by phone. Here the selection is made. Some of our clients use testing to help choose between the two finalists (although we've found that fewer than half tend to do this). Rather, many companies feel confident at this point that they've achieved a distinctive sound that truly conveys their essence and values. Some present to upper management, while others just go ahead and make their decision as a team. The final selection is based, not on musical likes and dislikes, but on what would be best in achieving the brand's goals.

How to tell if you have a strong audio brand

Here is a handy rubric for judging your audio brand. Some of the questions might not be appropriate now, but the first ones you can begin using right away:

- Does it reflect the brand values and convey the brand's story?
- Does it help the brand stand out from the competition?
- Does it include an audio logo that stems from the overall brand music?
- Is it used coherently across touchpoints beyond advertising?
- Does it allow flexible adaptations within a structure rather than merely repeat itself?
- Is it used consistently over time rather than changing with ad campaigns?
- Do you have a working Audio Style Guide that lays out usage guidelines?

Touchpoint adaptations and an Audio Style Guide

The audio DNA by itself then becomes the inspiration for real-world adaptations. Every company gets started in its own way depending on what is most urgent or important to them.

These first applications can come from any angle. A large energy company, for instance, urgently needed meaningful music for a global meeting. On the other hand, a city began using its audio brand with its booth at a very critical convention (a convention for the people who plan conventions). To kick off the year's campaign, a packaged goods firm shared its new audio DNA with its international marketing teams to guide music scores for TV commercials. A pharmaceutical group first began using their new audio brand in their corporate social responsibility videos that were placed on their corporate website. A car company needed to create an immersive in-person experience to launch a new line at an international car show. A hospital wanted to replace its expensive licensed music in its commercials with branded music before it had to pay a licence renewal fee. A beverage company needed a brand video to reveal the new direction its evolving brand was taking. So as you can see, audio brands make their debut in a myriad of ways.

At the same time, a company will begin to plan for the medium and long terms, creating a practical music library and a plan to expand its audio universe, if not all at once, at least in stages.

Before the adaptations begin to spread, though, the company needs to know how to get the most of their audio brand and the boundaries of use. This is accomplished with an Audio Style Guide.

Similar to the one you should expect to receive from a visual-branding firm, this comprehensive piece captures the reasons behind the musical choices, the guidelines for use of the music, the different applications for each piece of music, and, finally, explains how to create mix-and-match adaptations using the pre-composed tracks and transitions.

The Audio Style Guide often exists as a part of the brand's online marketing toolkit, though a booklet version is often shared at launch. Many clients prefer that the Audio Style Guide be interactive so employees and agency partners can listen to the tracks and examples and see best practice examples for its incorporation.

Internal launch planning and roll-out

Your brand's unique audio identity has great power to foster employee pride and unity. It gives you a reason to reaffirm your long-held values or underscore your new positioning.

It shouldn't be sprung on a company's employees or dribbled out piecemeal. Rather, the launch of your audio brand should be treated as a reason for a celebration. Therefore, if possible, your employees should be introduced to it before it's launched with consumers.

The journey that led to this new brand asset's creation provides a compelling story that reinforces that which makes your company special and can be retold at the celebration (as well as used with the press when announcing your new audio brand).

One of the ways Sixième Son draws the employees of the company into the journey is by documenting the process in a 'Making Of' video. These videos vary from the informal to the highly produced. With them, employees are treated to a behind-the-scenes view of the lively discussions, the decisions made (including why), the musicians involved, and the resulting musical identity that casts new light on the brand.

Another way to involve employees is to hold a contest to let them give a name to the overall composition.

To foster engagement and build anticipation even before the launch, you can let the team vote on aspects of the music prior to its creation – an exercise that is similar to the mood board exercise but simplified down to a couple of choices.

A particularly helpful way to present the brand is in a company meeting into which good sound design has been incorporated. The walk-in music gently suggests the new brand identity as people assemble; then as the first speaker is guided to the stage, it becomes more prominent; it is woven into the musical transitions between speakers; and when it's finally presented, preferably by the CEO, it already feels familiar and natural. The brand video works to create an emotional bond among the audience and their company.

Support and extension

In the first year, especially, you can help root your audio brand among your teams and agencies by holding audio brand discovery sessions with the potential users, either in person or by remote meetings. Your audio-branding agency should be able to help lead them and answer questions.

These discovery sessions shouldn't be limited to marketing people. For instance, the HR team may become a heavy user of the branded music library for their training and recruitment videos, for their workshops and employee education sessions, and for corporate meeting and events. The people responsible for your company's call centre, too, will benefit by knowing how they can implement pre-pickup and on-hold music and thereby improve service perception.

In a technology company that needs sounds for its devices, platforms, software, or even hardware – think Apple's start-up chime – the engineers should also be briefed. Please keep in mind that they may need assurance that they have access to a sound vocabulary that's more meaningful than the standard beeps and buzzes.

You may want to appoint an audio brand champion or audio brand team to answer people's questions, hear their concerns, share best practices and guide appropriate usage. This team can also regularly update the company on the ways the audio brand's influence is spreading.

You can have your audio-branding agency provide a help desk for your employees. Also, set up a monthly call to check in on progress, give new assignments or suggest refinements, and hear about other clients' successful implementations that can guide your own.

Ongoing, you will need feedback from your organization on what's working and what's missing (perhaps a more rousing adaptation for sales meetings or a substantial variation on the audio DNA for a new line extension).

This feedback can be gathered through roundtable discussions, surveys, interactive website, conference call or as part of a regularly scheduled marketing meeting. What's key is to plan it into the year's calendar. The goal is to create a two-way forum for all stakeholders who are using the audio brand assets. Besides being your partners, they, as 'the walking brand' also provide an additional medium through which to extend brand influence.

But now that we have taken you through the process of creating your audio brand, we have one more step: its marketplace launch. While we spend a little time exploring it in this chapter, the next chapter will be focused entirely on the launch, as this is among one of the most important steps. So join us to learn how you can ensure the success of your new audio brand.

GUEST PERSPECTIVE Neil Gains

The rhyme and rhythm of branding: using sound to build the sense, symbol and story of your brand

How does sound contribute to a brand's story? To find out, we asked Neil Gains, founder of TapestryWorks and author of Brand esSense: Using sense, symbol and story to design brand identity *(Gains, 2013). Here is what he had to say (and to know more about this area, we recommend his book).*

Sound is often the most neglected of the senses when it comes to branding, although it is only second to the visual senses in terms of its importance and has a very specific role that helps the brain to create stories from cause and effect.

There is more to using sound in branding than music and song, important as they are. Of course, music and song are particularly powerful in creating links to specific emotions. However, in the esSense® framework outlined in *Brand esSense*, other aspects of sound can also contribute to building a brand through the senses, symbols, and stories.

The overall sound of a brand is important in our overall sensory experience. Our sense of hearing has more 'bandwidth' in the brain than any other sense apart from vision, relating to its important role in helping the brain organize the world and our experiences into a sequence of events in time. Hearing helps us understand the rhythm of the world, and to pinpoint 'when' events happen (while vision helps us understand 'where' they occur).

Sound shapes both our mood and physical state, but is also an important component of the intensity of our experience. Can you imagine watching your favourite film (assuming it's not a silent movie) with the sound turned off? Just as what we see influences what we hear, our hearing also shapes our vision. This is why car manufacturers have had to make electrical car engines less silent, as too many pedestrians were not 'seeing' them on the road. Clothing retailer Abercrombie & Fitch are known for the 'intensity' of their brand experience, which is why the lights are low and the music volume is high in their stores (or at least it was, as they are in the process of rebranding as I write this).

Sound can also contribute to the symbolism of a brand, through the brand name, the language the brand uses and sonic icons. Sonic icons have been used very successfully by Intel, increasing its awareness from 24 per cent to 94 per cent in the first year it was introduced. Nokia was also very successful in creating a sound signature, although less successful in keeping its product line as innovative. Many car manufacturers are now creating sound signatures for their brands and the Harley-Davidson engine roar has long been a key signature of its rebellious personality (so why did they ever consider a silent electric-powered bike?).

Names and language are particularly important for what they mean and also for how they sound (in Western languages the sound of a name is particularly important, whereas visual symbolism is more important in Asia). The sound of 'Cracker Jack', a brand of popcorn candy, invokes the product itself. In a similar vein, the shortening of Federal Express to FedEx makes the business sound faster, reinforcing ideas of speed that are also symbolized by the typeface of the logo and use of an arrow symbol between the last two letters.

Because of sound's role in helping us understand the relationship between events and time, and therefore cause and effect, sound's biggest role is in telling a brand's story. That is also why music can often have such a direct physiological effect on the body. Our body will speed up to match a fast rhythm and slow down (and even physically droop) when it slows. We can feel happy or sad depending on the tempo too, and also the key of music.

Songs and music tell stories by themselves, a topic well covered in this book. Songs are often part of rituals that are linked to a brand's story (think of communal singing at a rugby or football game or the New Zealand All Blacks' 'Haka'). Music and song have often been used by drinks brands, most famously Coca-Cola, as an integral part of their branding, and this is also true of many alcohol brands, be they Heineken and their music festivals or Stella Artois using classical music to communicate its class and heritage as a brand.

People are more likely to buy brands and products that are associated with music that they like (Gorn, 1982) and song has a particularly strong role in linking to the identity of the consumer and the brand. Thus music and song can help you link your brand to the right emotion and the right audience.

Ambience in retail is important to creating a mood, and music plays an important part in this along with the talent that work for you and the way they behave and interact with customers. As mentioned earlier, Abercrombie & Fitch create a very specific mood and ambience with their talent, behaviour and audio environment, and Virgin Atlantic (and other airlines) are another example of creating an ambience using people and sound.

In summary, TapestryWorks' esSense framework contains a total of 30 elements that contribute to the sense, symbols, and story of a brand. Sound comprises a major part of more than one-third of these elements, reflecting its huge potential contribution to brand identity. Sadly, many brands are not yet making the most of the potential of audio branding, and this offers a huge opportunity to leverage our sense of sound to strengthen brands. If you want to build the rhyme and rhythm of your brand, then *Audio Branding: Using sound to build your brand* is a great place to start.

Guest biography

Neil Gains is the founder of TapestryWorks and author of *Brand esSense*, and helps clients to weave sense into brands. Neil is also an associate fellow of the Institute on Asian Consumer Insight, hosted at Nanyang Technological University in Singapore. He worked for Cadbury Schweppes for more than 10 years in R&D and sensory research, before moving to Asia with AMI (later Synovate) to manage their Asia Pacific innovation practice, setting up TapestryWorks in 2010. He has lived in the UK, Indonesia, China and Singapore and has a doctorate in Consumer Psychology and Sensory Science. He loves travelling, reading detective novels, and sharing ideas.

CASE Atlanta Convention & Visitors Bureau (ACVB)

Even cities can have their sound: how the ACVB built its identity

Every city has one: a convention and visitors bureau. And their missions are essentially the same: to attract conventions and tourists to their city. So in 2014, when the city of Atlanta was the would-be host to an extraordinarily important convention, the ASAE Annual Meeting and Exposition, attended by convention planners and association executives from all over the country, the Atlanta Convention & Visitors Bureau (ACVB) knew they had a unique opportunity to fulfil their goal of attracting conventions and tourists to Atlanta.

Andrew Wilson, now the Executive Vice President and Chief Marketing Officer of the ACVB, along with his marketing team, shouldered the task of making the Atlanta brand stand out and communicating what makes Atlanta an inviting destination. A central island booth was planned for the exposition trade show floor and they would showcase a spectacular new film about the city, as well as interactive terminals and animations of the city's high points based on their print ad campaign.

From there, the idea took shape of creating a unifying brand sound that truly captured Atlanta's unique attributes and values and could be used to unify the various video collateral elements. Sixième Son began the process of creating the audio identity that would eventually begin at the convention and ripple outward for years to come.

As part of the brand briefing, the marketing team shared the paradoxes that they faced:

- Atlanta is a popular destination for conventions with an excellent airport/highway system and all the convention facilities and amenities; nonetheless, the direct competition is perceived as having more activities and nightlife.
- Though Atlanta has a young and educated workforce, 49 universities, and supportive community, it isn't widely known as the entrepreneurial hub that it actually is.
- It does have the aura of southern hospitality but that comes with a downside, the perception that the south isn't as progressive as the rest of the country.

The ACVB marketing team articulated their perspective concerning the values and attributes embodied by the city.

Atlanta is open, it's inclusive of diverse people and lifestyles, open to newcomers, open to new ideas, open to the world via a vast highway and railroad network, and the world's busiest airport serving 225 destinations. The city is filled with opportunity from thriving entrepreneurs to global headquarters, new initiatives supported by the community, and their universities combine with business to create possibilities.

What's more, the population is optimistic, entrepreneurial, forward-looking, and with a thriving and energetic newly arrived workforce. The offerings are eclectic. There's an extreme variety in music, food, and entertainment as well as businesses and people.

Like the rest of the south, Atlanta is welcoming and warm and its welcome extends to businesses as well as visitors. It supports new ventures and nurtures its businesses. With the goal of attracting convention planners, young professionals (especially the creative class), and tourists, the ACVB strove to portray the city as the progressive and open-minded oasis that it is. A dynamic new logo made a powerful statement about vibrancy and leadership.

With that, the competitive research began. The music associated with other convention city competitors as well as their brand positioning were examined. This research helped underscore the fact that many cities in the south leaned on southern hospitality and leadership, but few emphasized the promise of diversity and eclecticism. In the end, the distilled brief for the music strategists identified three areas to explore musically:

1 diversity, eclecticism, surprise;
2 warmth, hospitality, community support;
3 dynamism, leadership, authority.

The Sixième Son strategy team began to comb existing music for different musical ways to express each of these clusters of ideas. At the same time, Andrew Wilson pulled together a diverse listening committee comprising marketing and PR professionals and a professional singer and musician, to participate in guiding the next step of the process.

For this workshop, three audio mood boards were created, each one a playlist containing different musical approaches to describing one of the three sets of values. During a facilitated meeting at the ACVB headquarters on Peachtree Street, the listening committee began to carefully concentrate upon each selection of music. Their goal was to decide whether each selection conveyed the value to them and, more importantly, whether it conveyed it in a way that was consistent with Atlanta's brand.

The ACVB listening committee observed that what often is warm can also sound too beachy and casual, that certain excerpts connoting power were too aggressive and off-brand. They noted that smoothly blended sounds didn't express their diversity as well as layers of different instruments with strong identities of their own. As to human sounds, the group gave clear direction: whistling was out, choral voices were a possibility, clapping was welcome – as it echoed both the sounds of gospel music and the sense of encouragement from the community.

This sorting exercise made it possible to fine-tune the creative brief before beginning the creative development process. The music design team in Paris took over and at the end, five compositions were created. And the listening committee convened again.

In this step, the group was surprised to learn that they agreed on what *colour* the music was. They had written their answers on worksheets. In one case, the group found they had described the music as 'blue', 'blue-green' or 'turquoise' and in another, they found they had chosen 'yellow', 'orange yellow', 'orange' and the outlier 'brown'.

The listening committee winnowed the five down to two musical ideas that were developed and refined. Then came a small parting of the ways. The consumer team leaned toward one composition and the B2B team leaned toward another. Andrew Wilson broke the tie by moving the discussion to a higher ground. He asked, 'Where do we anticipate the greatest growth for the city will come from?'

The answer was this: 'From changing the perceptions of the convention goers and the referral business following the initial convention impression of Atlanta that would extend to their families and friends.' In this way, the audio identity was decided, not on a musical basis but on a business one; the group chose the brand expression that would support the greatest growth.

Today, the Atlanta Convention & Visitors Bureau's custom-tailored audio identity is rooted in the city's rich musical heritage and includes vocals. It distinguishes Atlanta by conveying the city's warmth and hospitality along with its authority and dynamism. Its unique sounds and rhythms tell the story of eclecticism and capacity to surprise.

The audio DNA that emerged from this process is not a song, but a guiding score that set the foundation and brought audio consistency to the many compositions that followed.

The ripples

The ACVB audio brand has proven extremely adaptable. Although its first uses were in the business-to-business realm, it has since also guided the development of consumer-focused productions.

First, in the convention booth, the audio DNA informed the score for the beauty reel and three interpretations for animated short features highlighting nature, nightlife, and technology.

As a logical next step, the ACVB created videos to be used by convention planners to encourage attendance to Atlanta conventions, the music reflecting that heard at the Atlanta expo booth.

A glittering version of the music was adapted for a video that underscores the glamorous delights of Atlanta's chic, upscale neighbourhood, Buckhead, which was designed to appeal to both convention planners and leisure travellers.

And in early 2015, musical adaptations were deployed in different culturally adapted scores to support foreign language videos in Latin American Spanish, Brazilian Portuguese, French, German, and British English. These are now in use on the ACVB website, in international sales efforts, and at the baggage claim in the international terminal of Hartsfield-Jackson International Airport.

Once conventions have been attracted and convention attendees and their families encouraged to come, the next clear goal became to get the visitors to partake of more of the city's attractions and discover the diversity of the city's offerings. A new set of videos was created to underscore the surprising and eclectic nature of the city. The ACVB commissioned videos for each neighbourhood in Atlanta featuring the specific attractions offered, with both English and Spanish voice-overs. The music has been interpreted in new ways to reflect those neighbourhoods: Eastside, Westside, Downtown, and Midtown now, like Buckhead, have their own interpretation of the Atlanta audio DNA.

Summing up his experience, Andrew Wilson said, 'Audio branding is as cathartic and rigorous a process as any visual-branding exercise. If not more. You have to dig deep into the understanding of the core values of the brand and the target audience or consumers. You have to make choices. Your brand can't be all things to all people and the process brings clarity to that truth.'

Atlanta's marketing team has been strategic about drawing convention planners, convention goers, families of convention goers, and other tourists. Beyond that, they've worked to deepen their immersion in the city and to bring these valuable visitors back. The ripples are still expanding. It's no wonder that they have risen in the ranks of convention cities since the original project began.

References

Gains, N (2013) *Brand esSense: Using sense, symbol and story to design brand identity*, Kogan Page, London

Gorn, GJ (1982) The effects of music in advertising on choice behavior: A classical conditioning approach, *Journal of Marketing*, 46 (Winter 1982), pp 94–101

How to launch your audio brand   08

Congratulations, you have your audio brand. You even have some plans on how to launch it and maintain it, arguably two of your most important steps in the branding process. Just think: branding elements are only as good as their consistent deployment, so they're only as strong as the people who manage them. While we touched on basic tools for launching your audio brand in the previous chapter, let us spend more time on it here.

When thinking through the launch, we recognize that every organization presents its new audio brand in a way that is rooted in its own culture and is based on both its immediate and long-term needs.

As we mentioned in Chapter 7, some companies introduce their audio brand gradually by, first, using it to create the score for a brand video or even an ad campaign, then properly launching it over all of their touch-points after it has had a chance to create an earprint.

Others like to bring in their audio brands with great fanfare, introducing them at a global corporate meeting, pre-selling them with employee or community involvement activities, creating games and ringtones to encourage engagement with the sound of the company or product, or other awareness-building programmes.

There's no cookie-cutter approach to kicking off your audio identity.

Your audio-brand launch provides the chance to involve your employees and make them feel part of a unified company that has positive, forward motion. Beyond grasping the music's intentions, employees can come away with a deeper understanding of the company's essence, values, mission, and promise as well as with a more personal connection to their fellow colleagues.

Music gives your media relations team something new to communicate to the press, too, and the launch provides a news angle that you can leverage.

Many companies use the launch of their audio brands to enliven long, offsite corporate meetings. This allows meeting organizers to refresh the audience by introducing a multisensory experience that engages a different part of the audience's mind, while staying relevant to the proceedings at hand.

We have found that attendees appreciate the mental shift and get a lift from the energy it creates.

While we provided some examples in Chapter 7, for inspiration, we'll explore four different approaches taken by different companies in different sectors. One of these should be right for your organization.

Launch approaches

An engaging teaser for an upcoming launch

At a pre-release event of an audio brand in Rome for the one of the world's largest energy companies, Enel, the launch team incorporated a nifty DJ mixing table called Reactable. To help them prepare for the event, the Sixième Son team deconstructed the audio DNA into eight of its component parts, including guitar, piano, and percussion and loaded them into the Reactable programme. (Meanwhile, it's important to note that the audio logo stayed intact.)

The event audience then emerged from the meeting room to encounter the innovative electronic musical table, which enabled them to remix the brand's sound, change its structure, and be creative in an engaging and intuitive way. Finally, after the attendees were done playing with the music, a professional DJ began to mix with the Reactable and the party started.

It's important to note that this type of event can be very helpful in realizing all of your marketing goals. As identified in *The Activation Imperative: How to build brands and business by inspiring action* (Rosen and Minsky, 2017) events can be motivating to both employees and customers and can even fuel sharing of information on social media, a goal you might want as you première new branding elements. Why? One reason is that 'Millennials and Gen Z place an extremely high value on obtaining experiences, particularly those that are unique or exclusive and aligned with their interests and values' (Rosen and Minsky, 2017).

A launch focused on unifying two disparate teams

Perhaps the most dynamic and inclusive audio brand introduction was for Pfizer Animal Health. Two different companies had recently been merged and, as a result, very intense management meetings were required among large teams (who didn't know each other) for the merger as well as for the creation of the audio brand.

To help kick off the audio brand, the launch team involved three different divisions of the company in a dynamic, interactive creative task. The meetings took place in Monte Carlo, Monaco at a famous hotel overlooking the Formula One racetrack. And these audio DNA events were sprinkled throughout the weeks of business meetings.

Though the branding team had already settled on an audio DNA for the company overall, each division – cattle, pets, and chicken/swine – had the opportunity to create a uniquely tailored version, based on that DNA, to represent itself.

The meetings took place over three weeks, one division per week. Voting technology was installed at the seats. On successive Mondays, each division en masse gave their input by using joysticks to answer questions about the music. By the following Friday, the audio-branding music, now incorporating their collective guidance, was presented along with a package of custom ringtones representing the division. So, beyond customizing the music to their own divisions, people had the opportunity to further choose which ringtone suited their personal style.

By allowing the divisions to create something together, the audio brand helped unify the two companies' teams into one. The Nice airport rang with the Pfizer Animal Health mobile ringtones for an entire month as Pfizer Animal Health teams came and went.

A revitalizing event for the brand

In keeping with their close ties to the entertainment world, the French telecom company SFR used their audio-brand launch to make a splash by creating a contest for recording artists. DJs were invited to liberally remix the sounds of the SFR audio brand as long as the new musical pieces respected the audio logo and the beats-per-minute. The participating musicians could download the SFR audio-identity elements such as theme, guitar, whistles, drums, and percussion from a dedicated SoundCloud location. They were then asked to upload their creation onto the SFR Young Talents website. The winner was determined by a jury composed of professionals including SFR Jeunes Talents team, the executive editor of a French music magazine, and an artistic director.

The winner's composition was played for the opening of a giant SFR event boasting 6,000 attendees at the Grand Palais in Paris, it was used in the 'Making Of' video shown during the event, and it also was the score for the 'best of' film that was the event's grand finale. Fittingly, this event celebrated SFR's many festival and band sponsorships.

As part of her prize package, the young woman who won the contest was featured in an article in a famous underground electronic music magazine, was given a €3,000 credit to spend on instruments at a famous music store and had her composition included in the electronic magazine's compilation CD.

A launch that proved a deep bond with the core audience

MACSF, which provides insurance for healthcare professionals, launched their new audio brand in a way that was completely faithful to their values and personality. The company has a reputation for warmth and mutual support. They had finalized a new audio identity that succeeded in capturing that message in a friendly and contemporary way. The group felt that the music hit the nail on the head and were very pleased to roll it out.

To make it a special event for the MACSF associates, Sixième Son created an orchestral score of the music and commissioned the Orchestra of the Hospitals of Paris (Orchestre des Hôpitaux de Paris) to perform the composition.

A 'Making Of' film was then created to shed light on the creative idea behind the audio brand and, importantly, gave an exclusive inside look into the recording of the orchestral performance by the musically accomplished medical professionals.

The MACSF audio brand was then launched at a theatre and included a live performance by the hospitals' orchestra. Employees left the launch party with a CD recording of the performance as well as a choice of ringtones with which they could personalize their mobile phones. Because the orchestra represented the very clients the company insures, the circle of mutual support was complete.

As you can see, the launch of your audio brand may be in person or through a webcast, it may be serious or entertaining, it may be one-way or interactive. Whatever you decide, the inclusion of a 'Making Of' video is a good way to give people context and help them build trust by sharing a behind-the-scenes look at the process.

But some companies don't go that far. They merely add their new audio-branding materials to their brand assets site and send out a memo, but as they begin to include the music in corporate social responsibility videos and new initiative announcements, and play it in company meetings – pretty soon it begins to be felt as part of the unique sound of the company.

More on the mighty Audio Style Guide

For this to happen on a long-term basis, and for your audio brand to become a recognized equity, you need to take into consideration one more audience segment – your marketing partners. And to ensure proper usage among this key group, we need to return to our discussion on the use of your Audio Style Guide, which we had started in the previous chapter.

After all, as we all know, companies may rely on both various internal departments and on a dozen marketing agencies and suppliers for the creation of marketing materials, including their experiential, digital, social, advertising, public relations, e-commerce, on-hold marketing, investor relations, and other marketing partners as well as their direct relationships with production studios.

These partners tend to understand the value of branding to varying degrees.

But in many cases, it is the agencies who choose the music for their materials – video news releases, branded content, sales videos, and advertising – and often these selections are based merely on the arbitrary tastes of their audio engineers, creative directors, and editors. Now, however, your audio identity can become a vital resource for them all.

First, they need to know the many musical options they have at their fingertips, as well as understand your rules of the road. To keep your audio brand from becoming diluted, you especially need to communicate what is flexible and what is sacred.

Enter the Audio Style Guide. As hinted at in Chapter 7, this style guide should include a detailed explanation of your audio brand and the values on which it is based. It should also identify the tactical adaptations of the audio brand and suggest how to use them, so the brand is protected.

Your Audio Style Guide could be a free-standing piece or it could be embedded into your overall brand guidelines. Either works. Ideally, it should contain links to all the music available as well as some best practice examples of the audio brand in use.

What follows is an example of the contents of a hypothetical Audio Style Guide. It's made up of a combination of guides currently in use by different companies.

Audio Style Guide: an example

1. The audio identity

An audio identity is an original composition anchored by two elements – the audio DNA and the audio logo – which communicate the essence, values, personality, and aspirations of the brand. Our audio identity establishes a distinct audio vocabulary that, when employed properly as well as consistently, strengthens the impact of our brand's communications by conveying meaning across all touchpoints.

For [product], it is an expression of hope and enthusiasm about the promise of this breakthrough. It conveys not just science but the community that has worked and will continue to work together, always looking to a brighter more fulfilling future.

2. The audio DNA

The audio DNA is the basis of [product's] musical universe. The [product] audio DNA has been composed and arranged to embody the brand:

- the introduction creates a sense of anticipation, propelling the audience into the future;
- the melody is driven by acoustic instrumentation, mainly a bright piano, accompanied by subtle synthesized textures to create a feeling of scientific advancement;
- the composition focuses on a feeling of community strength, evident in the overall optimism, hope, and excitement conveyed in the melody.

Rules of use:

- The audio DNA serves as the brand's audio guidelines and is not intended as a music bed to support promotional vehicles.
- As with the brand's visual style elements (such as fonts, colours, shapes), the audio DNA composition is not to be modified or changed in any way. Should an evolution in the sound be warranted (possible reasons could be a change in brand strategy, positioning, lifecycle, competitive environment etc), the composition will be updated.

3. The audio logo

Two short musical signatures (3-second and 2.5-second) have been extracted from the audio identity, which in a few seconds, convey optimism, teamwork, and scientific advancement. Highly memorable, these signatures become our brand's sonic seal of recognition. They enhance our identity, reinforce people's memory of the communication, and increase its attribution to the brand. These musical signatures have been specifically adapted to the visual animation of the logo. They must systematically and consistently accompany the end frame.

The ending is intentionally surprising and abrupt to convey the authority of our brand and to accentuate adrenaline and passion. It also helps to distinguish our commercials from others in the category.

Rules of use:

- Every communication should be endorsed with the audio logo. Whatever music you use in the body of the communication, the audio logo must end the communication. It is important to ensure a good transition between that music and the musical signature.

- The signature must not be adapted or distorted. The signature is composed of a four-note melody. This sequence must never be interrupted, broken up, speeded up or slowed down. No other element or voice-over may be added to it.

- Unless the piece is scored using the audio brand and a natural musical transition, you must leave a pause in transitioning to end frame. It is critical to leave a short pause, without music, before the arrival of the signature. Ideally, there should be between 0.3 and 0.5 seconds of blank space between the commercial's music and the signature. This breath will allow you to easily integrate the end frame sound, regardless of the music chosen for the body of the advertisement.

- Treatment of promotional messaging. In the case of advertising with a promotional message at the end, the audio signature should be placed at the end of the first part of the advertising before the promotional message. The promotional message must not encroach on the end frame. In the case of advertising with promotional messaging, it is also important to maintain a certain consistency with music. Whatever music is chosen for the body of the spot must be the same music for the promotional message at the end. And in the case of a spot without music, promotional messaging after the audio signature must, likewise, be left without music.

Suggested usage:

- Videos, meeting/event music, convention booth environment, on-hold music, mobile apps, web, radio, and TV ads.

4. Adaptations

Each touchpoint has its own context and communication purpose and therefore requires a specific audio adaptation. The [product] audio identity has thus been adapted to each need while living in the musical universe established for the brand.

A. End frame

The end frame is the official 3- to 4-second animated visual paired with the audio logo. Its purpose is to appear at the end of branded video content – both internal and external – to reinforce brand messaging and recognition.

The end frame should be included at the end of all branded video content. It should not be altered in any way.

Suggested usage:

- Corporate and product videos, presentations, convention booth content/videos, website, mobile apps, digital sales tools, etc.

B. Meetings and events package

The meetings and events package is composed of six distinct audio elements. As a whole, the package has been produced to support a variety of experiential situations by helping to create a powerful, memorable and branded experience.

1. Opening: 1 minute *Purpose: to give a feeling of anticipation and support the start of the main event.*

2. Enter stage: 10–15 seconds *Purpose: to introduce the first speaker or the main event about to happen on the stage (or main floor area).*

3. Transition: 7–10 seconds *Purpose: transition between action or speakers on stage (or main floor area).*

4. Exit stage: 10–15 seconds *Purpose: to give a feeling of closure as the last person leaves or action takes place on the stage (or main floor area).*

5. Closing: 1 minute *Purpose: to give a feeling of closure to the main event. To be played after the exiting stage music – perhaps as people are leaving and before one might start the background music again.*

6. Background: 3 minutes *Purpose: Background music provides ambience during the event – either for a reception or as guests arrive/depart and is meant to change or vary in the DNA melody throughout the sequence. It's not a focal piece – people will talk over it, be moving, etc – it's for subtle exposure.*

Rules of use:

- You may use the complete set or a limited mix of audio elements (eg 'background' music and 'enter stage' music), depending on the circumstances.
- The composition of each element should not be modified musically (ie do not add instrumentation or create a new version of the music); however, each component can be cut/faded out, to support the specific timing needs of each event.
- The 'transition' element should be used to combine package components and link to the audio logo.
- The 'background' music is designed to be looped and can be concluded by mixing in the audio logo.

Suggested usage:

- Internal meetings (salesforce, marketing, company-wide), employee events, external meetings, symposia, dinners, trade-show booths.

C. Ringtones

These adaptations of the audio identity are provided to foster a sense of belonging, formatted for customized brand ringtones. Internal audiences, partners, and prospects can download and set them as ringtones on mobile phones:

1. Ringtone 1 – starts simple and crescendos.
2. Ringtone 2 – starts dynamic and adds variations to the melody.
3. Ringtone 3 – incorporates unexpected sounds to stand out from background.

Suggested usage:

- Internal distribution, giveaways to partners and suppliers, take-home gifts from conferences and trade shows.

D. Custom score for brand film

Custom scores are developed to support and enhance the intention of a brand film. Detailed attention is given to transitions, such as those found in a voice-over, topic and/or images, so as to highlight key moments. Overall, the objective is to produce a final product that has a clear impact and coherent brand link.

Example: introductory film Custom score highlights the transition between the before and after reveal of [product]. The film begins with surprising numbers and statistics and its seriousness is reflected in the overall serious mood of the music. After [product] is revealed, the musical intention changes in coherence with the excitement and hope that the product offers.

Modular set of audio beds for videos The modular set of audio beds for videos provides on-brand music compositions each at least 30 seconds in length, designed to be looped or cut and repurposed, providing music for a range of internal and external brand videos:

1 calm;

2 walking pace;

3 hopeful;

4 inspiring;

5 lively;

6 jubilant;

7 rocking;

… plus, transitional element: the transitional audio element exists to connect modules together or lead into the audio logo at the end.

Rules of use:

- The modules have been designed to loop, as well as attach to one another or link to the audio logo. A transition element has been provided to help connect the audio components.
- The instrumentation of composition should not be modified.

Suggested usage:

- Internal and external video footage such as: corporate films, salesforce videos, recruitment videos, training materials, trade-show content, web, mobile videos.

Follow the suggestions in this chapter and you will be well on your way to having a successful audio brand. But strong brands actually get better with age, because, as we all know, you can build up greater equity over time. The catch? This takes great care and nurturing, not just for the visual aspects, but for all aspects of a brand. And managing your audio brand long-term has some unique considerations as well. What are they? Stick with us and we will explore them in the next chapter.

GUEST PERSPECTIVE Ellen Byron

The search for sweet sounds that sell: household products' clicks and hums are no accident – light piano music when the dishwasher is done?

The small sounds consumer products make – whether a snap, click, rustle or pop – can be memorable and deeply satisfying, often suggesting luxury, freshness, effectiveness, or security. Companies, in their endless drive to motivate customers to buy, are paying more attention to these product noises and going to great lengths to manipulate them. Sound is emerging as a new branding frontier.

While your audio logo is perhaps the most important element of a traditional audio brand programme, sound contributes to the overall branding in other ways. Indeed, more and more companies are discovering that the sound a product makes can convey subtle information about its quality and influence purchasing decisions.

To give you a sense of these opportunities, we asked reporter Ellen Byron if we could reprint a piece she wrote on the topic for the Wall Street Journal, *which was published on 24 October, 2012. She graciously said yes and, after clearing permissions with the publisher as well, here is the piece. We hope it inspires you with ideas on the various ways you can expand the sound of your brand.*

Subtle auditory cues can make a big difference to shoppers choosing from several brands, companies say. Occasionally a product pitches its unusual sound directly: remember 'Snap, Crackle, Pop' for Kellogg's Rice Krispies, and Alka-Seltzer's 'Plop Plop Fizz Fizz'? Sound, for the most part, isn't the first thing consumers notice about a product. But when it's good, they quickly come to appreciate it, marketers say.

'These little touches can really separate you from the other guys', says Ted Owen, vice president of global package design at Clinique, an Estée Lauder Co's line. 'We call them the intangibles.'

Last month [September 2012] Clinique introduced High Impact Extreme Volume mascara, which produces a soft, crisp click when the top is twisted shut. The click reassures users that the package is closed and the liquid mascara won't dry out. But more subtly, Mr Owen says, the click conveys the elegance of the $19.50 formula.

Mr Owen and his team fiddled with some 40 prototypes of inner parts of the mascara tube, paying particular attention to the tiny, curved plastic tab, called a 'nib', that emits the click when the top twists over it. By adjusting the slope of the curve and a corresponding tab located inside the top, designers could alter the click's tone. A steep curve made a high-pitched click, which the team thought sounded cheap. A flatter curve made a dull sound. 'We sweated that detail,' Mr Owen says. 'You have to pay attention to it and manage it through all the materials you consider and all the manufacturing steps to be sure you get it right.'

Getting it wrong can bring major consequences. Hoping to tout its SunChips brand as environmentally friendly, Frito-Lay, part of PepsiCo Inc, introduced a compostable chip bag in 2010. Consumers found it noisy and complained. Sales fell, and Frito-Lay eventually went back to the old bags. 'The packaging of the product is a multisensory experience for our consumers,' says a Frito-Lay spokesman.

Even product sounds that happen just once may be treated with reverence. Snapple, owned by Dr Pepper Snapple Group Inc, says the pop a consumer hears when unscrewing the top from a new bottle of Snapple is a cue that it is fresh. The company calls it the 'Snapple Pop' and says it builds anticipation and offers a sense of security, because the consumer knows the drink hasn't been opened before or tampered with.

Snapple was so confident about the pop's safety message that in 2009 it eliminated the plastic wrapping that encircled the lid. It saved on packaging costs and eliminated an estimated 180 million linear feet of plastic waste, the company says. 'We were a lot more comfortable making that decision because we knew there was this iconic pop,' says Andrew Springate, Senior Vice President of Marketing.

Discussions of sound in corporate meetings brings linguistic challenges. 'We're not quite as bad as when you go to the mechanic to try to describe a car problem,' says Lisa King, Vice President of Insights & Innovation at Newell Rubbermade Inc, maker of Sharpie markers.

Company executives call the sound a Sharpie marker makes as it moves across the paper the 'scritch-scratch'. When they consider making a product innovation, they check for the scritch-scratch. 'It's part of the experience of using that marker', Ms King says. 'The sound of your product can be as distinctive as the look.'

Despite the growing attention, it's still rare for ads to boast about product sounds. In May, Volkswagen introduced a commercial praising the 'thunk' of the door on the Jetta. (A guy shuts his car door, and the thunk makes things – a football, a kite, a doll, a cat – fall out of a tree.) 'We were looking for a metaphor to convey quality and well-built,' says Tim Mahoney, [formerly] Volkswagen of America's Chief Marketing Officer.

Some annoying product sounds are overdue for an update. General Electric Co's appliance division is overhauling the abrasive buzzers, dings, and beeps that clothes dryers, ovens and microwaves have been making for decades.

GE worked with a sound designer who composed a 'soundtrack' for each of its four major brands. Instead of beeps, rings, and buzzes, the appliances play snippets of their song. Turn on a machine and hear the music crescendo; turn it off, and the same snippet decrescendos. For time-sensitive alerts, like a timer, the music becomes increasingly urgent.

Each brand's music is meant to appeal to the target customer. Hotpoint, a budget-friendly line, will have a grunge-rock tune. The Monogram line, GE's priciest, will feature light piano music. 'This is more Aaron Copland', says David Bingham, GE Appliances' Senior Interaction Designer. 'Very forward-looking and elegant-feeling'.

As home-appliance design becomes more minimal, GE says, elements like sound are more important. The new sounds are set to hit the market in two or three years.

Some products strive for silence. Tampax Radiant, the tampon line Procter & Gamble Co launched in April [2012], has a textured plastic wrapper that won't make loud crinkling sounds.

The wrapper is targeted at women, especially teens, who say they want more privacy in public restrooms. 'They are trying to keep the secret and the wrapper wasn't able to do that', says Alex Albacarys, Associate Director for global Tampax research and development. 'On this wrapper we took it to the next level in terms of sound avoidance.'

P&G researchers measured the noise of the new wrapper in the company's sound laboratory and found there was a 25 per cent decibel reduction with the Radiant compared with Tampax Pearl, which was previously P&G's quietest tampon wrapper.

Household brand Method Products puts its bottles to a 'trigger tester' to be sure they can withstand some 10,000 sprays without emitting what Don Frey, Method's Vice President of Product Development, calls 'chatter'.

In recent months, Method has been evaluating new packaging suppliers and bottle nozzles to keep up with growing sales. A squeaking or chattering nozzle usually indicates a mechanism that isn't put together well. 'It creates images in consumers' minds of how well it's going to work, and how well it's made,' Mr Frey says.

Dyson, the appliance maker, has been paying more attention to machine noise in recent years. Globally, the company wants its vacuums to have a pleasing, low tone, which it says sounds more upscale.

In the US, Dyson says consumers have been fairly tolerant of loud vacuum cleaner noise, but there are signs they are becoming more sensitive. In March, Dyson introduced the DC-39, its quietest full-size vacuum available in the US. The motor is attached to sound-dampening mounts, and polyurethane helps absorb sound energy.

'There has started to be more demand from the US for quieter, better-sounding products,' says Rachael Pink, an acoustic engineer at Dyson. 'People now expect products to sound good – not just sound quiet, but have a nice quality.'

Guest biography

Ellen Byron is a news editor for *The Wall Street Journal* and writes about consumers and the companies that chase them. Since joining the *Journal* in 2000, Ellen has covered consumer-product makers, retailers, advertising and human-interest tales from the Midwest. Prior to *The Wall Street Journal*, Ms Byron worked for ABC News. She is a graduate of Carleton College.

CASE Renault

Getting up to speed with Renault's audio brand

The automotive sector is extremely competitive and in France three of the top five advertisers are auto brands: Renault, Peugeot, and Citroën. Of these, the top advertiser is Renault. And, to say the least, competition is tough, not only from domestic manufacturers but from the mighty German brands next door.

In the 2000s, Renault began to undergo a transformative process. First the company refocused on a design-based approach, then it committed to a guiding set of values that would underlay their new approach: vibrancy, connection to people, strong and passionate orientation toward the future.

The company had also set its sights set on moving upmarket.

In 2011, their concept cars began to reflect an inventive new look, starting with the distinctively designed Captur, which served as the focal point for the repositioning of the entire car brand. As Ramón Vives Xiol mentioned in his guest perspective in Chapter 4, the sound for each of the lines in the huge expo booth was designed to stand alone or to blend with the others.

And they were sequenced to describe the stages of life that a car owner would experience. This was Sixième Son's first step into creating a unifying, but flexible musical brand expression, for Renault.

In 2014, a new positioning, visual identity and brand tagline appeared as a natural result of the brand's evolution. The company replaced the long-standing line, 'Drive the Change', with the more stirring sentiment, 'Passion for Life'. Once these branding elements were developed, the brand turned its attention to its audio identity.

An audio audit of the car category revealed that many advertisers used the same type of audio vocabulary, often based on the sound of the vehicle or the metal itself, and were, thus, hard to distinguish from one another. Worse, the positioning of most car companies seemed to always default to the same tired notions of power, safety, or technology. Renault was no different. The audio logo that had existed since 2003 had a cold and metallic sound and wasn't very engaging. And it certainly didn't express either 'passion' or 'life'.

The good news was that the company was willing to risk breaking from the traditional sounds of automotive category. The first task for Sixième Son was to create the composition that would reveal the new vehicle, the Renault Kadjar, and highlight the company's changing dynamic. The new sound created for that event included an actual song with original lyrics, a very uncommon practice in the category and, indeed, in Sixième Son's own work. The film that introduced the, now iconic, Kadjar at the Paris Auto Show in 2014 bore a fresh musical stamp: colourful, vibrant, and full of emotion. It set the course for the audio identity to come.

This revealed itself during the step of the audio-branding process in which the audio mood boards are evaluated, as described in Chapter 7. One of the strategic musical selections presented anonymously among the selection of musical clips was an extract from the music composed for the Kadjar film. The listening committee immediately noted that this selection had captured the Renault brand's unique mixture of values and contrasts. Both rich and yet simple, its captivating sound became the jumping-off point for the development of the ultimate Renault audio identity.

The audio identity that was born from this parentage brought Renault a sound vocabulary like no other. It works seamlessly with the restructured brand and communicates its future-facing vision and its passion.

The mould-breaking audio logo sums it all up. The little breath that introduces the signature brings to mind humanity and passion; it also has the practical advantage of making it easy to bridge from other music into the branded finale. The following notes ride on the breath and add an alluring quality. The voices, both male and female, complement each other. They break the cold and technological image of the previous signature and reinforce the emotional differentiation. The final thump brings the audience back to the reliability of the brand.

A quick test showed that it had a positive effect on the brand. Brand perception among consumers under 35 revealed the following impressions:

65 per cent 'more modern'

62 per cent 'more enthusiastic'

60 per cent 'more unique'

65 per cent 'more momentum'

At another motor show in the spring of 2015, the entire new identity was unveiled with ringing success.

To gain acceptance of a change of this magnitude, the message needed to be delivered with great clarity and confidence both inside and outside of the company. Renault used a series of executive meetings to launch the audio brand and gave the management full responsibility for spreading the word to their organizations.

The tools provided for this job included an Audio Style Guide, like the one described in this chapter and a film created to unify the company behind the initiative. These were accompanied with specific guidelines for the brand's agencies along with tailored explanations to help them understand the reasons for the change.

The company took a holistic approach to the diffusion of the new audio brand. In the first year, implementation of the new musical territory of the brand spread widely:

- At headquarters, the music in the reception area and the on-hold music for the customer service line was reworked to introduce an adaptation of the new audio identity. This enabled consistency in the brand's voice and sent a clear message to the officers, staff, and shareholders alike. They wanted everyone to understand the importance of this initiative.

- Ringtones: several mobile ringtones were adapted from the audio identity both unifying people around the common sound and allowing for personal choice. These empowered employees to embrace the evolving corporate culture in a personal way.

- Renault Captur introductory app: this app accompanied the launch of the model at the Geneva Motor Show. Adobe named it App of the Week and featured it on their Adobe TV saying, 'The Renault Captur has built a brand engagement iPad app using the Adobe Digital Publishing Suite. The app features engaging slideshows, images, and video to illustrate details of the car, to showcase the design process from concept to reality, and communicate its consumer lifestyle message' (Adobe, 2016). In the video, they point out that the opening page features a video with music that can be played throughout the app but explain that it's left up to the user's choice whether or not to play the music. They recommend that people activate the music to see how it adds to the experience.

- Point-of-sale: Renault dealerships are among the most intimate points of contact with the customer, as they provide a welcoming place for discussion and decision-making. Their role is to immerse customers in a trusted universe that's in tune with their brand values. Sixième Son created a detailed retail Audio Style Guide to establish the types of musical selections that their dealerships could employ to create an appropriate experience for the customers.

- Music library: not every film needs a bespoke score. Videos for social media campaigns and 'budget' videos must come out fast and economically. These are often treated catch-as-catch-can and, from a musical point of view, can distort the image of the brand. The music grabbed is often rights-free, and does not convey Renault's values or support the communication of its message. To replace these meaningless clips of generic sound, the Renault music library provides for a range of music that's freely and quickly available without compromising on brand consistency.

- The audio at auto shows: since 2011, Renault has shown a purposeful approach to the sound in their impressive booths at shows including Paris, Geneva, Shanghai, and Frankfurt. Based on the audio vocabulary of the brand, this sound has been enriched over time to achieve high levels of sophistication. The events can be musically scripted, dividing the space into several areas to offer a distinct musical atmosphere to each or, movingly, to join all parts together to form a powerful whole that highlights the massive scale of the space.

- Musical staging of press presentations: Renault invests heavily in auto shows both to defend its status and to present its wide range of vehicles. These auto shows are often punctuated with press events in which new vehicles are revealed, which in turn requires dramatizing the positioning and style of new vehicles without losing the overarching sound of the brand.
- TV advertising: the brand's goal is to gain auditory brand consistency while avoiding locking its advertising into a style that limits expression. Renault considers outside music brought by the ad agency but may also commission, for comparison, a score based in the audio DNA, which is tailored to the script.
- Radio: Renault is ubiquitous on the airwaves in many countries including France and, of course, the music helps bring consistency among all their spots.

With all the audio touchpoints, most brands would experience the potential problem of having the sound become annoyingly repetitive. But Renault proactively solved that potential problem with subtle variety. Sometimes the music plays within the territory of the overall brand, without the melodic line or the usual signature. In other words, the sound stays just close enough to the audio DNA for the listener to recognize it, but not close enough to eventually create boredom.

Renault's new sound identity emerged quickly, not only because it fit the brand like a glove, but because the launch was executed comprehensively and confidently, making sure the audio brand is firing on all cylinders: a great lesson for anyone wishing to launch their sound and ensure that it sticks quickly.

References

Adobe (2016) http://tv.adobe.com/watch/digital-publishing-customer-showcase/app-of-the-week-renault-captur/

Rosen, W and Minsky, L (2017) *The Activation Imperative: How to build brands and business by inspiring action*, p 115, Rowman & Littlefield, Langham, MA

Maintaining and evolving your audio brand

09

A strong brand name and image that evolves as the times and needs change can last for what is considered forever in the business world. Just look at Coca-Cola, Siemens, Dial Soap, Fiat, Mitsubishi, and Cadbury. Brands are essentially corporate religions (Hanlon, 2006); look at how long Judaism, Catholicism, Islam, Buddhism, and other religions are continuing to thrive as they have evolved. It is conceivable that brands can do the same.

Observing organized religion (with utmost respect), it's easy to see that, in many ways, it forms the structural roots of branding; religions' values are communicated and their reputations are built in more ways than just their well-known visual iconography of stars, crosses, crescents, and yin-yang circles, but also through the other senses; just think of the smells (incense and spices), the tastes through the various foods and wines served in services or on the holidays, and most of all, the sounds we hear during the chants, prayers, and songs at services.

While the audio-branding specialty is still in its early days, audio identities can also last for decades – if not longer – if they are adapted and evolving in their sounds, but don't completely change every two or three years, the way typical ad campaigns do. Rather, it makes more sense to take the brand management approach you use with your visual assets.

Your audio identity and audio logo can continue to support the long-term brand through its changes in advertising campaigns, just as your graphic assets do. The music, almost always, based on your brand's audio DNA, is then scored to dramatize the storyline and adds the appropriate brand emotions at the right times.

As a rule of thumb, the longer and more consistently you've been using your audio brand, the more room you have for interpretations – because audiences will have been educated to recognize its unique texture, its recurring motif, its rhythm, its quirks, and its charms.

Michelin, for instance, can afford to unleash a dubstep version of its audio brand for a big US auto show precisely because the company has been highly disciplined in employing its audio identity throughout advertising in every corner of the world, in its employee communications, global company meetings, customer service line, and even its ringtones. Otherwise, with such an exaggerated change in musical style, the connection to the brand would be hard for people to recognize.

As we explored in the SNCF case in Chapter 1, a brand can evolve in response to changing trends in the concerns and needs of the audience and still be recognizable. For SNCF, the idea of 'leadership with a human face' came first, but as passengers became more concerned about the environment, the ecological aspect of travelling on a train was stressed. The music became more acoustic. Then, as passengers became focused on speed and efficiency, a different sound, that suggested a 'whoosh', was introduced within the same brand tune. But the core notes remained the same.

In these cases, the process of creating the new interpretation takes less time and budget than it did to create the original one because the team already understands the brand and its resulting music. The task then is to keep what's important and find a way to integrate new information into it through a shift in the rhythm, the instrumentation, or through other musical devices. At Sixième Son, Paris, the word they use for this work is 're-lift' and, in general, it takes place every three to five years.

This approach keeps the brand in mind while still allowing new meaning to emerge. And that has value because in the audience's mind, the unique sound of the brand can often provide the most emotional and influential connection with it, not only for the audience but for the employees as well.

United Airlines: a long off-and-on-again relationship with *Rhapsody in Blue*

Perhaps the most comprehensive and long-term relationship between a US brand and its music has been United Airlines' with George Gershwin's *Rhapsody in Blue*, a composition that has many qualities that make it useful as an audio brand. Surprisingly, the piece didn't begin as a formal symphony but as a musical idea created by Gershwin and arranged by Ferde Grofé. They collaborated in much the same way that a creative team works together at an audio-branding agency.

As does a good audio identity, the music has a recognizable theme. And, being rooted in jazz, it has lent itself to interpretations by musicians over the years, starting soon after it first appeared on the scene. This variety has conditioned listeners to expect it to pop up in different guises. So, in a marketing context, it's perfectly permissible to reinterpret the music without 'desecrating' a classic. In fact, interestingly, the symphonic arrangement that is now considered the definitive *Rhapsody in Blue* didn't appear till 1942, 18 years after the original performance of the piece (Bañagale, 2014a).

Rhapsody in Blue showed up at United in the mid-1980s as the airline was suffering the consequences of a damaging pilots' strike and a steep decline in customer satisfaction. The airline intended to infuse 'quality, elegance, and class' via the music and the images that accompanied it.

The music soon began filling an ever-greater role in the United Airlines customer and employee experience. As mentioned in Chapter 1, it was played on entering and landing the planes, it was heard on their safety videos, and graced the long moving walkway corridor at O'Hare's Terminal One, among other places.

After the 2010 merger between United Airlines and Continental, United's use of the music diminished. But then, in 2013 the famous music came roaring back into their TV commercials and reappeared in its safety video, 'Safety is Global'. In fact, it may have been found to be among the strongest brand assets in the portfolio of the combined brands.

One of the ways this music has stayed fresh is through the delightful variety with which it's used. A good example of this is the 'Safety is Global' video. The movie takes place around the world and there are light touches of local instrumentation that signal where the action is taking place. Ryan Raul Bañagale, writing in the Oxford University Press blog, stated that:

> While in France, a pair of accordions play the introductory bars of the piece while a pilot welcomes us aboard and reminds us to heed instructions. The flight attendant hops a cab to Newark Airport (United's East Coast hub) to the strains of a jazz combo setting of the love theme. A tenor saxophone improvises lightly around this most famous melody of the *Rhapsody* while she provides instruction on how to use the seatbelt from the bumpy backseat. Finally, a gong signals a move to Asia, where we encounter the ritornello theme of the *Rhapsody,* but it is being played on a plucked zither and bamboo flute.
>
> Source: Bañagale, 2014a

Curious? We invite you see it, so you too can experience the music's ultimate flexibility (Bañagale, 2014b).

We find it interesting that the emotional attachment to *Rhapsody* was still there after the pause, as evidenced by this enthusiastic article:

> Imagine my delight when in 2013 United reintroduced this timeless classic. The piece is galvanizing, soaring... I was in Chicago recently and went through the tunnel connecting terminals at ORD. There is something magical about all that neon, the colours, the moving sidewalk, and *Rhapsody in Blue* playing. *Rhapsody in Blue* IS United.
>
> Source: Airline Guys, 2014

Counter-intuitive but true: protect your audio brand by not playing it

United manages its audio brand with great sensitivity. According to Herman Tiemans, regional manager, marketing communications until 2006, United mindfully withdrew the music during two critical times. One was after the 9/11 World Trade Center attack in 2001. That was a time when employees and travellers were very anxious about getting back on airplanes and into the air. The airline had to communicate serious information to a jarred audience. Another time was immediately after the carrier's 2002 bankruptcy filing (Fahey, 2016).

How you use and maintain your audio brand, of course, depends on your unique goals, situation, and competitive actions. But there are steps you can take to extend longevity. Let us take a look at some of them.

Some best practices for maintaining your audio brand

- Share it with the employees. Don't keep it within the marketing department under the guise of protecting it. We are living in an interactive age, where your various audiences have as much control over your brand as you do. So you need to make sure they convey your brand in the ways you want and employees are your first line of defence. Help the key internal audience – they are your 'walking brand' – understand its genesis and purpose. Again according to Herman Tiemans, the employees wholeheartedly embraced *Rhapsody in Blue* and were a force behind its reinstatement on the planes, in the waiting areas, and other areas after it had been withdrawn.

- Create plenty of variety. The audio DNA shouldn't be a straitjacket; rather, it should be a guide, so the audio brand has life and expansiveness, just like people flex and change according to the situation, but are still undeniably identifiable as themselves. Use the music in creative, relevant, and even whimsical ways to keep the message both familiar and surprising and to keep the brand conversation alive.

- Keep your employees updated on any new developments. Through their employee newsletter, AXA provides its global employees with quarterly updates on the new musical interpretations being used in global TV commercials and the new musical additions available in the audio library. Just think: the best way to get employees thinking about how to use the audio-branding elements is to let them know they exist.

- If your brand has taken on a new characteristic, consider a 're-lift' (a modification that still preserves the recognizable sound but adds a new layer of meaning). This is preferable to recreating the entire composition or creating an entirely new audio brand and, in both of these options, losing the brand equity you've built. In addition, these re-lifts are not as costly and time-consuming. So, your company will win on the cost and the benefit sides of the equation.

- Regularly update and refocus attention on your Audio Style Guide. It is the first line of defence in protecting your brand, particularly in light of the typically high turnover rate among brand managers today and whose replacements often want to toss out the work of the previous regime, so they have attainments to boast about on their resumés. (It's been said in packaged goods companies that the first sign of inexperienced brand managers is that when they come into the positions, they immediately want to change the packaging, the very guide consumers use when searching for the item in the store.) The same can be suspected when it comes to the audio DNA and music, even if the same person would not dare consider tampering with the visual-branding elements due to their longer familiarity with the value of coherence in this discipline.

- Though senior management must convey its support for the audio identity, it is useful to have an identified champion and manager lower in the ranks, someone who acts as a branding watchdog and facilitator. Ideally, this person should have strong cross-functional skills and can also gently nudge other departments into the adoption of the audio brand for new and expanded uses, whether it is in areas of a new building, introducing a new employee training initiative, or other places and times sound can be used to enhance your brand.

- If you are a heavy advertiser, like a grocery retailer for instance, consider creating an audio logo *system*, instead of repeating the exact same sound several times a day. Nobody wants to turn brand recognition into an annoyance. Huggies took the system approach in creating its audio logo. Their main audio logo ends in the sound of a toddler's delighted squeal. But there's also an audio logo with the same music but without the voice. And, there are other iterations already waiting in the wings, some that contain the voices of babies in other stages of maturation from newborn to toddler.

- Bring your key advertising, public relations and other marketing agencies into the loop. They should help you brainstorm the possibilities, either together or on their own, as well as work in tandem with each other and your audio-branding agency to get the most out of the vast potential of having your own distinct and meaningful sound.

The hard work is now over. You have an audio brand and a plan for maintaining it over the long term. So you are good to go. But there's one more topic we want to cover in more detail: the strategic employment of audio brands in public spaces – shopping malls, retail environments, entertainment arenas, stadiums, hospitals.

As more services become products and more products become services and both seek to create more engaging environments through the use of events, pop-up stores and flagship stores – think the Hershey's store that first premièred on Times Square, the club-like auto showrooms on the Champs-Élysées, or the competing tech playgrounds run by wireless carriers on Chicago's Michigan Avenue – we think this chapter would be of interest to all marketers. Join us. After all, we believe that it will help you think through all the possibilities with your new audio brand.

GUEST PERSPECTIVE Janet Borgerson and Jonathan Schroeder

Hawaii: a historical exemplar of audio branding

As we saw in the case study featuring the Atlanta Convention & Visitors Bureau, audio brands are for more than just products and services. They are for locations as well. And one of the first locations to benefit from having a distinct audio brand is Hawaii. So we asked Janet Borgerson, a Fellow at the Institute for Brands & Brand Relationships, and a Visiting Research Fellow at Cass Business School, City University London, and Jonathan Schroeder, the William A Kern Professor in the School of Communication at Rochester Institute of Technology in New York – both experts in different theoretical aspects of branding – to give us their perspective on the historical audio branding of Hawaii. We hope you find it instructive and we believe that even branding professionals in the product and service arenas will find it instructive.

Hawaii evokes a repertoire of sounds, songs, and south-seas sonority, presenting a strong brand identity and providing an illustrative example of audio branding. Indeed, the marketing of popular music with distinct sonic characteristics, such as steel guitar, ukulele, exotic birdcalls, and crashing ocean waves, reinforced these audio assets as essentially Hawaiian. Audio resources suggested an 'authentic' cultural and natural history for the Hawaiian brand, and aided in Hawaii's transformation from a so-called primitive paradise into the 50th State. In this way, market-created fantasies intersected with associated acoustics to form powerful auditory brand value.

Hawaii, and what the branding of Hawaii has deemed her 'lilting call', lure us to an ultimate audio brandscape. Like AT&T's chimes, IBM Windows' sonic start-up 'logo', MGM's roaring lion, and Nokia's familiar cellphone ringtone, Hawaii was strategically linked with certain sounds. As liner notes from RCA's classic vinyl record *Hawaii in HI-FI* from 1959 state, 'In music, a body of undulating songs have been more effective causes for vacationing Americans choosing Hawaii than all the illustrated brochures of the travel agencies.' In some ways, the Hawaii created through aural atmospheres is more easily identifiable than the landscapes of these South Pacific islands. Certainly, more people have heard Hawaiian music than have visited Hawaii, and the paradise promises of the Hawaii brand exist mainly in the imagination and in marketing campaigns. Hawaii and her audio-brand extensions still reach our ears.

Hawaii remains an important tourist destination, strategic military outpost, and 'tropical paradise', and much of the related music is still available: online, on CD, and on new and reissued vinyl LPs, smartly repackaged as Hawaiiana, exotica, and retro lounge (see Figure 9.1). These days, 'Hawaiian' sounds often stand in for any tropical island resort, providing something of a challenge to brand distinction. Here, we provide a brief case study on the decades-long audio branding of Hawaii, and her brand extensions, drawing upon developments in branding thought generally, including audio, or sonic branding (Gustafsson, 2015), brand culture (Schroeder and Salzer-Mörling, 2006; Schroeder, Borgerson and Wu, 2015; Wu, Borgerson and Schroeder, 2013) and retroscapes (Brown and Sherry, 2003).

The Hawaiian craze
A Hawaiian craze swept the United States after World War II, and much of this was musically motivated, fanned by the tourism industry, popular films, and broadway shows, such as *Blue Hawaii* and *South Pacific*, and

Figure 9.1 *Hawaiian Holiday*, George Wyle Orchestra and Chorus, Imperial Records

the Hawaiian Chamber of Commerce. Hula dancing, backyard luaus, tiki-totems, tropical drinks, and Hawaiian shirts became the rage. The 'lure of the islands', often a scantily dressed brown-skinned woman, posed on waterfalls and decorated with flowers pleasingly represented Hawaii's qualities as a sensual resort paradise (Canniford and Karababa, 2013; Costa, 1998). Airlines, travel agencies, and the Kodak Film Company worked to develop visions of Hawaiian paradise: stately palm trees, the white sand of sunlit Waikiki beach, and hula girls in grass skirts with flowers in their flowing dark hair. Tourist sites like the 'Kodak Hula Show' offered idealized island highlights, including 'natives' performing in colourful attire to embody the sonorous exotic qualities of tropical Hawaii.

Many marketing campaigns not only relied upon a visual representation of Hawaii, but also presented a Hawaiian sound. Native drums, steel guitar, and tropical birdcalls provided the acoustic backdrop for pineapples, Pearl

Harbor, and impending statehood. Preparing Hawaii for mass consumption meant transforming these islands into a brand that could be associated with attractive flora and fauna, exotic peoples with colourful rituals and celebrations, and distinctive music and sounds – both vocal and instrumental. Sound emerging from each of these arenas, such as waves crashing on the beach, the characteristic sound of the ukulele, or songs sung in Hawaiian, offered a broad range from which to draw elements of audio brand-building. Music served as an aural image of Hawaii, for example, as provided by the US government's support of the long-running *Hawaii Calls* radio broadcasts. What became known to the US mainland, and in many cases the world, as 'Hawaii' resonates with these sounds, calling forth an earlier era, and invoking a complex legacy of culture and history, tourist management and nostalgic hype. 'Packaged Hawaii' emerged as island paradise, tourist destination, and honeymoon resort, crucially supported in all areas by audio aspects.

Hawaiian popular music helped animate Hawaii as a brand. Hawaiian music provided a window into the conceptual state of Hawaii, allowing the uninitiated mainlander access to the spirit of Aloha. The genre provided sonic sources for familiarizing US mainlanders with this distant chain of islands and served as a central element in the tourist industry's campaign to attract visitors to Hawaii. Moreover, Hawaiian popular music mobilized the potential of modern sound recording and dissemination technologies, including the hi-fi record album and radio programmes.

The audio branding of Hawaii

As part of cross-promotional campaigns, Hawaiian record albums were often distributed by travel agencies (see Figures 9.1 and 9.2). Deluxe packaging for these albums might include five or six blank, or lined, pages that could be filled with personal reminiscences, or snapshots of the laughing hula girls, the white sand, and the lush island paradise – much like a proto-Instagram feed. Other features of these souvenir records included colour photos of key visitor sights, attraction maps for each island, as well as the vinyl LP of songs and sounds, including pounding drums and evocative birdcalls. These inspirational visual and aural images presented the Hawaiian experience, whether one eventually travelled to Hawaii or found satisfaction simply sitting in the living room with the LP and a record (Connell and Gibson, 2008).

The Kodak Hula Show, which provided a touristic highlight for decades, offers an iconic example of the efforts to audio-brand Hawaii, as hula dance calls for hula music. Kodak photo film was sold near the show,

Figure 9.2 *Destination Honolulu*, Sam Kailuha and the Islanders, Cavalier Records

which offered many picture-taking opportunities, as it was staged outdoors expressly for tourists to photograph; the performers wore brilliant green 'grass' skirts, yellow leis, and red flowers – perfect Kodak colours.

The hula girl and her musical accompaniment form a foundation of Hawaiian branding, helping to make Hawaii instantly recognizable the world over. Indeed, the iconic hula dancer became a stock image and common trope of native sensuality repeated in sheet music graphics, Hollywood movies, television, and of course on vinyl record album covers of the era. 'Hula girls' appear in hundreds of images; and most Hawaiian vinyl records feature at least one song about a caricatured and sexualized hula dance. In one frequently recorded song, listeners are teasingly instructed to keep their eyes on the dancers' hands during a hula performance, and not be distracted by musical rhythm-induced

Figure 9.3 *Authentic Music from the Kodak Hula Show*, Waikiki Records

movement of 'the lovely hula hips'. Related marketing communications, such as the photographed covers of vinyl LPs, served to re-inscribe the visual image of Hawaii, and included an audio-branded soundtrack on the record within. Figure 9.3 shows a 1960s era LP, *Authentic Music from the Kodak Hula Show* from Waikiki records, that supports a noteworthy integrated marketing effort, promoting photographic film, tourism, and vinyl LPs in one package (Borgerson and Schroeder, 2017).

Popular singers also released Hawaiian albums infused with steel guitar, ukulele, and a smattering of Hawaiian language lyrics. For example, Bing Crosby's *Blue Hawaii* from Decca Records features Bing singing the standard Tin Pan Alley-penned Hawaiian tunes such as 'Blue Hawaii', 'Sweet Leilani', and 'Tradewinds', backed by Hawaiian choruses. The album cover shows a tourist brochure shot of an endless sand beach, an outrigger canoe, a lone palm tree and Diamond Head – the distinctive landmark of Waikiki beach. We are reminded by a small note printed along the bottom of the front cover that Hawaii is 2,394 miles from the USA via Pan American World Airways. One of the first big stars to release a Hawaiian album, Bing started a massive trend.

The familiar face of Elvis Presley adorns one of the best-known Hawaii albums, the soundtrack of Hal Wallis's film *Blue Hawaii* from RCA Victor. This hit record introduced the classic ballad 'I Can't Help Falling in Love' as well as Elvis's hiccupping versions of the Hawaiian standards 'Blue Hawaii', 'Aloha Oe' and 'Hawaiian Wedding Song'. The classic 'Rock-A-Hula Baby', a game attempt to blend the Hawaiian sensibility with rock 'n' roll, was another hit from the album. Martin Denny, of course, is well known for his musical 'exotica'. He released several specifically Hawaiian-themed albums for Liberty Records in the 1960s, including *Hawaii Tattoo*, *20 Golden Hawaiian Hits*, and *Hawaii Goes a Go-Go*. Arthur Lyman worked with Denny and is often credited with introducing exotic birdcalls into standard popular songs, along with a wavering vibraphone tropical lounge sound. Les Paul and Mary Ford's *Lovers' Luau* from Columbia Records shows the pioneering musical couple seated at a lush luau table looking a bit out of place among the bananas, flowers, and hula girls. The LP includes some Les Paul originals, with the rich twangy sway of steel guitar sounds.

Webley Edwards created *Hawaii Calls*, the most successful radio show of its kind (Smulyan, 2007). In a profound audio-branding moment, Edwards opened each *Hawaii Calls* show intoning, 'the sounds of the waves on the beach at Waikiki', as the surf slapped against the sand in the background. First over the radio, then later through 28 popular record albums featuring well-known Hawaiian singers such as Alfred Apaka and Haunani Kahalewai, Edwards was influential in engaging a worldwide audience with a carefully constructed image of the Hawaii brand.

Hawaii Calls, partially funded by the United States' legislature, broadcast live every week for almost 40 years from the 1930s to the 1970s, and was perhaps the most influential force in making mainlanders Hawaii-conscious (with the exception of Pearl Harbor). As notes on one *Hawaii Calls* vinyl record cover state:

> beneath the Banyan tree … at the Moana Hotel on Waikiki Beach, Hawaii calls the world by radio every Saturday morning. In that lovely tropical setting, more than a thousand happy, gaily clad islanders and tourists gather as Webley Edwards conducts *Hawaii Calls* – a program that is carried on the mainland's

Mutual Broadcasting System, the Canadian Dominion Network, the Australia Network, the Armed Forces Radio Service, by short-wave to Africa, Asia, and Oceania, and over the Voice of Freedom to Europe.

Source: *Hawaii Calls*, Capitol Records

Edwards insisted that his show was the real Hawaii featuring real Hawaiian music; however, one need not be Hawaiian to produce it. In discussing their audience, one commentator suggested, 'To them, and millions like them around the globe, Web Edwards and the stars of *Hawaii Calls are* Hawaii' (from the Capitol Records LP *Hawaii Calls show, Webley Edwards presents*). In Edward's branding discourse, a song written yesterday in Peoria was as Hawaiian as something written a hundred years ago by a native if it had that 'Aloha spirit'. Of course, also at work were copyright laws and royalty payments. Most of the songs on the *Hawaii Calls* shows were written – or at least copyrighted – by whites. From 'primitive' rhythms, Hawaiian music was transformed and modernized, for Western consumers. By recording the tropical – and primitive – sounds of Hawaii on the latest in advanced recording equipment, the recording industry offered up Hawaiian music as part of the latest achievement of modern technology, and the state of Hawaii as the latest achievement of modern democracy. In other words, *Hawaii Calls*, its music, voices, and tropical sounds stood in for Hawaii, helping create a distinctive and powerful audio brand.

Conclusion

Hawaii's audio-brand image vibrates through strings of steel guitar on the ubiquitous 'Aloha Oe', or ukulele and coconut shell bongos on famous favourites 'Little Brown Gal' and 'Lovely Hula Hands' that appear on thousands of 'Hawaiian' vinyl LP albums. This popular Hawaiian music genre captures a primitive past – with seashell drone, wood block clicks, and sharkskin drum thuds – a vision of paradise and an escape from the modern world. Tropical location-associated sounds infused Hawaiian music and provided a soothing soundtrack for backyard luau parties, Hawaiian dinners at home, and other pupu platter-centred, tiki-themed environments popular during that era – and enjoying a resurgence. Hawaiian music served as a sonic resource that lends the Hawaii brand an 'authentic' history that draws on cultural, mythical, and stereotypical resources – about Hawaiian natives, paradise, and fallen monarchies. Hawaii's audio branding lures us to what we have called the ultimate 'retro-escape' (Borgerson and Schroeder, 2003).

Hawaiian cultural codes, historical and fantastical, have provided resources for building brand meaning, including visual and aural images to suit huge varieties of contexts and purposes, such as international trade, profitable tourist escapes, and imaginative cocktail bars (Cate and Cate, 2016; McKnight-Trontz, 1999). Hawaiian music provides a spectacular case for analysis of the way music, brand culture, and retro-appeal cooperate in audio branding. Of course, what became known as Hawaiian music was often familiar easy listening created mostly by white mainland songwriters with little or no connection to the islands. Nevertheless, the marriage of modern technology and 'authentic' sounds was a potent force in the audio branding of Hawaiian paradise. By associating certain audio elements with Hawaii and capturing these on the latest advanced hi-fi equipment, the radio and recording industries offered up a Hawaiian sonic experience as part of the latest technological achievement, promoting paradise as a sound as well as a place to visit. Hawaii provides an early, memorable example of a powerful audio brand.

Guest biographies

Janet Borgerson is a Fellow at the Institute for Brands & Brand Relationships, and a Visiting Research Fellow at Cass Business School, City University London. She works at the intersections of philosophy, branding, and culture. She earned a BA (Philosophy) from University of Michigan, Ann Arbor, and MA and PhD (Philosophy) from University of Wisconsin, Madison. Her research has appeared in a broad range of journals, including *Consumption Markets & Culture*, *European Journal of Marketing*, *Journal of Brand Management*, *Philosophy Today*, and *Sociological Review*, and she is co-author of *From Chinese Brand Culture to Global Brands* and *Designed for Hi-Fi Living*.

Jonathan Schroeder is the William A Kern Professor in the School of Communication at Rochester Institute of Technology in New York. His PhD is from the University of California, Berkeley. He has published widely on branding, communication, consumer research, and identity. He is the author of *Visual Consumption*, co-author of *From Chinese Brand Culture to Global Brands* and *Designed for Hi-Fi Living*, editor of *Conversations on Consumption*, and *Brands: Interdisciplinary Perspectives*, and co-editor of *Brand Culture* and the *Routledge Companion to Visual Organization*.

CASE AXA

AXA off to a strong start: more to come

AXA tops the global rankings in the insurance sector. A business built through acquisition of companies in different countries that, due to regulation and market differences, doesn't deliver the same products and services everywhere. With over 150,000 employees, the company sought to assert its power to lead the industry and set the standards for the category. They developed a unique global advertising model in which they use branding musical advertising assets across markets.

Facing increased competition, the brand expected its audio communication strategy to meet four major challenges:

- stand out from the competition through a distinct and unmistakable identity;
- convey the new communication goals;
- clarify and amplify the change in position;
- create a more specific but universally consistent brand experience.

The overall audio audit revealed ample room to optimize the audio-branding strategy. For instance, an analysis of the company's global music use revealed that, in lacking a set of brand audio guidelines, each country would select songs varying in musical styles and genres. Sixième Son also found that some songs were paid for and then only used one time, a costly behaviour for the brand.

At the same time, the audit revealed a pattern of sameness in the category. Three major music styles dominated financial services communications:

- grandiose classical instrumentation: heavy strings and brass; sometimes use of popular classical tracks (eg Bach, Beethoven);
- musical theatre/cabaret music: naïve, bouncy piano melodies, choruses;
- 90s' popular rock song scoring, which had the ability to create connection but no strong personality to transmit to the brand.

To help the brand stand out, the design of the audio DNA and audio logo was focused on positioning AXA in a musical territory that would break these trends.

In 2008, the company launched its new brand positioning around the world. The brand's aspirations were expressed in the tagline, Redefining Standards.

The initial solution: AXA audio DNA, audio logo, and creative toolkit
AXA established its leading position and natural authority with a distinctive audio DNA and very unusual audio logo: heavy, strongly assertive, with an unsingable melody, and endowed with an uncompromising sound texture and powerful, definitive ending. This audio identity with its distinctive five-note audio logo left a strong earprint.

When the audio DNA and audio logo were approved, AXA and Sixième Son focused on creating tools to facilitate the consistent and coherent global use of audio over such touchpoints as radio, events, customer service call centres, and meetings.

Being the most familiar item to AXA ad agencies, the end frame was the tool that was adopted most quickly, but that wasn't enough to bring a total brand experience to TV spots. Agencies could still buy single tracks for a one-time use. This practice didn't maximize the communication of the brand values and nor did it optimize budgets.

The expanded solution: adding the AXA global advertising audio library
The company decided to go beyond the usual adaptations to offer a unique turnkey tool to support the dissemination of the audio brand: a unique musical library designed to support the dramatic arc of various storylines and convey a wide variety of moods.

A truly breakthrough approach to their audio identity, the AXA advertising musical library was a resourceful invention that served the communication needs of all their diverse businesses across the continents.

AXA invested in an off-the-shelf library of music based on the new audio identity to make it easy for any market that needed to create a commercial to get exactly what they needed. Sixième Son scored music segments based in the brand's audio DNA to convey and which were designed to support the emotional content of almost any story.

The idea was simple. As the films are divided into problem/solution scenarios, the music had to be too.

The complementary musical elements from two different sets of music gave the markets the power to instantly score hundreds of commercials, all of which had pre-approved music. Besides the speed and ease provided by this solution, an additional barrier to decision-making and production time was removed. The markets neither needed to calculate nor pay any licensing fees because those had been covered under a global licence by the parent company.

How the library works
The music in the first group of compositions sets up the problem or situation. In the second group, the music evokes the kind of emotions that might result from

the resolution of a problem: confidence, dignity, enthusiasm, hope, strength, serenity.

The user selects one from the first group and one from the second, an on-brand audio transition is provided to connect one half to the other – and all the spots end with the punctuation of the strong audio logo.

This gave the agency and teams some freedom to choose which combination of Groups 1 and 2 to use. Table 9.1 provides some examples:

Table 9.1   The music library: composition options

Group 1: Problem Music		Group 2: Solution Music	
Serious	expresses quiet concern	Enthusiasm	reminds you of happiness and harmony
Music Box	reminds you of the sounds of your childhood and conveys a nostalgic mood	Confident	conveys a serious and trusting atmosphere
Soft	carries a rhythm based on the ticking of stopwatch	Hopeful	encourages you to believe in the future, like a promise
Enigmatic	builds suspense and creates an uncertain atmosphere	Strength	reminds you of bravery and power
Unsettled	creates a cautious and uncertain mood	Dignity	reminds you of pride and humanity
Suspense	creates a feeling of the unknown	Serene	provides a peaceful but dynamic moment
Intrigue	suggests a scheming atmosphere		

SOURCE Sixième Son (with permission of AXA)

TV commercials tell wide-ranging stories as diverse as a man running through a gauntlet of closed doors, another learning to ride an elephant and a family having trouble scanning groceries. The music successfully enhances each of the stories.

An Audio Style Guide details the various selections available and provides advice and boundaries to the use of the library and other audio-brand communication tools. The whole system not only offers choices but assures high quality and coherence.

After seven years of the audio brand's existence, its effects have been extensive:

- Over 100 campaigns in places as diverse as France, Germany, Hong Kong, Nigeria, Saudi Arabia, Thailand, and the USA have successfully used the library or have commissioned related music to create the soundtracks for spots.
- More than 150 TV campaigns endorsed by the audio logo in 59 countries around the world.
- Eight million views of content containing the AXA audio identity on YouTube by 1 April 2016.
- Savings seen by AXA in terms of the purchase of musical rights alone amount to over $500,000 per year.
- Early research in 2008 showed increased perception of leadership based on the comparison of the new end frame (the logo animation plus the audio logo) and the previous one: the 'leadership' rating increased by 21 per cent.

The pragmatic but sweeping implementation of the AXA audio identity system brought savings, consistency and power to the brand. Brand power that promises to build one touchpoint at a time, over many years.

Said Marc Raisiere, former VP of Marketing Communications, 'We act as a leader, we look like a leader, we talk like a leading company that's changing the rules for the benefit of its clients, partners, employees, and shareholders. Now, we sound like a leader and that sounds like no one else.'

CMO, Paul Bennett sees branding's role growing

AXA Chief Marketing Officer, Paul Bennett, has ambitious goals for the brand. In his estimation, the value of brand in the insurance sector has far to go. Today the AXA brand drives about 20 per cent of consumer purchase decisions, which Bennett says is in line with the category. This, he says, contrasts with the banking business in which the brand contributes 30 per cent to sales and the mighty luxury category, where the brand can contribute 70–80 per cent of sales.

Because, in insurance, the role of the company's agent is diminishing and the role of the insurance aggregator is growing, the role of branding has become more critical. In an aggregator situation, prospects might be shown a list of 20–30 companies to choose from, so it's vital that the insurer cultivate brand affinity and nurture a direct brand relationship.

Bennett intends to move AXA from a transactional- to a relationship-based brand, and foresees the day when the AXA brand will contribute as much as 35–40 per cent of sales.

One difficulty in building a brand today, according to Bennett, is in maintaining brand consistency across the increasingly fragmented touchpoints. That task has become more important today than it was 20 years ago.

The key challenge for AXA along with awareness will be brand differentiation. Not just differentiation in what is shown on TV but what the customers experience and feel. For instance, does the customer's call centre experience match up with the TV experience? The other critical touchpoints and interactions along the spectrum need to be managed strategically.

Bennett believes the role of music as a brand tool has become more important because marketers are trying new ways to cut through and to make something memorable. He says that as the company seeks an emotional connection with its customers, the ad agency can no longer choose music by asking, 'Do I like it?' Today music should be considered at the brand level because, when used consistently, it is a very powerful tool for creating that memorability and staying at the forefront of the customer's mind. But it is also about positioning your brand, a task that can be done with words but makes a stronger emotional impact with music.

He feels that AXA has done reasonably well in using music to drive a stronger consistent global brand but has yet to unleash the potential of what its audio can do.

References

Airline Guys (2012) 6 reasons why United should reintroduce the 'Tulip', https://airlineguys.com/2014/08/03/6-reasons-why-united-should-re-introduce-the-tulip/ [accessed 11 December 2016]

Bañagale, RR (2014a) *Arranging Gershwin*. Oxford University Press, New York

Bañagale, RR (2014b) United Airlines and *Rhapsody in Blue*, OUP blog, http://blog.oup.com/2014/08/united-airlines-gershwin [accessed 11 December 2016]

Borgerson, JL and Schroeder, JE (2003) The Lure of Paradise: Marketing the retro-escape of Hawaii, in *Time, Space and Place: The rise of retroscapes,* ed S Brown and JF Sherry, pp 219–37, ME Sharpe, Armonk, NY

Borgerson, J and Schroeder, JE (2017) *Designed for Hi-Fi Living: The vinyl LP in mid-century America,* MIT Press, Cambridge, MA

Brown, S and Sherry, JF Jr. (2003) *Time, Space and the Market: Retroscapes rising,* ME Sharpe, Armonk, NY

Canniford, R and Karababa, E (2013) Partly Primitive: Discursive constructions of the domestic surfer, *Consumption Markets and Culture* 16, pp 119–44

Cate, M and Cate, R (2016) *Smuggler's Cove: Exotic cocktails, rum, and the cult of tiki,* Ten Speed Press, Berkeley

Connell, J and Gibson, C (2008) 'No Passport Necessary': Music, record covers and vicarious tourism in post-war Hawai'i, *Journal of Pacific History,* 43, pp 51–75

Costa, JA (1998) Paradisal Discourse: A critical analysis of marketing and consuming Hawaii, *Consumption Markets and Culture* 1, pp 303–46

Fahey, C (2016) Personal conversation with Herman Tiemans

Gustafsson, C (2015) Sonic Branding: A consumer-oriented literature review, *Journal of Brand Management*, pp 20–37

Hanlon, P (2006) *Primal Branding: Create zealots for your brand, your company, and your future*, Free Press, New York

McKnight-Trontz, J (1999) *Exotiquarium: Album art from the space age*, St Martins, NY

Schroeder, JE and Salzer-Mörling, M (2006) *Brand Culture*. Routledge, New York

Schroeder, JE, Borgerson, JL and Wu, Z (2015) A brand culture approach to Chinese cultural heritage brands, *Journal of Brand Management*, 22 (3), pp 261–79

Smulyan, S (2007) Live from Waikiki: Colonialism, race, and radio in Hawaii, 1934–1963, *Historical Journal of Film, Radio and Television*, 27, pp 63–75

Wu, Z, Borgerson, J and Schroeder, J (2013) *From Chinese Brand Culture to Global Brands: Insights from aesthetic, fashion and history*, Palgrave Macmillan, Basingstoke, UK

Music and sound design in environments 10

Ever noticed that many retailers, restaurants, shopping centres, other brands with physical locations as a component of their offering or experience – even sports teams – have a disconnected approach to the music with which they present their brands? They take one approach to it in their advertising and a completely different approach in their live environments such as the store. Go from one retail establishment to the next and the story is virtually the same: at branch, in salons, in restaurants, and at dealerships.

As we saw in Chapter 5, when music is perceived as a good fit for the brand, the user perceives the brand as more authentic. One way to make sure it is seen as a fit is to ensure that the music in the environment is coherent with the tailor-made branded music in your communications efforts. After all, a brand constitutes a promise to behave a certain way. When the audience arrives in your environment, they should experience that place as consistent with your total brand identity and your values as possible.

Unfortunately, brands that are clearly striving to transmit the idea of authenticity in their TV commercials or branded content fill their stores with the slightly metallic sound of voices altered by Auto Tune. We've seen – or, rather heard – 'natural ingredients' restaurant chains who feature acoustic instrumentation in their advertising confuse customers by using synthesized instruments and mechanical drum machines in the restaurants themselves. Retailers promising elegance, craftsmanship, and style blare voice-forward teenage pop stars more appropriate to those that offer tween accessories. (We suspect that the music, in the latter case of the high-end, elegant store, supports their sales of impulse-purchase baubles, rather than their carefully crafted leather goods.)

Alternatively, playlists may be too generic and predictable with no attempt to convey any distinctive message about the brand (and subsequently come across as ubiquitous). This indifferent approach happens in environments beyond retailers, too. You will find it in airports, for instance. With such a convenient opportunity to create a sense of feeling welcoming to a specific place, some opt for a standard playlist that often says they don't care.

One day, while travelling south, Michaël Boumendil noticed that the same music he had heard in the corridor of Atlanta's Hartsfield-Jackson Airport was what he was hearing in Miami International. Yet Atlanta and Miami are both such great brands! These cities come with strong musical heritages of their own, and both compete hard for convention and tourist business, but they didn't infuse any local flavour into the atmosphere of their corridors or lounges that were busy with travellers arriving, departing, and making connecting flights.

Then there's the problem of announcements.

Most airports solve the problem of getting people to hear announcements by pushing up the volume, not by providing a pleasant attention-getting signal. Most in-store messages don't take into account the sounds of trolleys, conversation, and HVAC. For instance, at one French supermarket, a survey revealed that only 5 per cent of their customers were hearing the messages. In other words, their announcements of specials and events were blending in and when they were noticed, according to our client's research, were often perceived as radio, not as a communication to customers from the store they happen to be shopping in – clearly a wasted opportunity but not a terribly hard one to fix.

A trendy taco restaurant in Chicago, for another example, is carefully decorated with bright Mexican tiles and tequilas, serves its guacamole in earthenware cazuelas to their English and Spanish speaking patrons, and plays a Pandora Radio selection based on the music of indie rock band, Cold War Kids (except when they play a Jay-Z/Kanye West combination to end the day). When employees asked the manager why he doesn't sprinkle in some Latin American rock bands, like Maná, he won't hear of it. They suspect it's just a result of the manager's personal taste.

Internet streaming has brought the opportunity for more variety into the world of in-store music. No longer does music have to be shipped to stores on CDs or downloaded onto local computer hard drives. This variety is a boon to employees and to customers, both. But it still needs to be managed in order to support the brand.

The trapped audience for environmental music: the staff

The most affected audience for in-store music is your employee team. If the music is too repetitive, too loud, or too grating, they suffer. And, oh boy, don't get them started about holiday music. Frequently, it is a very short playlist of often smarmy songs which repeats incessantly from October till 24 December. 'Honestly that's the worst', said an employee from a chain drugstore, according to one client's research. Her comments were echoed by many. Let's agree that these are cruel and unusual working conditions.

One thing to also note is that the customer-facing staff have strong opinions about whether the music in the store suits the shoppers' tastes, because they get to hear the compliments and complaints first-hand.

Listen to your employees

Here is an excerpt from an interview with a sales associate at a high-end Toronto department store, 18 July 2016. As you can see, employees understand the audio needs of their customers:

'Seven years ago when I started, the music was a mix. It wasn't bad, it was a little bit of everything: classic rock, R&B, dance mix music, nothing too annoying to me. It was a wide variety and it wasn't too loud either. But as the years have progressed, it's getting worse because they're playing Top 40.

'It's very inappropriate for our clientele because it's a luxury retailer. Especially because it's on all four floors. It might be OK for the contemporary and, maybe, even main floor but it's absolutely not appropriate for the floor of people buying designer pieces well into the four digits.

'I get complaints every single day. Every day. Especially from the ones who are spending the money. They ask, "Why is this type of music being played?" "Who are they targeting?" A typical customer complaint is, "What is this garbage they're playing?" "Oh, my gosh, it's too loud." It's too loud for the store. We are trying to have a conversation. It's like I am in a nightclub.

'I feel whoever's choosing the music isn't thinking about who the clients are. They may be choosing the music they like or what they think is trendy right now. The clients are an afterthought.

'It's on a loop. I hear the same song over and over. I even know some songs that I wish I didn't because they play it so often.

'They play Christmas music in late October, even before Halloween. And the clients say, "Isn't it a little early?" Some of the carols may be religious. And a lot of our clients are Jewish, they don't like it. It's too early and, then, the people who enjoy the carols are not in the store yet.

> 'They think the retailer is trying to force it on them. Like, "You've got to buy Christmas products now!" They're not thinking of it for enjoyment: it's just a marketing strategy to get people to buy presents early.
>
> 'You don't need all that crazy beat. Some more pleasant music could be played, something that's not dominating the shopping experience. It should be putting you in a relaxing mood, not an annoyed, frustrated mood. Maybe if you're in a Zara and Forever 21, it's OK.
>
> 'I'm open, I like all genres of music, I'm open-minded but there's a time and a place… and a certain volume as well.
>
> 'There are some very, very high-value clients who do actually have the power to get them to turn down the music a little bit. But it still it goes back up again.'

What to do? Sorry to sound like a broken record: it's all about values

So how do you manage the brand experience, the need to address specials, warnings, and announcements, the employee state-of-mind, the tastes and aspirations of the shopper?

One approach is to choose music that fits your brand values, essence, and personality.

If audio branding can help you find your way to the brand identity and guide your various tactics, it can also guide you to your wider brand territory of music at retail and in other environments where your brand lives. You can have distinctive, unexpected, and brand-supportive music in-store if you lay your groundwork first.

The approach we use is to create a sample playlist for each of the key values the brand intends to express and then, based on the importance of each value, choose the right proportion of each type of content.

One brand's values and music filters: authenticity, intimacy, audacity, and virtuosity

What follows are short summaries that illustrate how four values-based sample playlists would guide the music selection for a prestigious men's leather goods and clothing retailer:

- **Authenticity:** Here, noble, acoustic instruments such as cello, double bass, upright piano, or woodwinds were explored. These classical instruments, however, have been played in a modern and contemporary way, favouring a light and positive approach rather than one that's impressive and imposing. They help create a warm atmosphere that's both elegant and welcoming.

- **Intimacy:** The goal here would be to recreate the magic moments of a private concert. Some live songs were included, but not overly dramatic ones. As in a private club, the sound would be sophisticated but not 'trendy', creating a convivial and friendly atmosphere.

- **Audacity:** The brand includes culture as well as creativity, and the intellectual playfulness that entails. So the music offers dashes of Italian optimism and French charm. The selection of music in this group would add a feeling of energy, creativity, and playfulness, and contain references to art, in order to bring out the child and the artist in everyone in the store.

- **Virtuosity:** Because of the specialized craftsmanship found in the products, some short warm-up exercises used by classically trained musicians provide a recurrent punctuation throughout the playlists. The sound of instrumentalists practising their complex exercises on a piano or a cello invites the customer to a privileged place, the heart of a craftsman's atelier.

Let's contrast that to the jewellery store we also saw in Chapter 4, but this time we will take it to a later stage of the process. The brand stands for elegance, luxury, and beauty. Imagine the strategy and music selection have been approved and the project has moved to launch. The handiest way to keep the global teams aligned with the strategy is the Audio Style Guide. This guide has two functions: to help staff understand the reasoning behind the selection; and to set parameters. But it also allows for some flexibility at the store-level: '…an eclectic selection, both classic and contemporary, whereby arts, sensuality and creativity have been explored. Hints of cinema and opera, exceptional voices as well as timeless songs of French musical heritage and avant-garde pieces of music. A daring mix, for a unique and innovative musical ambience.'

This music had been pre-programmed so a shuffle option enabling any playlist to be played randomly at any time of the day. However, employees could modify the pre-set selection and programme the broadcasting. They had the option to control the musical ambience in their boutique or let it run by its own. Some 50 hours of music were provided with quarterly updates of 14 hours of additional music:

- Playlist 1 offers soft and soothing music for a voluptuous atmosphere.
- Playlist 2 provides a selection of rhythmic music.
- Playlist 3 combines calm music balanced with more rhythmic tracks.

And a children's boutique has a different set of values that the music has to evoke: purity, kindness, respect, and innocence. By now you know that each one will inspire its own musical exploration and mood board.

Bringing the shopper back to the spirit of the brand

Beyond establishing the brand territory of the selected music, we also strongly believe in using sound to bring shoppers back to the brand after every few songs. This can be done with a light touch, so it adds pleasure to the customer experience rather than beating them over the head with repetitive communications. The brand, in this example, is reinforced by what we call 'winks' or 'commas'. They can't be bossy and they shouldn't intimate that 'We're the management here and don't you forget it!' (This tendency is particularly prevalent among transportation systems.) The winks suggest a friendly relationship with the customer. After all, a little bit of humour, nostalgia, or reassurance doesn't hurt:

- For a luxury women's brand, these special brand sounds consisted of a collection of pieces that began with a 6- to 7-second glittering fountain of diamonds and then led into a snippet of a song by an iconic actress or singer from the 40s and 50s. This approach underscored the twinkling, glamorous heritage of the brand.
- For Fiat Motor Village, each auto line was given its own audio footprint. These short pieces all live within the same musical universe but each reflects the special personality of that distinct brand: Alfa Romeo, Abarth, Lancia, Maserati and Jeep. There's also a short, evocative musical piece that weaves in the sound of an early motorcar and underscores the long heritage of the umbrella brand, Fiat.
- For French clothing manufacturer Petit Bateau, the brand pulls you back with snatches of children's voices counting, questioning, conversing, and, sometimes, just exuberantly shouting, 'Petit Bateau'.

- For a previously mentioned elegant men's shoes and clothing brand, the musical winks underscored their craftsmanship. Sprinkled among the musical selections, you could hear the sounds of instrumentalists practising their scales or working on their fingering in short exercises that classically trained musicians use. The idea: to highlight the practice that goes into mastering a craft and to create the sense of intimacy that might occur in a master's studio.

Closely related to branded 'winks' are signals that precede any announcement. But, in contrast, their purpose is to draw your attention to a piece of information, rather than to charm you into a smile or a feeling of belonging. In the SNCF case that we described in Chapter 1, we discussed the importance of being sensitive to your audience's needs and potential anxieties in creating the signal that precedes announcements. It's not necessary to project the voice of authority; you might do better to create affinity. In cases where there are many announcements to be made, you may even want an interrelated system of signals. For example, one for basic, repeating announcements, one for real news, and one for emergencies.

There's no need to use your audio-branding firm to manage in-store execution

Some clients want hand-picked music. If you are one of those, depending on how many hours you're open and how long people stay, you will probably need about 60 hours of music. And you will need to update it regularly with between 10 and 20 hours of music. Your strategic audio-branding firm can do this work but there are plenty of other firms who can provide third-party music that is either rights-cleared or covered by contracts with the artists. And they have systems that let you include your branded moments and your announcements, as well.

After the foundation is laid out by your audio-branding strategy, you will have guidelines with which to manage a specialized resource or to provide parameters to your own local management teams. Or, you can let the audio-branding agency manage the resources or company teams for you.

A word to the wise: it needs to be said that music is protected by copyright law. Don't let your in-market management teams assume they can use their iPod playlists or even the radio (although, in the United States, some small establishments can use the latter). The company could end up getting fined. Since the rules are different in different countries, it's best to learn them for your locale. Your music supplier will be able to guide you or you may want to get help from a lawyer who has experience in this area and knows how to negotiate licences. Using professional music services is not only a matter of enhancing the customer experience, it's also important for your protection.

Zoning and dayparting: creating specific moods within the same environment

Customers may have very different music needs in different parts of your establishment. Take a hotel, for instance, where the same guest may respond to the same music differently depending on whether he or she is in the fitness centre, the business services centre, the elevator lobby, or in the bar. The practice of breaking the space down into key zones helps the music planner think through the specific spaces and preferred ambiences.

The guest also may prefer different moods at different times of day. For instance, enjoying a relaxing lunch and a beer. But in the evening, it's more likely to be party time at the bar, calling for not just a more lively, spirited style of music but a change in music volume as well. That is where dayparting comes in. A good plan will take into account the shift in atmosphere needed, especially in social areas (the business centre and the fitness centre may not need varied approaches, as the guest's goals there don't usually change between the daytime and evening).

All of us have been in establishments in which the music is mismanaged. No amount of interior design, technological marvels, or even customer service can help override it. This sensitivity is underscored by personal experience. In a business hotel one night, the staff saw fit to play 'The Ride of the Valkyries' for the edification of the bedraggled transatlantic travellers checking in after a very late night flight. That night, any small irritation resulted in angry outbursts or frustrated tears. Exhaustion may have played a role but, you and I both know, the tumultuous and piercing music was largely to blame.

This brings us to another best practice in the world of environmental music design: not only should you provide examples of the kind of music that is appropriate, you should also give examples of what's *not acceptable* – especially if your business is being run by franchisees, remote managers, or rotating leaders. In the case of the business hotel above, perhaps the team believed that they were supposed to play selections from the 'Western classical music tradition' but the guidelines had neglected to exclude certain types of sections that might be inappropriate, if not downright painful.

Along the same lines, an establishment may wish to support different products or services with different musical moods. Imagine a store that sells jewellery in one department as well as warm winter coats in another. Chances are the visual environment in each section has been designed differently to support the product mix. But what about the sound?

With the use of music, it's possible to create a stylish, sparkling atmosphere in one and a comforting, cozy atmosphere in the other while staying within the brand's guardrails. As music has a way of raising sales of the products that are perceived as being congruent with it, the better the fit, the stronger the effect. Imagine playing nostalgic 1950s music in the tween section. It wouldn't work. But it might in the section selling pleated khakis and golf clothing.

Need some examples on how to provide the instructions? To help, here are some excerpts from the music guidelines created for a hotel chain. They aimed to create an ambience in which people came to meet and to mix together in a place that provided both comfort and energy. So the guidelines recommended a balance among four categories: 1) *friendliness and warmth*, through positive, comfortable music; 2) *modernity* by using today's music; 3) *elegance* using refined musical genres; and 4) *regional variation* (within boundaries).

It also describes what music should make up the total experience and defines the type of music for specific areas of the hotel: lobby, bar, restaurant, fitness and spa lounge, and executive lounge. For instance, the recommended mood for the reception, waiting area, meeting areas, and elevator lobbies during the daytime was 'discreet, soothing, conducive to working and relaxation' with a music selection of 'light, ethereal, pop, folk, electro, easy listening, lightly orchestrated jazz and classical music' played at a soft volume. Conversely, the bar in the evening had the goal of creating a rousing, spirited atmosphere via modern, rhythmic dance-like music. Here the recommended genres were 'electronic, electro-jazz, lounge, and rhythmic pop' played at a high volume.

The 'Do Nots' of the guide also tell a lot about what to expect by warning against music that is:

- aggressive and intrusive;
- experimental and irritating;
- inelegant and vulgar;
- too heavily orchestrated;
- loud singing;

as well as to:

- avoid those musical genres that are specific niche styles (hip-hop, techno, folk, New Age, etc);
- avoid radio hits (except in the evenings in the bar and the lobby).

These recommendations were accompanied with music playlists demonstrating examples in each genre that indicated what was too baroque, too cliché, too ethnic or too showy.

Environmental sounds: great opportunities for wit and humour

Michaël Boumendil, whom you first met in Chapter 1, often counsels his team that 'the music should *play* with the architecture and design'. And, what better way to create a sense of relationship with customers than to surprise them with some little unexpected moments of humour or delight?

Thus, mermaids sing in the ladies' room of a mall at the confluence of two rivers; a plant wall is transformed into a tropical rainforest waking in the morning, settling down for the night, or visited by a freak thunderstorm; the clacking of local stork beaks provide the percussion for a town's shopping centre; and some waiting area chairs lead you through a relaxing meditation. You never know what will be around the next corner.

These artful touches show your humanity and your interest in delighting your customers. And by adding pleasure to people's journey, you create more affinity for your brand. After all, isn't that the goal of branding – creating affinity? So if you are branding a mall, retail environments, restaurants, entertainment venues, sports stadiums, hospitals, or other places where people congregate, think what you can do make the experience even a little better through the sounds of your brand. So why don't you get started today? After all, soon your brand will be singing the songs of success!

Some tips for music in environments

To help you get started, here are some of the key points to remember:

- have at least 60 hours of music so as not to drive staff mad;
- choose music with voices set back a bit;

- include *brand winks*;
- create a signal to catch people's attention for announcements;
- vary the dynamics;
- refresh at least 15 per cent of the music every quarter;
- have a POV on 'Do Nots' as well as 'Dos'.

GUEST PERSPECTIVE Mickey Brazeal

Audio branding in physical spaces

As there is with the use of sound and music, there's lots of research into the use of music in physical spaces. To help us explore that rich area, we asked Mickey Brazeal, whom we met in Chapter 5, to provide us with his thoughts and research. Enjoy!

An important consideration in audio branding is the *environment* in which it takes place. Audio branding takes place in the corporation, at retail, and in other environments. Different environments offer different opportunities for the brand to interact with the customer. And different environments create different limitations on how musical ideas can be exposed, how they will be attended to and how they will affect the actions of the hearer.

To employ audio branding effectively, in the retail space, we need to understand three things. First, we need to understand some strengths and weaknesses of music as a vehicle for persuasive communication. Second, we need to understand the needs, opportunities and limitations of the retail space, in order to find the best theoretical opportunities. Third, we need to understand previous experience in solving these problems: experience derived from research and from the activities of early users.

1. Music as persuasion
Music is the expression of an idea, an expression as direct and sometimes as influential as a verbal expression, or the expression of a visual idea.

This form of expression has different strengths and weaknesses than other forms, and must be designed and focused to accomplish what it does best. Here are some examples.

A musical idea is not as cognitively explicit as a verbal idea. It cannot be reasoned with, or be part of an argument which might persuade the hearer to take a particular action. The other side of this is that a musical idea cannot be argued with. One does not hear a melody and think, 'Oh that's not true. In fact, the opposite is true.'

Yet a musical idea may persuade just as certainly as a verbal idea may persuade. It can express a spirit that its hearer wishes to join with. If a hospital wants to make itself feel like a warmer and more soothing and reassuring environment in which to endure a high-anxiety experience, verbal messages won't get it done.

But music surely can. As you're already heard, music can express values that its hearer wants to subscribe to and support. Most of all, it can provoke an emotional response that enlists the heart of the hearer. It has at least as much power as the most eloquent words to move us to laughter or to tears. And this strong emotional power may induce action on its own, or it may make us more responsive to persuasion by visual or verbal means.

While a musical idea may be less explicit than a verbal idea, it has a much greater power to differentiate. In the crowded categories of commercial persuasion, many of the most relevant messages are already associated with another brand. But we never run out of new music. Variations on an already known theme are recognizable, and the recognition is enjoyable.

Communicators work hard to come up with words that will be memorable, and they don't always succeed. But pieces of music will stick in your mind, and pop up again and again.

In the meantime, visual ideas can be quicker, near-instantaneous, but musical ones have a wonderful ability to build intensity through duration. And a musical message carries the presumption of enjoyment. It doesn't feel like an imposition, or something you try to get rid of. When a moment of melody has been associated with a pleasant experience, it brings to mind that experience each time it occurs.

Music can evoke your membership or relationship with a group. It can evoke ethnicity, age cohort, social class, region, or nation, all without being offensive. What's more, it can be cosmopolitan and universal, as the communicator decides.

Music works with both active and passive listening, and may clearly communicate an emotion in either mode. It doesn't require you to divert attention from what you are doing.

Music's message is not subject to legal restriction. You can express whatever values you wish, without making any regulated claim.

Music can magnify or accelerate other forms of persuasion. It can intensify a verbal message or a visual message or both together. It can draw new attention to a verbal message that has been around for a long time.

Outside of mass media, it is sometimes difficult for music to be confined to a particular physical space. Music played in a particular supermarket aisle, for example, will leak over into adjoining aisles.

The pioneers of audio branding have found that they can create a repeatable musical mini-event that expresses the values that a brand uses to build a relationship with its customer. If a brand is 'a promise about the customer experience', music may be able to communicate that experience more emotionally, more authentically, more believably than a verbal assertion can. As brands move more and more beyond a proposition to an experience, music becomes more and more important in communicating what the brand is.

2. Persuasion issues in the retail space

The retail environment has needs, limits and opportunities that are different from the mass media space and the corporate space. The following are some of them.

First and most important, retail spaces allow for instant action in response to persuasion. Even a relatively small and temporary persuasive event can produce a transaction. The distance between choosing to act and not choosing to act is nowhere else as small as it is at the retail point-of-sale. And yet a small change in the conversion rate – the percentage of visitors who make a transaction – is an earth-shaking event for the retailer. What is more, in many categories, a first transaction has a large effect on attitudes toward the brand. Most musical experiences in *mass media*, even online, do not provide such an instant opportunity to act.

The retailer's goals include both differentiation of the retailer, and differentiation of brands within the retailer. Either or both can provoke action. Either or both can grow the business. Each is available to the persuasive power of music. It can be directed at the identity of the store. It can be directed at the identity of a department within the store. Right now, some supermarkets try to differentiate their high-margin imported foods section. And music is a logical tool for that.

Or, in a department store, for example, it can be focused on a section that showcases a single designer brand. This will not work where the brand has only a tiny space – a facing on a shelf – but it is common for designer brands to have a small section of their own, and a musical brand can work in that space.

Differentiation between retailers is largely emotional. Competitors deliver similar services, but customers develop strong preferences for one or the other. Where differences are primarily emotional, emotional persuasion can have a powerful and immediate effect on behaviour.

A retailer's brand identity has a powerful effect on its margin. Some stores can charge a lot more for arguably similar products. Where musical persuasion can change or intensify a retailer's brand identity, it can create or sustain a margin advantage.

In many categories, retailers struggle with scepticism about explicit verbal claims. 'Best value', 'longest lasting', 'finest craftsmanship' are all empty words. A need is created for a kind of message that does not provoke disbeliefs. The kind of value statements made in a brand's music do not trigger scepticism or disbelief. But values are recognizable in an audio brand, in the moment of music that a customer is exposed to in-store.

A critical problem in retail operations is creating a consistent experience. Retailers have to 'live the brand'. But the theatre of retail is performed by fallible human beings, in real time, with all kinds of personal or mechanical or supply-chain issues that threaten the consistency of the experience. Audio branding provides a part of the experience – an emotional part of the experience – where consistency is easy to produce.

It is not a contradiction to say that, in addition to providing a consistent experience, the retailer is constantly asked to create the sense of a special event, a momentary difference in the experience that is a special opportunity for the buyer. You can always put up another 'Sale' sign. But on an emotional level, you can also help to create the sense of an event with a change in the music environment. It can be within the bounds of a musical brand, but new and different and more intense. It can magnify other verbal and visual communications of the special event. It can fit in with the visual imagery of the event. And it leaves room for other special events down the road, each one different from its predecessors, unless the marketer wants them to be the same.

Sometimes a brand at retail has to encompass a whole bundle of unlike things. This is an obstacle for visual communication, because a picture needs to be a picture of one single thing. It can be difficult to make a picture of the brand essence, of the values held in common by the various products in a brand. That kind of visual is not often seen at retail. But musical persuasion is well-adapted to this task. It can sing the brand no matter how many or how diverse the products are.

A problem at retail is the amount and density of verbal and visual messages. A supermarket aisle is intense visual popcorn: messages on almost every square inch of shelf space, often the same size and shape as dozens of others in the category. If you want to add a message to that maelstrom, it probably cannot be another verbal or visual message – there is no power to grab attention from what's already there. But you can add a musical overlay – like the exotic background a supermarket might provide for its imports section – for the audio space is wide open and uncrowded.

The United States is grossly over-stored. In big cities and suburbs, the competitive environment is brutal. If you could magically make every fifth store disappear, in almost every category, the shopper would hardly even be inconvenienced. There would still be someplace close, someplace that speaks to your segment, someplace that carries pretty much exactly what you want. And so, for the retailer, now more than ever, differentiation is a survival issue. A clear, distinct and desirable brand identity is almost as critical as a competitive price-point. Audio branding is the differentiation tool that has yet to be employed in most competitive categories. It can communicate a difference in style and values that magnifies and intensifies everything you do with merchandising and store décor and signage and brand choices. And like every other innovation at retail, in will deliver its richest value to the early adopter.

3. What can we learn from what has already been done?
Though audio branding in its current form is a recent development, retailers and people who study retailers have experimented and tested alternative forms of musical persuasion for years. Their experiences and findings close off some pathways and open lots of others.

Dr Philip Kotler of Northwestern did early work on what he called 'atmospherics' (Kotler, 1974). His conclusions help to frame a lot of the work that came later. Kotler said people respond to the whole experience of buying and consuming a product, including 'atmospherics', and that in making choices, atmospherics can be more powerful than the characteristics of the product itself. He found atmospherics to be most powerful at the place where the product is purchased or consumed, and more important in decision-making where product or price differences are small. Kotler found that atmospherics modify both the information the consumer collects and the consumer's affective state. He traced effects in attracting attention, in message creation and in emotional response creation. Han, Back and Barrett (2009) found 60 different academic studies in which changes in atmospherics changed consumer behaviour.

The psychologist Janishevsky studied low-involvement decision-making in buying and consuming products. He asserts that attitudes can be formed about a product without conscious thought (Janishevsky, 1988). He describes a phenomenon called pre-attentive processing, in which people monitor sensory inputs to detect where they should shift their attention – without being consciously aware of doing so. His research found support for the idea that preferences for one brand or perhaps one retailer over another can be generated independent of conscious thought. If this is true, then it is important for the audio brand-maker, because music could presumably be a powerful way to form pre-conscious emotional ideas of a brand. Numerous other studies have replicated the effect of strong musical influence on purchase behaviour in low-involvement situations.

Mehrabian and Russell proposed a structure for measuring the effects of atmospherics, a structure which many others have adopted, called PAD (Mehrabian and Russell, 1974). It proposes three responses to atmospherics:

- pleasure/displeasure (P);
- arousal/non-arousal (A); and
- dominance/submission (D), by which they mean a perception by the shopper that he or she is or is not in control of the experience.

The P dimension is associated with time spent. A higher P score means more time spent in the store. The A dimension is associated with interest in, or focus on the product, and willingness to explore. The D dimension seems to control satisfaction with the experience of a retail store visit. The idea is that the marketer should be able to measure the effectiveness of his in-store atmospherics, and modify them to produce desired changes.

Donovan, Rossiter, Marcoolyn *et al* (1994) used the PAD instrument to get shoppers' perceptions of a store's retail experience after five minutes in the store. The scores significantly predicted liking, enjoyment, friendliness, willingness to return, and expectation to spend more than expected.

The pleasure/displeasure part alone predicted most. The dominance factor was not predictive. The scores were shown statistically to be 'additional' to cognitive factors like price, quality, and perception of value. Changes in store liking (50 per cent) were greater than extra spending (12 per cent), but both were clearly connected to the PAD score. The same study (along with several others) associated a positive musical experience with spending more time in-store. In some retail categories, more time spent predicts more purchases (Donovan et al, 1994).

Several studies (North et al, 2004; MacInnis and Whan Park, 1991; Dubé and Morin, 2001) have demonstrated that music is a statistically significant factor in impulse buying and that changes in music will change impulse buying behaviour.

Two studies (Beverland et al, 2006; Mattila and Wirtz, 2001) suggest that mistakes in choosing atmospherics can produce negative changes in behaviour. What appears to be most important is 'fit' with expectations, brand perceptions, and the other atmospherics.

Two studies (Areni and Kim, 1993; Dubé and Morin, 2001) have suggested that music will usually be the primary influence among the atmospherics. Factors within music were genre, style, voice, tempo, and lyrics.

Building on these studies, Ballouli and Bennett (2014) found several consistent effects on consumers from music experienced at retail:

1. Shoppers who hear brand-specific music will perceive a higher degree of 'fit' than shoppers who hear generic music.
2. Different shoppers have measurably different levels of responsiveness to music in the retail experience.
3. Shoppers who perceive a 'fit' between the music and the brand/store had a more positive evaluation of the environment, and therefore of the shopping experience.
4. Perception of 'fit' increased satisfaction with the experience, which produced an increase of positive attitudes toward the brand.

The Areni and Kim (1993) study referenced above describes a specific experiment in which a wine shop played on alternate occasions classical music and music described as 'Top 40'. At a statistically significant level, they found that the classical music occasions were associated with larger purchases – not more bottles, but more expensive wines. A similar wine shop experiment associates a shift from French music to German music with a shift in purchasing toward more German and fewer French wine purchases (Ballouli and Bennett, 2014).

Finally, a controlled experiment, run by the Audio Consulting Group (Langeslag *et al*, 2011), exposed visitors to a supermarket chain to in-store music which included a well-established and well-known audio brand for a particular wine. During the period of the experiment, sales of the sparkling wine category grew (as year-end holidays approached) by about 18 per cent. But sales of the brand whose brand melody was included in the music increased by 48 per cent, more than twice as much.

In other words

As brand communicators, music messages work quite differently than do verbal or visual messages. They have different strengths and weaknesses, and so must be used differently. Strengths include a power to differentiate, a power to deliver clear and compelling emotional messages, and the ability to make a particular environment or experience more pleasant and more satisfying for the hearer.

Musical messages are particularly effective in the retail space, and can be matched closely with basic retail strategic objectives, including the differentiation of a store from competitors, changes in shopper behaviour while in the store, such as time spent, impulse buying, the level of involvement with specific products, pleasure and satisfaction with the shopping experience, and attitudes toward brands formed while in the store.

A large cohort of peer-reviewed and published academic and business studies demonstrates and quantifies the power of persuasion via music. It includes such effects as creating, clarifying, and intensifying emotional responses to products, creating pre-conscious attitudes toward low-involvement products, increasing impulse buying, intention to return to the store, and others. Several elaborately controlled experiments show quantifiable sales changes produced by changes in the musical environment at retail. Results are replicated over and over again by many different researchers.

Now let's look at other service environments with audio branding.

Designers of the customer service environment can learn a lot from the retailer's experience using music as a way to increase customer satisfaction. But there are also three enormous opportunities specific to the service sector.

1. Music as a vehicle to brand the service experience

Consider the hotel. Most of what it offers is pure commodity. But subtle differences in the guest experience are the key to differentiation, preference, and the loyalty that is key to profitability. Many hotels have learned to play background music in their public spaces. But now a few have begun to use music strategically, as a tool for branding. Mangini and Parker summarize research that measures their successes (Mangini and Parker, 2009).

Background music has been shown, in a long series of studies (Mangini and Parker, 2009) to increase verbal exchanges, and other affiliative behaviours between customers and service representatives. A positive interaction with service reps will generalize to the brand, and may be a key to preference.

Hotels, like many service environments, have occasions for customer anxiety, about scheduling, coordination, and other details of the service experience. There is evidence that background music can reduce anxiety during waiting situations, and increase the presence of a relaxed state (Mangini and Parker, 2009).

Several studies say people spend more time in environments where music is perceived as congruent with the desired experience. For hotels with lounges and restaurants and so forth, that time is money.

Brand personality can be a differentiator, a driver of trust, a source of preference and loyalty. It can be a sustainable competitive advantage. For hotels, the physical environment, more than anything else, expresses the brand personality, creates a mood, forms and alters perceptions and attitudes. The strategic use of music is a simple and powerful way to tailor the customer's perception of the environment. In an experiment, a restaurant's shift to upscale, classical music made customers perceive the restaurant as more intelligent and more decorative. Music that consciously reflects a chosen set of brand values should be able to help make the experience more consistent and more differentiated.

There is a critical role for music on the website of a service organization. The website has become the first resort, the front line of the service experience. Now, a website is not like other media. To an extreme degree, the customer using a website is engaged simultaneously in a media environment and an unmediated environment – on the site and in the physical world. Experiments with music on a website demonstrate more interest in the content, more emotional arousal, and less attention to the physical environment (Mangini and Parker, 2009). Another study says that music can improve access to Csikszentmihalyi's 'flow state', 'intrinsically enjoyable' and 'accompanied by a loss of self-consciousness' (Hoffman and Novak, 1996). An increase in the flow state has been shown to increase information retention, and is associated with more positive perceptions of the website experience.

2. Music for anxiety reduction

A common characteristic of the service environment is that the customer is not in control. Outcomes might be more desirable or less desirable, and the customer's ability to determine outcomes is limited. A large number of tests over a broad range of circumstances illuminate the role of music as a reducer of anxieties.

The extreme situation most frequently studied is anxiety in a hospital's pre-op waiting room, where patients spend time before a surgical procedure. There is an ongoing increase in 'day surgery', where a patient comes in for a procedure and leaves the same day. Day surgeries have significantly longer pre-op waiting times. They produce higher anxiety because the patient is in this new environment without much time for orientation (Cooke *et al*, 2005). Now, this kind of powerful anxiety is medically significant. Anxiety creates both mental and physical discomfort. It affects cognitive abilities. It slows recovery and increases post-operative pain. It can be addressed with drugs, but hospitals don't want to give anxiolytic medicines to people who will be released soon (Lee *et al*, 2012).

An experimental study by Lee *et al* (2012) attempted to measure changes in anxiety in response to music, as measured by heart-rate variation, and a traditional measure, a visual analogue scale (VAS) in which the patient describes his own anxiety level on a 10-point scale. The study used music, delivered via headphones in the pre-op waiting room. The experimental group got the music and a control group did not. The experimental group experienced significant reductions in heart-rate variability and in the VAS score. The control group did not. The experimental group also got significant reductions in low-frequency heart-rate variation, and in the ratio of low-to-high heart-rate variation. They got an increase in high-frequency heart-rate variation, which is seen as a positive. (It is associated with deep, even breathing.) The control group did not.

Fourteen similar studies were reviewed by Cooke, Chaboyer, and Hiratos. All but two found significant anxiety reduction, and significant differences between experimental and control groups, including various physiological measures and the proven 40-item STAI anxiety measurement questionnaire (Cooke *et al*, 2005).

It is not useful to overstate the relationship between pre-surgery anxiety and the milder anxiety you might experience at the auto repair shop, or some other service location. But it does appear that appropriate music has demonstrated a powerful ability to reduce anxiety, and that there is a clear case for experimentation in other places where service anxiety occurs.

3. Can music reduce the annoyance of service waiting time?

Waiting time has an almost perfect negative correlation with satisfaction in the consumer service environment (Bailey and Areni, 2006). Managers try to address it with improvements in operational efficiency, but that is seldom enough. Service operations have tried many ways to manipulate perceived waiting time. There are studies of environmental colour schemes, entertainment, tasks to complete while waiting, reassurances from service personnel. Results are not definitive.

One small bright spot is waiting time on the telephone, on hold. It's easy to experiment here, and people have. Results seem clear (Ramos, 1993). Change your tune and you change the number of hang-ups.

But experiments with music involving in-person, on-premise waiting time don't tell a very coherent tale. North and Hargreaves, building on earlier research, tried to find the appropriate level of complexity in music that might reduce perceived waiting time (North and Hargreaves, 1999). Their experiment exposed four groups of waiting respondents to different musical experiences: music of very low complexity, music of moderate complexity, and very complex music, plus a group that got no music at all. The no-music group had three times as many people who left early, but the three music groups had roughly identical patience.

Bailey and Areni (2006) propose a model with two countervailing factors. If music works to shorten perceived waiting time, perhaps it works by reducing attention you pay to monitoring passage of time. Less temporal information is encoded by the brain, and perceived time spent is shorter. If that's true, familiar music will work better. However, the more things recalled as having happened during the waiting period, the longer it is perceived to be. So if a lot of musical events are specifically remembered, the perceived duration of the wait will be longer. Then the ideal would be music that is liked, but perhaps not noted in detail. Sounds like a problem not entirely solved.

But a third study (Stratton, 1992) suggests that, independent of perceived time, respondents waiting with music find the wait less stressful.

CASE Barnes-Jewish Hospital

The future of audio branding in healthcare and beyond

Way back in Chapter 1, when we were giving examples, we talked about a hospital. We invited you to walk into the admissions area and hear the clatter of trolleys, the chatter of announcements, the buzz of phones, everything that says, 'You're in an institutional environment'. Nothing that says, 'Welcome, friend'. No sounds to help convey the experience you wish for the patient, family, or staff, such as confidence, optimism, teamwork, or scientific rigour.

Let's revisit this hospital. We bring this up because hospitals present more audio opportunities than do most brands.

Would you like to make people feel they have waited less time on hold? Could you make their walks down long corridors more pleasant? Would you like to help patients relax as they get out of their cars at the car park? Want them to feel your brand values, even if they're not actually paying close attention to the TV or video when your organization's ad runs?

These are just a sampling of the places where you can put custom-tailored audio to work for your organization to create a unified and coherent experience that builds your brand in dozens of subtle ways.

In hospitals, besides the advertising and masses of branded content, there are car parks, corridors, customer service lines, treatment rooms, and community events. In fact, these days, hospitals create so many videos about nutrition tips, brain tumour care, nurses' week, hospital tours, patient stories, and 'Why Dr X loves working at Hospital Y' stories that they own a built-in platform to build a long-lasting brand earprint. Some hospitals we've researched have more than 700 pieces of video content online. Imagine if they all merely began and ended each video with their own brand's audio logo. As NBC does with its famous three-note chime (G, E and C), a hospital can easily distinguish its content from that of its competitors with an audio logo as well as other audio-branding tools.

Twelve places a hospital marketer can capture the value of its audio brand

The hospital has more places than most brands to turn a casual touchpoint into a brand experience. These include:

1   advertising;
2   videos;
3   podcasts;
4   on-hold music;

5   car parks;
6   corridors;
7   waiting areas;
8   health fairs;
9   treatment rooms;
10 website;
11 mobile apps; and
12 shuttle services.

Barnes-Jewish put its music where its brand is
Barnes-Jewish, a large teaching hospital in St Louis, which is known for its excellence in medicine and its innovation, has done much to enhance the patient experience. From the facilitation of communication in 90 languages, to concierges from 5-star hotels, and night noise-level reductions to a less-confusing check-out process, they are constantly looking for ways to improve their encounters with patients and their families.

At the same time and unlike many other hospitals, they have looked deeply into creating distinctive music that can help carry this message of care and compassion along with the confidence of their medical expertise. And with an eye to the long view, they assembled a cross-functional group including corporate, nursing staff, cancer centre, marketing, and agency to help define the audio vocabulary that expresses their evolving brand.

The result is a distinctive sound within the hospital category. Still new to the world, it's being used in their new TV commercials and will replace the music in their older ones, creating coherence and saving them the cost of renewing music licences.

Though the commercials are scored differently according to their narratives, they carry a coherent and recognizable audio sound throughout their musical scores. For instance, one spot tells the touching story of a victim of nerve damage who had the use of his arm restored, starting with very poignant and slow piano and building in instrumentation and tempo to a triumphant conclusion; the other follows the bicycle ride of a man who used to suffer from a heart condition, in which the music is treated more rhythmically. When the logo appears in both commercials, the audio logo underscores it, leaving a memorable earprint.

So often, when logos appear in TV, the music either stops dead or flows along almost pointing your attention *away* from the logo and tagline. Distinctive audio should support and punctuate the appearance of the logo in the end frame.

This music is destined to move beyond commercials and, following the 12 points we identified above, into the holistic brand experience. Since the hospital is challenged with speaking in more than 90 languages, their move to using the universal language of music is yet another way to make itself understood.

The future of music in the healthcare sector

While creating the desired image for your organization is one important goal for your audio efforts, it is also important to know that, moving forward, sound may also have some other tangible impacts as well. For one instance among many, researchers with the Bill Wilkerson Center at Vanderbilt University Medical Center have received a grant to explore music's impact on brain functioning and determine how it can be used to treat a variety of illnesses and conditions. While more work needs to be done to fully understand the connection, this is an exciting field that holds much potential.

What this all means is that perhaps in the not-too-distant future, music and the use of other sounds may move beyond being an identifier and messenger to actually a method of treating ailments.

By then, the smartest healthcare systems will have their own established audio identities from which to build new (and identifiable) music treatments.

More importantly, smart marketers in virtually every field can learn from this in the use of music direction and discover ways they can use music and sound to truly add value to their efforts. Come along with them and see what you can do with sound for your brand and your customers. Once you do, you just might be playing a new tune in brand equity and customer satisfaction.

References

Areni, CS and Kim, D (1993) The influence of background music on shopping behaviour: classical vs top-forty music in a wine store, *Advances in Consumer Research*, vol 20, pp 336–40

Bailey, N and Areni, CS (2006). When a few minutes sounds like a lifetime: Does atmospheric music expand or contract perceived time?, *Journal of Retailing*, vol 82 (3), pp 189–202

Ballouli, K and Bennett, G (2014) New (sound) waves in sport marketing: do semantic differences in analogous music impact shopping behaviours of sport consumers?, *Sport Marketing Quarterly*, vol 23 (2), pp 59–72

Beverland, M, Lim, EAC, Morrison, M and Terziovski, M (2006) In-store music and consumer-brand relationships: Relational transformation following experiences of (mis) fit, *Journal of Business Research*, vol 59 (9), pp 982–89

Cooke, M, Chaboyer, W, Hiratos, MA (2005) Music and its effect on anxiety in short waiting periods: a critical appraisal, *Journal of Clinical Nursing*, vol 14, pp 145–55

Donovan, RJ, Rossiter, JR, Marcoolyn, G and Nesdale, A (1994) Store atmosphere and purchasing behaviour, *Journal of Retailing*, vol 70 (3), pp 283–94

Dubé, L and Morin, S (2001) Background music pleasure and store evaluation: Intensity effects and psychological mechanisms, *Journal of Business Research*, vol 54 (2), pp 107–13

Han, H, Back, KJ and Barrett, B (2009) Influencing factors on restaurant customers' revisit intention: The roles of emotions and switching barriers, *International Journal of Hospitality Management*, **28**, pp 563–72

Hoffman, DL and Novak, TP (1996) Marketing in hypermedia computer-mediated environments: conceptual foundations, *Journal of Marketing*, vol 60 (3), pp 50–68

Janishevsky, C (1988) Preconscious processing effects: The independence of attitude formation and conscious thought, *Journal of Consumer Research*, vol 15, September 1988, pp 199–209

Kotler, P (1974) Atmospherics as a marketing tool, *Journal of Retailing*, vol 49 (4), pp 48–64

Langeslag, P, Santos, R and Schwieger, J (2011) The effect of branded acoustic stimuli on purchase behaviour, *Audio Branding Academy Yearbook*, 2011/2012, pp 151–61

Lee, K, Chao, Y, Yiin, JJ, Hsieh, HY, Dai, WJ and Chao, YF (2012) Evidence that music listening reduces pre-operative patients' anxiety, *Biological Research for Nursing*, vol 14 (1), pp 78–84

MacInnis, DJ and Whan Park, C (1991) The differential role of characteristics of music on high- and low-involvement consumers' processing of ads, *Journal of Consumer Research,* vol 18 (2), pp 161–73

Mangini, VP and Parker, EE (2009) The psychological effects of music: implications for hotel firms, *Journal of Vacation Marketing,* vol 15 (1), pp 53–61

Mattila, AS and Wirtz, J (2001) Congruency of scent and music as a driver of in-store evaluations and behaviour, *Journal of Retailing*, vol 77, pp 273–89

Mehrabian, A and Russell, JA (1974) *An Approach to Environmental Psychology,* MIT Press, Cambridge, MA

North, AC and Hargreaves, DJ (1999) Can music move people? The effects of musical complexity and silence on waiting time, *Environment and Behaviour*, vol 31 (1), pp 136–49

North, AC, Hargreaves, DJ, MacKenzie LC and Law, RM (2004) The effects of musical and voice 'fit' on Responses to advertisements, *Journal of Applied Social Psychology*, vol 34 (8), pp 1675–708

Ramos, LV (1993) The effects of on-hold telephone music on the number of premature disconnections to a statewide protective services abuse hotline, *Journal of Music Therapy*, vol 30, pp 119–29

Stratton, V (1992) Influence of music and socializing on perceived stress while waiting, *Perceptual and Motor Skills*, vol 75, p 334

GLOSSARY

Audio branding as a discipline is still consolidating its vocabulary. To help ensure we're speaking the same language, we've captured some of the most common terms, providing our definition of them.

Acoustic branding see audio branding

Audio adaptations The pieces of music that are derived from your brand sound and that specifically fit the unique psychological and contextual needs of each touchpoint.

Audio branding The big one! It's how you sound to the world. It's both a system and a discipline. You want people to recognize your audio brand, no matter where they hear it, whether their eyes are open or closed, whether they're listening to a radio spot, in one of your locations (or trade-show booth for a B2B brand), on hold with your customer service centre, or watching a how-to video.

To achieve this goal, you should create a system of music that conveys the meaning of the brand at each touchpoint. You manage it so your stores, your ads, your service line, and your customer support don't sound like four totally different brands.

It's also important to note that audio branding has also been called music branding, sonic branding, sound branding, and acoustic branding.

Audio DNA A short (under one minute) original composition that captures the values, personality, and core promise of the brand as well as defines the musical vocabulary of instrumentation, tempo, melody etc that the brand will use across your multiple audio touchpoints. It's your musical bible.

Audio identity The bad news is that you have one of these, whether you manage it or not. It's the sum total of the audio impressions your brand makes. And it impacts your visual brand as well. Cacophony or coherence? Take your pick.

Audio logo The hardest-working part of your audio DNA, your logo appears at the end of every piece of communication. It's the perfect partner to the animation of your visual logo.

To describe these short 2- to 3-second sounds, you might also hear the word 'mnemonic' used but the original meaning of that word refers to 'memory' or 'memorability' so we feel this usage is weak. At other times, people say 'sting', which sounds as if its role is attention-grabbing. But a logo is more profound. It performs both the aforementioned functions, but also conveys meaning, values, and personality.

Audio Style Guide This handy piece catalogues all the audio elements available that are based on your audio DNA and gives you the rules of the road. Some are interactive, so employees, partners, and agencies can hear samples of each piece.

Glossary

Audio touchpoints Points of employee and customer contact that create big and small brand experiences that are audio-enabled. An audio identity unifies them so that when you hear it, you attribute the positive experiences to the brand. Here are three examples:

- **Branded content** Like any show in TV or radio, a recognizable intro, a variety of on-brand musical interstitials and a memorable 'outro' helps your audiences remember that you provided the content without banging them over the head with announcements. (You will find a more complete list of touchpoints in Chapter 4.)
- **Customer service line** Branded music for pre-pickup and on-hold that aims to give your callers pleasant brand experiences and, in the best cases, discourages them from hanging up. Sometimes your on-hold includes ambient sounds and scripted recordings by voices that best capture the personality of the brand or meet the needs of the audience.
- **Meetings and events** In meetings, there's a real chance to subtly immerse your employees or other audiences in the sound of the brand. As they walk into your meeting they hear anticipatory background music, then more energetic music signals the event is about to begin. A further rise in energy introduces the key speaker, branded musical transitions between each speaker let people know there's a change coming, and exit music has them walking out carrying the emotion of the event.

Brand Another term for your product or service or what prospects and customers think about your product or service and what it provides to them functionally and emotionally. Some in the branding world also use this term to refer to the visual logo, a reference to a branding iron and the mark it left on the cow.

Brand essence The core of the brand – what the marketer wants the brand to represent. Often structured as two words bordering on the oxymoronic, it helps define the brand's outer boundaries and what it will provide the consumer functionally and/or emotionally.

Brand promise see brand essence.

Brand values The behaviours and beliefs the brand holds valuable, often aligning with the behaviours and beliefs of the brand's ideal consumer.

Environmental sound design Here we are talking about the soundscapes for physical spaces like shopping centres, spas, airports, or expos, where music and sounds are used to create the environment you desire. For instance, the soundscape is designed to make the audience feel comfortable, relaxed, awestruck, or amused. If you already have an audio brand, you can drop little hints of that into the sound of your environment.

Licensed music Typically, this music has been created for entertainment purposes rather than for branding. To use it on behalf of a brand, you have to pay a licensing fee. One thing marketers must also do when using licensed music is ensure that competitors aren't using that same piece as well.

Mnemonic see audio logo

Music branding see audio branding

Sonic branding see audio branding

Sound branding see audio branding

Sound design When we use this term, we often mean the manipulation of sounds or the addition of sound effects, but it's an evolving phrase. Another usage refers to creating the sounds that are used for devices or vehicles. And a third for changing the sound that an instrument makes. For instance, near a display of electric cars, you might manipulate audio to make the music feel more electronic and near petrol-powered vehicles let it sound more acoustic. Or, in a video, sound design can add the sounds of people eating in a restaurant or walking in a rainforest.

It also can refer to creating an appropriate sound for the medium – that sound will be different for a mobile phone than for a giant theatre.

Sting see audio logo

Winks Also called brand winks and clins d'oeil, are short reminders of the brand woven, now and then, among the music being played in brand environments. They often include the audio logo and a further sound, words, or song segments that bring out the personality of the brand. The intention is to lightly and, usually, playfully bring attention back to the brand.

INDEX

Note: *Italics* indicate a Figure or Table in the text.

Abercrombie & Fitch 38, 77, 132
AC Nielsen 93
acoustic branding 203
advertising 2, 3, 4, 5, 10, 16, 21, 66, 72, 81, 82, 94, 95, 113–16, 128, 145, 156, 157, 158, 162, 171, 172, 177, 198
  advertising awareness of 113
  aided and unaided awareness 113
Alka-Seltzer 149
Alstom 14
Apple 4, 9, 22, 33, 50, 130
apps 57, 155
Areva 6–7
Asian Paints 37
Atkinson, Rowan 4
Atlanta 70–71, 178
  Convention & Visitors Bureau (ACVB) case study 134–37
'atmospherics' 191–92
audio adaptations 203
audio brand launch 139–56
  approaches 140–43
audio branding 1–18, 27, 65–83, 90, 203, 205
  as a system 3–7
  brand launch 139–56
  cues 23, 28, 115–16
  deconstruction/layering 105–06
  differential through sound 23–24, 78–79, 80, 175
  digital age and 19–44
  do's and don'ts for marketers 89–92
  emotional responses 60
  environments and 5, 73–74, 187–98
  feedback 131
  lifestyle and 8–9
  maintaining/evolving 157–76
  process 121–22, *123*, 124–37
  protecting 160–62
  reasons for 51–52
  're-lift' 161
  role of senior management 161
  sharing with employees 160, 161
  tools 65
  variety 160–61
  see also music

Audio Branding Congress xiv–xvi
Audio Consulting Group xv
audio DNA 16, 23, 27, 41, 51, 59, 60, 61, 65, 66, 82, 88, 89, 90, 125, 127, 128, 130, 136, 137, 140, 141, 144, 156, 157, 160, 171, 172, 203
audio identity 2–3, 10, 41, 104, 129, 144, 157, 203
audio library 75–76, 77
audio logo 1, 66, 72, 90, 91, 118, 128, 145–46, 157, 203
audio logo system 161
audio 'mood' boards 124–26
  examples 125–26
Audio Style Guide 129, 143–44, 161, 203
  example 144–49
audio touchpoints 66–77, 91, 146, 204
AXA 6, 88
  case study 171–75
  global advertising audio library 172, *173*

B2B 29, 30, 52, 65, 113, 136
Baby Bell 6
Banagale, Ryan Raul 159
Barclaycard 4–5
Barňes-Jewish Hospital 198–200
Bennett, Paul 174–75
Bingham, David 151
BMW 8–9
Borgerson, Janet 162
Boumendil, Michaël 11–15, 17, 178, 186
Brace, Christopher 33
Brainjuicer 31, 36, 39
brand audio identity 85–101
  assessing strength 128
  leadership style and 85
  luxury and 87
  structure 86
  symbols 85, 86
brand briefing 122, 124
brand tracking 111–16
  design of 113–14
  insights from 112
branded content 204

Index

branding 2, 31
  auditory 50–51
  consumer value 46
  cultural differences 108–10
  example questionnaire 109
  metrics 29, 30
  organizational culture and 139
  purpose of 46
  rhyme and rhythm of 131–33
  sensory 45–64
  strategic role 20
  tactile 48
  touch 48
  US spending on 20
  visual 46–47
  see also audio branding, rebranding
brands 12, 19, 204
  audacity 181
  audio 24–29, 85–101, 128
  audio DNA 16, 23, 27, 41, 51, 59, 60, 61, 65, 66, 82, 88, 89, 90, 125, 127, 128, 130, 136, 137, 140, 141, 144, 156, 157, 160, 171, 172, 203
  authenticity 96, 181
  champion 130
  congruity 104
  DNA 27, 50
  see also audio DNA
  emotional engagement 35–36, 39, 80
  essence/promise 24–25, 122, 204
  internal launch planning and roll-out 129–30
  intimacy 181
  launch 139–56
  retailing and 76–77
  similarity to religions 157
  target audience 122
  touchpoints 66–77, 91, 146, 204
  values 50, 106, 157, 180–82, 195, 204
  virtuosity 181
Brazeal, Mickey 92–96, 104, 187–98
Budweiser 118
Burberry 38
Byron, Ellen 149–52

Cadbury 157
Cinnabon 37
Clinique 149–50
Coca-Cola 132, 157
Cochini, Laurent 97–99
Condiment Junkie 54
Continental Airlines 5, 15
'continuous partial attention' 22–23
copy testing 114–15
Costco 39
customer service line 204

Dengvaxia 6
Dial Soap 157
DiSanti, Ben 31–34, 76
Douroux, Jean 82
Dr Pepper Snapple Group Inc. 150
Dyson 152

Edwards, Webley 168–69
Enel 140
Eno, Brian 50
environmental music 177–201
  airports 177–78
  anxiety reduction 196–97
  as persuasion 187–89
  'atmospherics' 191–92
  audio branding and 5, 73–74, 187–98
  brand 'winks' 187, 205
  hotels 184–86
  humour 186
  impact on staff 178–7
  internet streaming 178
  learning from experience 191–92
  listening to your employees 179–80
  public announcements 178
  reducing annoyance from waiting 197
  retail space 189–91
  shoppers and 182–83
  sound design 204
  tips 186–87
  values and 180–82
  zoning/dayparting 184–86

Fabrigas 49–50
Fanichet, Christophe 17
Fat Duck Research Kitchen, The 54
FedEx 132
Fiat Motor Village 182
Fitch 37
Frey, Don 151–52
Fritz, Thomas 7–8

Gains, Neil 46, 49, 131–33
Gallup 36
GE 151
Generation Z 140
Gilmour, David 17, 71

Harley-Davidson 4, 50, 132
Harvard Business Review 29
Hawaii 162–70
  audio branding 165–69
  craze for 163–65
healthcare 198–200
Heineken 132–33
Hershey Company, The 32, 33, 34, 162
Hicks, Ken 31–34, 76

Index

Hobkinson, Caroline 55
Hoffman, Susan 25
household products 149–52
Huggies 6, 161–62
    case study 40–42
Hulten, B 45–46

IBM 2
Iddings, Drew 34
ING Direct 9
Intel 1, 4, 50, 72, 89
    case study 116–18
Internet of Things 74–75

James-Lundak, Molly 22
Janishevsky, C 192
jingles 3
Johnson, Angela 5, 41, 42

Kearon, John 39
Kellogg's 149
key performance indicators *see* metrics
Kia Motors 47, 49
King, Lisa 150–51
Koelsch, Stefan 8
Kotler, Dr Philip 191–92
Kraft Recipes 67
Kroger 34
Krug 56–57

La Roche-Posay case study 61
Lancôme Beauty Institute 6
Lewis, Lena 34, 39
listening committee 124, 125, 136
logos 2
    audio 1, 66, 72, 90, 91, 118, 128, 145–46, 157, 203
    visual 1, 24, 66, 72, 91, 118, 122
L'Oréal Group 61
Louis XIII Cognac 59–61

MACSF 142
Mahoney, Tim 151
marketing
    digital 20–21
    do's and don'ts 89–92
    landscape 20–24
    metrics 30, 103–19
    sensory 30, 45–64
    targeted audiences 21
    touchpoints 21, 66–77
Marriott Hotels 48
Max Plank Institute for Human Cognitive and Brand Sciences 7, 8
McDonald's 1, 25

Method Products 151–52
metrics 30, 103–19
    close rate 30
    company valuation 30
    perceived price/value 30
    unsolicited enquiries 30
Michelin 6, 88, 158
    case study 81–82
Microsoft 22, 50
Millennials 140
Minsky, Laurence 24
Mitsubishi 257
mnemonic *see* audio logo
Mood Media 49
music 67–68
    ambience and 133
    as persuasion 187–8
    brain and 87
    brand authenticity and 96
    brand 'winks' 183, 205
    branding the service experience 195–96
    colour and 88, 136
    conveying luxury 87
    copyright law 183–84
    cultural differences 7–8, 88–89, 108
    customer service line 67, 204
    decision-making and 95–96
    emotions and 75, 87, 94, 107
    environment and 73–74m 177–201
    expos/trade shows 70–71
    financial sector 9
    impact on sales 110–11
    licensed 66, 184, 204
    meaning and 87–88, 93, 106
    meetings/conferences 68–69, 204
    memory recall 94, 110
    messages and 93, 94
    mood/behaviour and 94–95
    new product reveals 73
    press events 73
    product sounds/signals 71–72
    purchasing intent and 96
    repetition 90
    research on effects 92–96, 106–08
    retailers and 76–77
    ringtones 69–70, 147, 155
    spicy 57
    storytelling 132
    surround sound 77
    TV commercials 93, 177
    videos 148
    worldwide language 7–8, 90
musical messages 12, 14

Nadal, Rafael 99
Nestlé case study 59
Neuro-Insight 110
Nike 25–26
Nokia 4
North, Professor Adrian 87

Ogilvy 40
   Ogilvy Argentina 42
on-hold 50, 204
   marketing 143
   music 2, 23, 67, 90, 91, 130, 146, 154, 198
Owen, Ted 149–50

Paris Auto Show 77–80
PepsiCo Inc. 150
Peters, Julia Tang 19
Petit Bateau 182
Peugeot 6, 8, 88
Pfizer Animal Health 140–41
Pink, Racheal 152
Presley, Elvis 168
Proctor & Gamble Co 151

rebranding 27–29
Remy Martin 60
Renault 9, 70, 78
   brand perception 154
   case study 152–56
RENFE 9
Resorts World Sentosa 49
ringtones 69–70, 147, 155
Robertson, Grant 117–18
Roland Garros (French Tennis Open)
        case study 7–99
Royal Air Maroc 88–89

Sabesp xv
Samsung Galaxy 4
Schroeder, Jonathan 162–70
Schultz, Howard 38
SCNF 9, 71, 103–04, 107, 114, 158, 183
   case study 16–17
senses 45, 131
   sight 46–47
   smell 37, 38, 48–50
   sound 50–51, 131–32
   taste 47, 55
   touch 48
sensory marketing 45–64
'sensploration' 57
SFR 141–42
shopping 19
   emotional engagement 36
   experience 31–34
   functional engagement 36
   impulse buying 193
   inspiration and 35–39
   multisensory triggers 36–39
   music and 96, 182–83
   storytelling 33–34, 76
Siemens 157
Singleton Sensorium, the 56
Sixième Son xvi, 11–15, 16, 24, 41, 65, 70, 76, 88, 89, 97–9, 105, 127, 129, 135, 142, 153
sonic seasoning 52–58
sound 54
   design 205
   household products and 149–52
   meaning and 1
   senses and 54
   taste and 55
Spence, Professor Charles 47, 52–57, 58, 92
Springate, Andrew 150
Starbucks 38
Stella Artois 133
Stone, Linda 22
synaesthetes 53–54
Syntegrate Consulting 33

Tagg, Philip 87–88
TapestryWorks 131
   eSense framework 133
Target 25, 31–32
Thomas Pink 49
Tiemans, Herman 160
Topper, Gene 104, 111–16
touchpoints 2, 10, 21, 22, 28, 38, 49, 51, 65, 66, 77, 91, 128, 139, 144, 156, 172, 174, 175, 203, 204
Trunk Club 47
TV commercials 72, 92, 93, 110, 156, 173, 199–200

Unibail-Rodamco shopping centre, Lyon 5–6
United Airlines 5, 158–60
   Rhapsody in Blue 5, 158–60
   'Safety is Global' video 159

Van Aelst, Geert 33–34
Vanderbilt University Medical Center 200
visual logos 1, 24, 66, 72, 91, 118, 122
Volkswagen 151
Volvo 78

Walking Brand xiv
Walmart 25
Werzowa, Walter 117
Wilson, Andrew 134, 136, 137
winks 76, 182, 183, 187, 205
Winther, Julie 22
Wrigley 33, 34

Xiol, Ramón Vives 77–80

YouTube 7

Zander, Mark 93
Zanna xv

Lightning Source UK Ltd.
Milton Keynes UK
UKHW020625120120
356774UK00003B/84/P